FRAMINGHAM STATE COLLEGE

3 3014 00026 2388

D1413759

APPROACHING DISARMAMENT EDUCATION

edited by

MAGNUS HAAVELSRUD
Institute of Social Science, University of Tromsö

WESTBURY HOUSE : GUILDFORD
in association with the
PEACE EDUCATION COMMISSION OF THE INTERNATIONAL PEACE
RESEARCH ASSOCIATION (IPRA)

Framingham State College
Framingham, Massachusetts

Published by Westbury House (the books division of IPC Science and Technology
Press Ltd), PO Box 63, Bury Street, Guildford, Surrey GU2 5BH, England

© IPC Business Press Limited, 1981, unless otherwise stated

All rights reserved. No part of this publication may be reproduced, stored in a
retrieval system or transmitted in any form or by any means electronic,
mechanical, photocopying, recording or otherwise without the prior permission
of the copyright holder, application for which should be addressed to the
publisher. The publisher is not responsible for the views expressed in the
following pages.

British Library Cataloguing in Publication Data
Approaching disarmament education.
1. Disarmament
I. Haavelsrud, Magnus
327.1'74 JX1974
ISBN 0-86103-043-5

Printed in Great Britain

JX
1974
A75

CONTENTS

iii

II Case studies in informal education

III Case studies in formal education

IV Epilogue

Preface

The work on this volume was begun in the summer of 1979 as the preparatory discussions for the UNESCO-sponsored World Congress on Disarmament Education were well under way. My understanding of the debate on disarmament education before and during the World Congress, which was held in June 1980, gave me an uncomfortable feeling that the tricky political issue of disarmament became even more controversial when it came to the questions of why and how disarmament *education* were to be developed. Paradoxically, however, the controversial aspects of this problem were kept at a safe distance, especially evident at the World Congress in which many hundreds of experts from all over the world met for almost a week. The unanimous adoption of the final document was, in my view, the result of a conference format in which, at least in the plenary sessions and in the commission on education, the speakers addressed themselves to the President and the Secretariat rather than to each other. Contradictions were not revealed but covered so that *disagreements* about fundamental principles were left largely untouched. This was mainly due to the lack of real dialogue amongst the participants.

This volume aims at showing a variety of positive approaches for disarmament education excluding approaches of a clearly negative and indoctrinating nature. Hence, most of the contributions view the problem of disarmament, or *negative* peace, in the light of social justice and development, or *positive* peace. Thus, I hope the volume can stimulate a discussion on the political realities of the problem and contribute towards keeping the 'game of disarmament', as Alva Myrdal has put it, away from the classrooms, television sets and newspapers. I hope therefore that the contributions included give the reader positive examples of education in the interest of disarmament and liberation from oppression, as opposed to pacification for the consolidation of present developments of militarism and suppression.

I would like to thank the contributors for their cooperation in the completion of this book and for many years of stimulating professional as well as personal contact, with most of them within the Peace Education Commission of the International Peace Research Association. Thanks also to my university for supporting the project.

Magnus Haavelsrud
Tromsö, January 1981

FOREWORD

Alva Myrdal, *Former Minister of Disarmament, Sweden*

This book will be of value in inspiring a new debate so as to alert public opinion towards greater consciousness of the ongoing militarization of our civilization. The contributions are of current interest and I definitely recommend the content to be read and discussed, in educational circles and also in the mass media.

What should be discussed is, of course, not only education but also miseducation. I take it as a common value premise that *disarmament* would be to the good of our world. Education for it must then not least be directed towards criticism of the miseducation that is promoted by schoolbooks and still more powerfully by the mass media, the press and particularly television.

I am personally not too optimistic about the effect of formal education in overcoming the drift towards acceptance of all kinds of war preparedness. Perhaps even the very word 'peace' has become something of an outworn cliche, not really raising any consciousness or still less conscienceness that the question is one of war and destruction. Perhaps the overdose of 'peace' terms explains some of the weakness of peace movements, the lack of real anti-war and anti-violence movements. Still, if public opinion *can* be awakened, we know from recent history that it can serve as a resistance movement, and succeed, as was demonstrated by its effect in stopping the Vietnam war.

Disarmament education must in the main be a training in critical awareness that events do not just happen but have causes. At present, in 1981, comparisons with 1914 give telling examples.

It seems to me that education can do two things. One task is to direct attention to the consequences of wars and preparedness for war in the arms race. This must be measured not just in terms of destruction, but of costs, for example, of inflation, the encouragement of oppressive dictatorships by weapons sales, and even of everyday violence by condoning the use of weapons; and not least the spread of a psychological climate of living in a weapons' culture.

The second task is to encourage a discussion of alternatives, giving greater weight to positive factors. To select just one example it seems to me a matter of concern that so little attention is given to international law, to the still *de facto* valid rules of war in the Hague Conventions, for example the agreement condemning the use of dum-dum bullets, which is at present grossly violated, or to point out, the much greater security for civilians against area bombing, which was solemnly agreed upon in Geneva in 1977 as a modernized addition to the humanitarian rules of war. This is a question for each nation: has yours ratified these protocols? Neither of the two superpowers has so far done so.

Even if a dialogue on disarmament matters appears be dilettante in an educational setting, it is highly valuable as an exercise in developing critical attitudes. We certainly need to make everybody better equipped to recognize false arguments — in a word, to make people propaganda-proof.

The task of education is not to give prescriptions to governments, since the premises change over time and in varying national and cultural environments. Its task can only be to cultivate the power and habit of criticism, involving diagnosis of the present, alternative visions of the future and strategies of changing the present. The linking of critical thought with a clear ethical view concerning disarmament processes may stimulate action initiatives necessary for such processes to be set in motion. And this book, not least because its teaching includes different and sometimes contradictory approaches towards disarmament education, should help in this important task.

Introduction:

Recent discussions on disarmament education

Robert Aspeslagh and Veslemøy Wiese, *Peace Education Commission of the International Peace Research Association*

This paper outlines recent discussions on disarmament education by pointing to some fundamental controversies, specifically related to the proceedings and the final documents of the World Congress on Disarmament Education. We shall also comment on some important points for future development of disarmament education.

Preparations for the World Congress

The term 'disarmament education' was first used in UNESCO at a meeting of experts in the field of 'obstacles to disarmament and the ways of overcoming them', held in Paris on 3-7 April, 1978. During this conference the participants called upon the Secretary-General of UNESCO to hold a world congress on disarmament education in 1980.

The decision to hold a world congress was taken by the 10th Special Session of the United Nations General Assembly in 1978, urging UNESCO to

> 'step up its programme aimed at the development of disarmament education as a distinct field of study . . . (aiming) to achieve disarmament education rather than disarmament itself, (the Congress should take) concrete steps to inform and mobilize forces capable of contributing effectively to the halting of the arms race and the transition to disarmament . . . increase the place given to disarmament issues in the educational process and encourage a critical and inquiring attitude among pupils and students so that they will be better prepared to resist propaganda for war and militarism and to apply their own judgement to the problems involved.'

As preliminaries to the congress, three conferences of experts were held: on 4-8 June, 1979, in Prague; on 14-16 January, 1980, in Paris; and on 26-27 January, 1980, in Vienna. In the course of these three meetings, the participants discussed how the concept 'disarmament education' might be put into operation. The final document of the Prague meeting emphasized that 'education for disarmament is an essential aspect of the more general notion of education for peace'. The most important results of the preliminary meetings, as laid down in the final documents, are a series of recommendations to UNESCO with respect to further elaboration of disarmament education, the setting-up of special commissions, and organization of special activities, such as a 'year of disarmament education', a 'world week for disarmament' and a 'special peace day'.

A full assembly of the Congress took place during the first two days and the last day and was divided into two commissions dealing with the following areas:

1. *Formal and non-formal education* at different levels: the training of teaching personnel, the working out of appropriate teaching materials, the revision of existing textbooks, particularly in history and geography, etc.

2. *Information:* the training of professional workers in the field of information, information ethics relating to questions of armament and disarmament, methods of informing the general public, scientific circles, military personnel, etc.

During these two days the situation of disarmament education was examined at all levels of education: primary, secondary and university levels, teacher training, adult education and non-formal education and education through the mass media. Commission 1 was scheduled to discuss on the first day, curriculum and materials, teaching methods, teacher training and teaching of military personnel, and on the second, informal education approaches, non-formal education, education within the family and education within trade unions. Commission 2 was scheduled to discuss formation of public opinion on disarmament questions through the mass media, approaches to problems of professional ethics in relation to disarmament problems and the development of audiovisual materials. Research, forms of cooperation and problems of documentation were to be discussed by both commissions.

Recommendations to the Director General of UNESCO in the final document of the congress* included:

1. initiatives to make adequate funds available for the significant development of disarmament education should be encouraged, by supporting in particular the proposal of the UN Secretary-General that one-tenth of one percent of military spending should be devoted to national and international efforts in favour of disarmament, including disarmament education and information;

2. social science research activities on disarmament, peace and international relations should be strengthened with a view, *inter alia*, to improving education and information programmes in these fields, in collaboration with the UNO and peace research centres;

---

* Part of the final document is given as an Appendix to this volume.

3. the possibility should be investigated of drawing up standard clauses whereby States as parties to arms control or limitation agreements would undertake, on the one hand, to foster the dissemination of the instrument in question and, on the other, to promote to the greatest possible extent, and by appropriate means, disarmament in general.

A question concerning the final document is, in what manner the concept 'disarmament education' is to be operationalized. The advantage of a term such as 'disarmament education', like 'peace education', is that the goal of the education is specified. It is, however, important to know just what is meant by 'disarmament', as well as by 'peace'.

Among the ten starting-points for disarmament education, the following description is given:

> For the purposes of disarmament education, disarmament may be understood as any form of action aimed at limiting, controlling or reducing arms, including unilateral disarmament initiatives and, ultimately, general and complete disarmament under effective international control.
>
> It may also be understood as a process aimed at transforming the current system of armed nation States into a new world order of planned unarmed peace in which war is no longer an instrument of national policy and peoples determine their own future and live in security based on justice and solidarity.

A second point is related to the substance of disarmament education. The final document states in article 4 that 'Disarmament education cannot, however, confine itself to the dissemination of data and information of disarmament projects and prospects nor even to commenting on the hopes and ideals which inspired them'. What *is* disarmament education then? The document lists a number of criteria of which three are given here.

1. Disarmament education requires the collection and dissemination of reliable information from sources offering the highest degree of objectivity in accordance with a free and more balanced international flow of information. It should prepare learners, in the strictest respect for freedom of opinion, expression and information, to resist incitement to war, military propaganda and miltarism in general. (article 3);
2. Disarmament education should be related to the lives and concerns of the learners and to the political realities within which disarmament is sought and should provide insights into the political, economic and social factors on which the security of peoples could be based. (article 4);
3. Disarmament education should provide an occasion to explore, without prejudging the issue, the implications for disarmament of the root causes of individual and collective violence and the objective and subjective causes of tensions, crises, disputes and conflicts which characterize the current national and international structures reflecting factors of inequality and injustice. (article 6).

The document thus establishes disarmament education as a distinct discipline *within* the broader fields of peace and development education:

> As an integral part of peace education, disarmament education has essential links with human rights education and development education, in so far as each of the three terms peace, human rights and development must be defined in relation to the other two.

This is in contrast to the view put forward by Pikas at the conference that disarmament education must be distinguished as a pedagogical discipline confined to the school system and should not 'bear the burden of all the values of "positive peace"'.[2] Burns point out that

> justice requires more than the recognition of development and peace as human rights, it is a statement about the maintenance, exercise and distribution of power.
> There are clear links between the arms race and the deflection of resources which could be used for development.[3]

Addressing herself to the problem of the link between disarmament and the transition to a disarmed world Stephenson said that

> The relationship between disarmament and security is a complex one. On the surface, many view disarmament as a withdrawal of security through arms. Alternative international security systems are a prerequisite to the halting of the arms race. . . Security in the most basic sense comes from attention to the basic needs of human beings including both needs for physical safety and needs for food, clothing, shelter and the like. There are many alternative security systems other than arms which can supply physical safety to an individual or to a nation. Reliance on these alternative systems would allow progress towards disarmament and consequent release of funds to meet other basic human and economic needs.[4]

Although the need for redeployment of production for military purposes to production of goods and services for development and the powerful interests involved in the sales and production of arms was touched as a problematic area of research by Stavenhagen in his address to the Congress[5], education for conversion, as part of disarmament education is not taken up in the document, nor the connections between development, human rights, human needs and the question of socially necessary production.

In the final document a cognitive approach is chosen, which goes no further than to study, research, comprehend, and draw comparisons with other educative goals such as 'education for human rights' and 'education for development'. Apart from the fact that, understandably, no attempt has been made at political analysis at the national and international levels, neither does the final document state just how these criteria should ultimately lead to disarmament. Thus the document makes pronouncements on the use and development of suitable methods of instruction, but says nothing about ways of converting attitudes and knowledge into skills; in other words, how to combine reflection and action.

In his paper for the conference, Randle emphasises this point:

> Peace action has a special place in the work of disarmament education because at its best it can symbolize the choices we are facing and directly challenge the militarism and irresponsible policies of governments. Like other instances of popular non-violent action, it also empowers people to take greater control over their own lives and the lives of their communities, a process which is at once the essence of any true educational endeavour, and the prerequisite for a world without war. . . the link between peace action and radical action for other social and political goals is close, just as the achievement of peace itself is inextricably bound up with the realisation of a social order and international system that eliminates domination and structural violence.[6]

Further work

The document stresses that disarmament education forms an essential part of peace education. Various participants expressed the fear that disarmament education might cost so much time, energy and money, that peace education would be neglected. It is our decided opinion that disarmament education if not associated with peace, human rights and development, will be doomed to failure. It would then run the danger of becoming a form of 'defence education'. For this reason it is good to see the final document clearly expressing itself on this point.

UNESCO has set an important process in motion, and one hopes that all efforts towards disarmament education, as part of a wider effort in peace education, will be supported. We suggest some important points in this future work.

Some of the main trends in disarmament education appear to indicate that its overall purpose is to contribute to the achievement of peace and justice, and to a radical change in the form of power relations applied in the conduct of international affairs. These two major purposes are related to other particular objectives, such as the development of a more wide-spread understanding of the arms race and contemporary efforts to halt or reverse its trends, as well as an understanding of human behaviour and moral values such as solidarity. However, these objectives are posed in too simplistic a form to comprehend the distinct and profound problems arising from attempts to educate for change in human behaviour. Education, even mass or popular education, is focused on the individual. Peace education is focused on the development of the conscious and verifiable intention of the individual to act for peace. It is also directed toward teaching political attitudes which are directed to the plight of the worlds' poor and oppressed and an understanding of the structural relations which lead to this oppression and exploitation.

The development of weapons and the arms race has not been caused by the individual and certainly not by those who make up the mass of world society, though indeed it is they who suffer most from the violence caused by arms.

Although the process of armament is strongly supported by competitive economic interests, disarmament must nevertheless be regarded as basically a political problem and must be dealt with by political means. Hence, disarmament education should not be construed in terms of 'national security' and 'national interest'; for such an approach would lead itself to manipulation by the ruling groups through its failure to challenge the very structures, both national and international, which produce the arms race. Rather disarmament education should be concerned with the 'security of people' and the 'human global interest'.

Disarmament education must not be used to cloak the purpose of so-called 'defence education' or civil defence which is emerging in the educational structures of various countries. Cast in this mould, disarmament education would run the risk of leading citizens to believe they could survive a war, even a nuclear one.

Disarmament education must not focus exclusively on the dissemination of the results of scientific research; for this approach would probably result in people turning away from the problem, Most research tends to show the problem in terms of an inescapable process, with mankind a helpless prisoner of events.

Each of these approaches — national interest and national security, civilian defence and dissemination of research — would reinforce the existing interest of the existing power groups and the structure through which they continue to pursue the arms race. A government could elaborate a programme of disarmament education based on any of these approaches and still steer away from true disarmament, having demonstrated its 'obligation' to defend the security of its citizens. Meanwhile the true threats to security in continued mutual armaments would grow even greater.

General and complete disarmament can never be achieved by education alone, but disarmament education is essential in creating the climate in which the goal can be pursued. General and complete disarmament could be achieved if people would refuse to serve any longer the interests of the ruling groups and refuse to continue the support of both national and international structures which keep those groups in power. People must become actively involved in the struggle to transcend the structures which maintain the arms race.

Education must therefore be linked to action. Such action is the vital connection between the political goal embodied in the concept of general and complete disarmament, and disarmament education as a general educational principle. Such a movement would be a tremendous force for disarmament and would be the most legitimate reason for disarmament education.

The concept of a mass movement reflects the basic idea that peace and justice will only be achieved when citizens participate equally in the decision making of their society and in the distribution of that society's resources. Disarmament education as a component of peace education must be guided by this principle, the principle of popular participation.

It must be kept in mind that arms are only a symptom of the larger problem of power. Eliminating and even reducing arms would not necessarily change the role of power in international relations, but it could induce a profound change in both international and national politics. It could be a significant step toward peace. But we need to be conscious that it is only a step, not full achievement of the goal. Disarmament education is only a part of peace education, not a substitute for it. Nor should the focus on the hard and practical problems of disarmament be used as an excuse to dismiss peace education as 'utopian'. Education for disarmament and education for peace are both necessary in the quest for social justice.

Notes and references

1. Secretariat background document
2. Pikas A. Disarmament education through teacher training. Conference background document, SS-80/CONF. 401/8
3. Burns R. Development education education and disarmament education: some comparisons and implications. Conference background document, SS-80/CONF. 401/18
4. Stephenson C.M. Teaching alternative international security systems. Conference background document, SS-80/CONF. 401/3
5. See also, Asquith P. Arms productions or unemployment — a false choice. Conference background document, SS-80/CONF. 401/14
6. Randle M. Peace action as a form of disarmament education. Conference background document, SS-80/CONF. 401/20

I. GENERAL PERSPECTIVES

1. Perspectives of women researchers on disarmament, national security and world order*

Elise Boulding, *Department of Sociology, Dartmouth College, USA*

Since disarmament and problems of national security and world order are not fields in which women scholars are generally considered to be prominent, the decision to make a survey of how women working in this field treat these problems immediately presented the challenge of how to identify enough scholars in the field to give a fair picture of their work. This survey therefore can serve two purposes: (1) to find out what specialists in the field do, and (2) to make these women visible to one another and provide the ingredients of an informal network for those who choose to use it. The isolation of professional women from one another as well as from colleagueship with men is one of the extra handicaps under which they work. Daniels has pointed out the crucial importance of informal contacts for professionals to get 'quick information — the best scholarly references, access to agencies of key informants in preparing a grant proposal, the crucial areas to find in technical reports when building a documented case about something.'[1] Women have good community network skills but are only beginning to develop the professional networks they need in order to work effectively. Such networks must of course include both women and men. At present, most professional networks are largely male. Facilitating women's networks should be seen as an intermediate step for women toward fuller involvement in public professional life, as well as an end in itself.

The informants
An initial list of 20 women from 10 countries was compiled on the basis of my previous knowledge of the field and association with scholars in the International Peace Research Association (IPRA), the North American Consortium on Peace Research, Education and Development, the USA based Institute for World Order, and governmental and non-governmental arms control agencies. All these organizations and agencies have a membership of social sciences scholars who work in an interdisciplinary way on world problems. The first two are known as peace research organizations. The purpose of IPRA is to advance interdiscipli-

*Previously published in *Women's Studies Internat. Quart.*, 4, 1

nary research into the conditions of peace and the causes of war through international collaboration between scholars. The Consortium on Peace Research, Education and Development links persons and institutions interested in scientific study, action-oriented research and education on problems of peace and social injustice. A third organization, the Institute for World Order, builds on the world law tradition found both in international relations and law and seeks to build workable models of a future world order through its world order models project. The Stockholm International Peace Research Institute (SIPRI), the US Arms Control and Disarmament Agency, and the non-governmental Arms Control Association were also sources of contact.

In response to my request for more names of women scholars from each initial and successive contact I eventually had a list of 63 names from 19 countries and received replies from 41 women in 17 countries. In my letter of inquiry I asked each woman

> to jot down your judgement of what research agendas should look like in the arms control and disarmament field, the extent to which you perceive existing research work to be relevant to that agenda, what your own particular research in the field has been in the last decade, and what you think is the most important piece of work you have done. For the purposes of this survey, arms control, disarmament, national security and world security, and any studies involving weapons systems and arms trade which are concerned with control, should be included. What do you personally believe to be the best approach to the concept of security? To make sure I don't miss anything you think is important, I would prefer that you yourself define the field in such a way that your work can be included. Please also mention what you are currently at work on, and what you plan to do next. Also, what are your personal estimates of the possibility of any major steps toward world disarmament by the year 2000? Can you recommend anything that has been written about what a disarmed world would look like?
>
> Are you aware of any particular characteristics that distinguish the way women approach disarmament research from the way men approach it? If yes, why — and if no, why not? Finally, add any comments you think are important that are not covered by the above questions.

Each correspondent was also asked to send her curriculum vitae (cv) and a couple of relevant reprints.

In addition to the written replies received from the 41 women, discussions on these questions were held with 10 of these same scholars who were present at the August 1979 IPRA biennial conference in Frankfurt, Germany, and with another 10 scholars present at the conference who did not send written replies. This makes a total of 51 women from whom I received information, representing 21 countries (Poland and Hungary are the countries from which I have received no written replies).

This is not a study of the women's peace movement. Since public

Table 1. Country of origin, age range, occupation and number of publications for women scholars by research orientation

Number of scholars	Countries represented		Age range	Occupation	Number who have served in government ministries, commissions	Range in number of publications
25	US Sweden UK Argentina, Australia Germany, India Nigeria, Romania, Canada	12 3 3 1 {from each}	23-78	New Conceptual Frameworks 7 professors 11 research associates (government or university) 5 administrator/researchers 2 free-lance researchers	14	1-21 books, monographs, pamphlets 2-100s articles and chapters in books
16	US Germany Denmark, France, India, Italy, Japan, Mexico, Norway, Philippines, UK	6 2 1 {from each}	32-52	New Social Order 5 professors 5 research associates 6 community organizers journalists	2	0-5 books, monographs, pamphlets 9-40 articles, chapters (for journalists, uncounted newspaper articles)
41	17		23-78	12 professors 16 research associates 5 administrators 2 free-lance researchers 6 community organizers, journalists	16	0-21 books, monographs, and pamphlets 2-100s of articles and chapters in books

13

opinion, both in and out of peace movements, frequently holds that peace is a special concern of women as wives and mothers, and that women have special skills and insights and clearer social vision related to peace and peacemaking than men, it will be interesting to see whether women scholars working as professionals in the field see their work and their role as researchers differently because they are women. This study reports their own perceptions. A systematic comparative study of men and women scholars would be necessary in order to state whether they are in fact different.

The 51 women participants (including the 10 who participated through discussion only) represent, I believe, some significant segment of the world community of women scholars working in disarmament-related fields. Preferring to err on the side of inclusiveness, I added some names of women working primarily in non-violence research and training to the list, in response to suggestions from the original 20 respondents. That process in turn created new gaps, but the deadline that had to be met prevented further additions of women who should have been included. Women doing community organizing were included only if they were also affiliated to a peace research organization and were published authors. Three women scholars that I considered as belonging in the field (one from Bangladesh) responded that they did not belong and so were not included — to my regret.

Since the research orientations of the respondents differ widely; and six of them are primarily journalists and community practitioners, it becomes important to differentiate among the orientations, categorize them, and discuss separately the women belonging to each group. Originally I had three categories to cover three different orientations: (1) Mainstream Traditions of International Relations; (2) New Conceptual Frameworks; (3) New Social Order. The more I read what the traditionalists were saying the more I realized that they too wanted new conceptual frameworks, so the original categories (1) and (2) were combined, leaving two groups: New Conceptual Frameworks and New Social Order. All classifications are arbitrary, and some women who have been placed in category (1) might also have been placed in category (2). I have tried to classify women according to where the main emphasis of their work lies, where their priorities are.

Table 1 gives the country of origin, age range, occupation and range of numbers of publications for the 41 women, by research orientation with summary totals for the whole group at the bottom of the table. The New Framework group is the largest, with 25 members; there are 16 in the New Order group. Although only the age ranges are shown in the table, in fact 32-35 seems to be the modal age for each group. The youth of many of the researchers is surprising, until one considers that women are probably now entering this field in larger numbers than before. There are more older women in the New Frameworks than the New Social Order category. Some of these are lifelong professionals. Some of them, however, are recent entrants into professional life after an earlier career of homemaking and child rearing. Others have combined child rearing and professional life. As cv's do not always mention children, the number of these women who have also been parents is not known; at least half of them have. First and Third World countries contribute similar proportions of scholars to the New Frameworks and New Social Order groups.

Twelve of the women are professors and seventeen are research associates, making a total of 29 of the 41 or a majority in those categories. The rest are administrators (4), free-lance researchers (2), and journalists and community organizers (6). (Only action-oriented journalists are included in this last category. Several journalists are affiliated to research institutes and are therefore included under research associates.) One fourth of the New Frameworks group are professors, and all but one of the women have served in government ministries or on federal commissions. One third of the New Social Order women are professors, but only two have worked with the government. The greater youthfulness of this group makes it less likely that they have had an opportunity for government work as yet; they may also have less interest in such work. It should be noted that there was a relatively poor response rate from women currently working in government offices. Had more of them answered, it is possible that a traditionalist category would have been justified. Those from government who did answer, however, fell clearly into the New Framework group. The alternative explanation is that relatively few women in this field are traditionalists.

The information on their occupational status and involvement in consulting with governments suggests that the majority of these women are fairly well established professionally. Their publication record bears this out. Only the *range* in number of books, monographs and pamphlets, as distinct from articles and chapters in books, is given for each category in Table 1. In fact only seven of the 41 women have not published their own books/monographs/pamphlets: 2-3 books was the most frequently reported number. (Pamphlets are counted with books rather than with articles because academic pamphlets are published in this field more than in other social science fields, and an important pamphlet may have the status of a book.) All the women have published articles, from two to several hundred, with 12 being a frequently appearing number. For the journalists, there have been numerous unrecorded newspaper articles. In short, every one of the 41 women has some kind of publication record. In many cases they have published in fields other than that of disarmament/security, but because it was not always possible to distinguish between titles on this topic and titles referring to other kinds of research, only the total publication record for each woman was noted.

It is frequently said that there are 'no qualified women available' in the disarmament and security field. This study explodes that myth. Alva Myrdal, who served as cabinet minister for disarmament in Sweden in the 1960s; Betty Goetz Lall, who served as special assistant to the Deputy Director of the US Arms Control and Disarmament Agency in the 1960s and is currently the US representative on the UN Panel of Experts on the Relationship between Disarmament and International Security, and Mary Kaldor, who serves on the Minister of State's Advisory Panel on Disarmament for the UK are perhaps the women experts best known internationally, and they tend to be the ones most frequently called upon, but there are many more as this study shows. Why are they not used? Regarding the US scene Lall writes

> Women are largely excluded from the SALT negotiating process. No women are members of the negotiation teams of the two sides. They do not constitute part of the back-up team in the United States which helps to prepare the rationale for policy-formulations. We do not know the composition of the Soviet teams. There are no women on the Senate Committees which will vote or participate in the hearings on SALT II and only one woman on the staffs of the Committees who will have any major role in preparing for Senate consideration. Furthermore, among the public groups to present Congressional testimony, few women are likely to be representative of their organization.[2]

Considering that half the women in this study are from the USA, the US record of utilization of women is not impressive. In Norway, by contrast, with no internationally known women disarmament specialists, the Consultative Committee to the government on Arms Control and Disarmament contains 4 women among 16 members, or 1 in 4, with 5 additional women serving as accredited observers.[3] Sweden continues its tradition of women's leadership in disarmament affairs with the work of Inga Thorsson, Swedish Under-secretary of State, who chairs the UN Group of Governmental Experts on the Relationship between Disarmament and Development. The recently appointed US Commission on Proposals for the National Academy of Peace and Conflict Resolution contains only one woman among nine members.

What kinds of priorities and images of the future do women researchers have? This is discussed under the following headings: research agendas and the relevance of existing research; current and planned research of respondents; concepts of security and images of a disarmed world; and perspectives as women.

Research agendas and the relevance of existing research

New Conceptual Frameworks perspective

The more middle-of-the-road researchers see nuclear non-proliferation, detente diplomacy, arms trade (particularly arms trade with the Third World), arms control policy, European security relations and regional security problems in important Third World regions such as the Middle East, as major issues. All deplore the quality of existing research.

There is a general feeling among New Frameworks scholars that there has been too much mindless data gathering, particularly in arms trade research and research on the technicalities of curbing the arms race. 'So much effort has been spent on a search for details without any hypotheses to make the answers worth having.'*

> The academic research coming from the left in the disarmament field some-times sends cold chills up my spine, from the waste of time and talent it belies. I think of one study which passed across my desk recently — a statistical discussion of the nuclear war equivalents of deaths from starvation around the world today. The point is well taken, but to my mind, could have been made briefly and impressionistically just as well as on the basis of who knows how much computer time and human energy.

Searching for new approaches, some suggest that disarmament should be explored in terms of inevitability: 'Are there inner compulsions on the major military industrial complexes to restrain their arms manufacturing efforts?' 'The military themselves have a stake in not letting arms levels get out of hand, and we should know more about military incentives for control.' Almost every respondent proposed research on the concept of national security itself. Most scholars want questions to be asked about the political, economic and social conditions that would make disarmament possible, to replace the focus on technical curbs. There is widespread concern that research perspectives on disarmament are too Western: 'War is still perceived as an outbreak in the European theater.' Arms trade is also viewed too much from a First World perspective, the respondents say, with too many assumptions about 'valuable spinoffs' from the military for the Third World, and no solid research on 'how militaries affect the allocation of resources within individual societies and thus shape the development strategy planned.' A lack of research on militarization in neutral and non-aligned countries as a distinct type of phenomenon in the world militarization process is pointed out.

---

*In order to respect the necessity for some of the respondents not to be named, all quotations are given without attribution.

Many focus on the need to understand the contexts in which disarming processes can take place, and complain of our ignorance of the cultures of other states and regions. The Soviet Union is cited as an example of the depths of the ignorance, in spite of decades of study of the Soviet Union by US scholars. 'We have no knowledge of the constraints and interests operating internally in Soviet society, of their perceptions of security.' Scholars study negotiation processes far too little, and pay little attention to developing models of peaceful settlement of conflict. (The US Congressional Research Service volume, *Soviet diplomacy and negotiating behaviour,* 1979, a history of diplomacy since the Greek city states, is cited as a notable exception.)

In general, there is a call to move 'away from the pseudo-scientific, pseudo-technical approach to arms control and concentrate on the issues that affect each of us. . . . It's not the response time of radar or the trajectory of ballistic missiles but the economic and social cost of military expenditures and the consequences of miltary solutions to political problems that matter.' 'I wish the research community would devote more resources to investigating *how* specific disarmament measures would function in the real world.'

There are some harsh words, too, for the peace researchers, 'who write in journals read by like-minded academics . . . and have had little or no impact on world arms or military policy'. One scholar who has set out to master both technicalities of strategic studies and peace research skills lays out the following research agenda:

1. study of the many functions of arms;
2. discrimination among functions, to understand how profound, and in what ways interrelated, the roots are, and to prepare a set of priorities for conversion;
3. dialogue between the military and arms control researchers on appropriate and necessary functions of arms;
4. take the initiative away from the military in planning for future military security, so that arms control design becomes part of the security design.

An additional area of study, on which most respondents agreed, was the vagaries and ambivalences of public opinion on disarmament versus defence and defence versus aggression, which parallel vagaries in national legislative bodies. The interrelationships of these shifting and ambivalent views with governmental policy-making need to be studied.

Alva Myrdal, the scholar who has been in the disarmament field the longest, emphasizes in *The game of disarmament* the interrelationships between secrecy and militarization, and the importance of publishing yearbooks detailing arms expenditures, military budgets and arms trade for every nation. Many of the respondents in this study are in fact contributing to that kind of documentation. Their very immersion in such data has led them to call for contexts in which the data can be put, hypotheses and models that will organize information meaningfully. There can be no argument that both are needed. Myrdal's own primary concern is precisely for context. She sees:

> the risk of an increasing militarization of the world. Nowhere is yet given the proper estimates of all effects of our pervasive preoccupation with military concerns, reflected in how we customarily — in press, parliaments, and even at universities — nowadays discuss foreign policy and international affairs more and more in terms of military strategies and capabilities.[4]

New Social Order perspective

The scholar who most clearly bridges what distance there is between the New Framework and New Order perspectives is also the one most often referred to by scholars in both groups: Ruth Leger Sivard. Her *World military and social expenditures* has been published annually since 1974 with the support of a consortium of foundations and organizations concerned with disarmament. Her painstaking and scholarly documentation also lays the basis for a profound questioning of the existing social order, which in the 1979 volume she calls a 'theatre of the absurd':

> There is an unreality about the world military situation in 1979 that begins with its sheer size. Few of us can follow with interest the incredible numbers involved: millions of people in peacetime armies; trillions of dollars in wasted resources; nuclear overkill sufficient to destroy every city in the world many times over.
>
> How much more difficult will it be for the historians of the future to find reality in this militarized world of 1979. How will their best computers deal with the balance of terror, the specialized language of the weaponeers, the gaming of megadeaths, the military grotesqueries of today.
>
> What kind of world was it, they will try to imagine, that celebrated the Year of the Child while adding to a vast pool of deadly nuclear waste that would be its most long-lasting legacy to hundreds of generations to come?
>
> Did their civil servants seriously play out war games that no one could win, but that required aggressor and defender alike to sacrifice hundreds of millions of their own people in nuclear deaths?
>
> When nuclear weapons were developed and there proved to be no defence against them, was it self-deception or a sense of irony that led governments to rename their war ministries 'defence' ministries?
>
> After the leading defence minister stated that nuclear war between the two superpowers would destroy in hours all that the two nations had built over centuries, where is the record of the public outcry against making even more such weapons?
>
> How did the nuclear powers plan to control the prevailing winds over

Europe to ensure that in event of war radioactive fallout would not blow back on their allies and themselves, killing them as freely as their enemies?

Who were the leaders who were prepared to march millions of young men against battlefield weapons that would blow them into radioactive dust?

Of course, the historians will conclude, it was not the real world of 1979, it was pure theatre, global fantasy, a diversion no doubt from intractable social problems.[5]

In general, there is a fairly complete rejection of current research approaches, even the most 'liberal' one, and an attempt to formulate new research priorities. That real issues are not made visible through the kinds of research undertaken is the general premise.

The new international economic order is not generally seen as offering fruitful research approaches. The basic needs approach to the world economic order, as utilized by Chichilnisky in her work with the Bariloche world model[6], is more congenial to this group. Generally, the search among these scholars is for new research themes that will dismantle the existing military industrial order without setting premature constraints on an emergent order. Kaldor's writings, for example, strike a theme representative of this group in pointing out the consequences of taking the position that social and political goals cannot be achieved through military means. The decision to opt out of a type of development based on the military industrial complex may mean a drastic shift in priorities

from capital-intensive to labor-intensive technologies, from town to countryside, and from international to local initiatives. Undertaken on a sufficiently wide scale, such a policy would induce a re-examination of the prevailing ideology among advanced industrialized countries.[7]

Localism is seen as a new approach to security, reducing dependence on large-scale systems. Localism is a strong research theme for this group, exploring structures and social roles that will make a disarmed world possible. The 'barefoot researchers' project of the Pacific-Asia Resources Center in Japan with which one respondent is associated involves creating a new role for researchers, conceptually analagous to that of the barefoot doctor role in community health in China; it researches existing military and economic dependency structures in Asia and seeks to make visible at the grassroots level the ingredients of a self-sufficient demilitarized social order for the communities of Asia. Our respondent acknowledges that she has few women colleagues because of the difficulties for Asian women of assuming such deviant roles.

Several women in this group move back and forth between the roles of journalist, community organizer and research associate in an academic research institute. In a different part of the world, one woman works with displaced farmers in a setting of considerable physical danger, where there is a daily possibility of disappearance by kidnapping, yet she also serves on international bodies of scholars. Her concern with disarmament is focused on a concern to disarm the oppressors, and to build local communities that are not dependent on oppressors. Another Third World scholar sees development as inextricably linked with militarization, and pronounces liberation, not development, as the name of peace. Terrorism of scholars and destruction of data files are not unknown in her part of the world. A student of how development has destroyed the capacities for local autonomy and local problem-solving in the rural areas of her region, her focus is on the development of local alternatives to dependency on the military/industrial complex. Among these respondents, the research orientation towards grass-roots capabilities is found equally among women in Third World, European and North American settings.

Another theme is that of building a new culture, free from patriarchy and the techniques of dominance associated with the male cultures of East and West, North and South alike. One strong set of new consciousness themes comes from Italy, home of much political violence, with a focus on the consciousness of children and how a new non-military order can be built with the knowledge that comes from research on children's attitudes. Women with experience in teaching in primary and secondary schools come to their later research roles with a keen interest in the learning process. They see this as central to the development of new curricula focused on social skills and understandings which will produce a generation capable of replacing military threat by a political diplomacy based on social insight and objective problem-solving competence.

A tendency on the part of some scholars to emphasize research on the values of a feminine as compared to a masculine culture in creating a disarmed world is countered by others, who point out that women are socialized to maintain the military culture as much as men, and that research is needed on the structures of power which create pathological female cultures. Research on the behaviour of *men* in war, and on the phenomenon of soldiers on the battlefield who deliberately aim not to kill, etc., is proposed to help dismantle premature linkages of maleness and war. Research on alternatives to the values and institutions of the military/industrial complex is also a major concern.

As one scholar, a specialist in non-violence, puts it

> the main issues in disarmament are not the technical ones to which so much attention is given, nor even political ones (in the usual sense of that term), but social and psychological. Yet practically nobody pays attention to these latter topics. Moverover, I think research on non-violent *alternatives* is crucial. When we have seriously explored some non-violent alternatives, we

may get some measure of disarmament. I don't think it will happen the other way around. By non-violent alternatives I mean such things as non-violent conflict resolution, non-violent (civilian) defence, unarmed peacekeeping, etc. — but also economic structures that do not destroy, new kinds of social relationships, etc.

I also am not sure how much research we need in the conventional sense of that term. I think we need to *think*. I think we need to act creatively (which includes experimenting with alternatives). I think we need to understand better the ultimate sources of our anxieties and fears (which may involve some 'research'). But I happen not to think that we will be saved by 'social science' as that term is ordinarily construed.

We suffer mainly from a paralysis of will. Most people do not think we are capable of creating a relatively non-violent world.

This same scholar goes on to point out that the number of weapons around do not determine how non-violent a world we have: 'arms are not the key thing: human behaviour is.'

Current and planned research of respondents

When it is considered that researchers are not necessarily free to work on their own preferred research topics, the research reported in Table 2 corresponds surprisingly well with their own earlier statements about the kinds of research that ought to be done. The topics are grouped under the themes (I) studies of the military, (II) development studies, (III) arms control and disarmament, and (IV) disarmament strategies, non-violent alternatives. Half the topics involve studies of the military and of arms control and disarmament processes. Development studies, closely linked both with military studies and with disarmament, provide another 11, and if the three are lumped together it could be said that ⅝ of the topics are centered on arms, arms control and development. This fits the general pattern of what peace researchers do. What is of special interest is that nearly 40% of the topics represent research on strategies for a disarmed world and non-violent alternatives.

Since in general the New Frameworks scholars listed 2-4 research topics and the New Order scholars 1-2, this means that a number of the New Framework scholars are looking seriously, together with the New Order people, at institutions, structures, processes and beliefs associated with disarmament as a strategy and a less violent world as an outcome; 11 are looking at some form of localism, 7 at alternative value systems and 5 each at behavioural skills and the curriculum required to learn peaceableness. These are also traditional topics for peace researchers, but not in such numbers.

There would appear to be a significant tilting of the research concerns of the respondents toward a study of that which is needed to

Table 2. **Current and planned research of respondents, rank ordered within research areas**

	No. reporting this category	Total
I. Studies of the military		
1 Arms transfer to Third World	5	
2 Nuclear proliferation, nuclear safety	4	
3 Worldwide military R and D programmes	3	
4 Trade in conventional arms	2	
5 Reporting of military expenditures	2	
6 Military education of youth	2	
7 Comparative economic structures in military establishments	1	
8 Nuclear arms race	1	20
II. Development Studies		
1 Disarmament and development	7	
2 Ecological impact of arms on development: food, environment	3	
3 Linkage of economic and military exploitation	2	12
III. Arms control and disarmament		
1 Alternative international security systems, UN reforms, world models	5	
2 Policy analysis: arms control impacts, security studies	4	
3 Soviet behaviour, US-SU negotiation, SALT	4	
4 Arms control diplomacy and military force planning	2	
5 Arms control and violence	2	
6 Economics of arms control	1	
7 Political strategies for disarmament	1	
8 Unilateral restraints in military force planning	1	20
IV. Disarmament strategies, non-violent alternatives		
1 Grass roots movements, localism, organized non-violence	11	
2 Alternative cultures, alternative value systems	7	
3 Behavioural skills of conflict management, non-violence	5	
4 Curriculum development, education for disarmament world order	5	28
Total		80

make a demilitarized world work. A study of the individual research biographies of respondents indicates that a significant number of them do, as one described, 'follow a zigzag approach', weaving back and forth between research at the macrolevel on structural problems, and research in the area of changes of values and behaviour. While the structural functionalists are in the majority and the neo-Marxists in the minority, a number of the women do not fit neatly into either of those categories. They tend to be more Meadian or social-psychological in their perspective, allowing for emergent processes and the creation of new reality through new imagery.

Concepts of security, and images of a disarmed world

All respondents agree that security must be redefined, and many feel that scholars have failed to research the phenomenon of fear and insecurity as experienced by the public and dealt with daily by policy-makers. A policy analyst suggested that security depends on the ability to avoid unpleasant surprises, and thus depends on a good two-way system of communication with other actors in the environment. Another suggested that it lies in knowing one has good problem-solving skills, good mechanisms for collaborative action, good trust-building capabilities; another that justice, and liberation from oppression are necessary for security. Others saw security as something for which individuals had to assume their own responsibility: 'Our security can't be turned over to others. It is a state of mind'.

No one suggested that security depended on arms. Many agreed that absolute levels of destructive hardware pose more dangers than the risks of military imbalances *vis-à-vis* other nations. Reducing present armed forces to the size of police forces, with strong inhibitions as to their use, was seen as a way to repair the concept of security in relation to military force. The general thrust of the comments was in the direction of developing problem-solving and communication skills to replace the use of force, and to redefining national security goals in the context of international security and wellbeing. New definitions of national identity, new awareness of a broader human identity and a reordering of value priorities which involves willingness to live with uncertainty, are seen as involved. One repondent saw the development of human rights doctrines and policies as assisting in this process.

Many respondents commented that it was difficult or impossible to visualize a disarmed world. Of those who could do so, several saw it as much like the present world, but minus military capacity and with a better functioning of economic, social and political capacities. Most of those who could visualize a post-military world saw it as highly differentiated, localist and egalitarian, in which human needs would be met by appropriate technology at the local level, with minimally functioning international organizations handling residual redistributive requirements. Communication networks would be of major importance. The post-military society would be the information society. The bibliography lists the books respondents mentioned as giving an image of post-military society.

No one thought major steps toward disarmament would take place by the year 2000. Most respondents saw a long difficult period ahead, with small gains possible at most. Their views are sober, realistic, yet without despair. 'This is the way things are, this is what we have to work with,' is the message.

Perspectives as women

Only 20 of the 41 answered the question whether women approached disarmament in distinctive ways. Several were clearly irritated by the question, and all, no matter how they answered, felt they had earned the right to be thought of as scholars, not women who were scholars. Nine gave an unequivocal 'no' to the question; of these, two said education erases gender differences. Several mentioned hard-line women colleagues, and pointed out that this was the way to succeed in the field. On the other hand, 6 thought there were differences, and 5 thought there might be differences, a total of 11, thus dividing the respondents fairly evenly into *pros* and *cons*. The 'maybe's' noted that women are outsiders in the arms control field, have a marginal status, tend to get less absorbed in the excitement of the power game, and on the whole appear more objective. In meetings and conferences their interventions are said to be more to the point, less embroidered with rhetoric. Those who had a clear feminist perspective saw women as having developed different skills and different sensitivities because of their social roles as women, and therefore as more likely to 'humanize' the data they worked with, attempting more interpretation and trying for more reality testing. They felt that women were more inclined to see the interconnections between militarization, violence and other features of social institutions. They would be more aware of the 'ridiculousness of the intense preoccupation with military superiority', as one put it.

Conclusion

The 41 scholars who responded to this survey are professionally active women with strong career commitments, representing two major research orientations toward disarmament and world order: (1) the search for new conceptual frameworks and a better use of social science disciplines in seeking solutions to arms problems for a society that is basically ameliorable, and (2) the search for new social structures and a new social order, rejecting the existing order as an obstacle to the achievement of peace and justice. Both groups see existing research as bogged down in meaningless detail and lacking significant concepts and hypotheses, and propose research that will be more global in orientation, less parochially Western, with more attention to the conditions for disarmament and to the complex interrelationships between the military and other aspects of society. They also propose more attention to process and to problem-solving and conflict-management skills. In general the New Framework scholars are engaged in trying to make data collection more meaningful, and in developing new models to describe military research and development, arms control processes, and successful international negotiation. In general the New Order scholars are focusing on alternative models of the world system with strong localist components, on the grass roots ingredients of a new order, and on the development of new institutions, new values, and new behavioural and problem-solving skills in the arenas of school, community, academia and government.

These women are not optimistic about immediate prospects for disarmament. They see the process as long and complex, but are willing to work for it over the long haul. They are divided on the issue of whether they have special perspectives as women, all uniting on the view that they have earned the right to be thought of as scholars, not women who are scholars. Those who felt a difference attributed it to their marginal status in the field and their different socialization experience, concluding that these factors made them more effective scholars, in that it enhanced objectivity and gave them more analytic power while also pushing them toward more attention to the interpretation of data in its human dimensions and its human consequences.

There are sufficient significant implications for disarmament research in the materials collected for this study to warrant closing with the suggestion that a conference of women scholars on disarmament, security and world order would be a productive enterprise for an international body to undertake, in collaboration with the appropriate UN agencies.

References

1. Daniels A.K. Development of feminist networks in the professions. *Annals New York Acad. Sci.,* 1979, **77**, (2). 215-227
2. Lall B.G. SALT and the coming public debate. *Women Lawyers Journal,* 1979, **65**, (2)
3. Hansen S.R. and Mykletum J. *Nedrustning: visjon og mulighet.* Flekkefjord, S. Bern Hegland AS, 1978

4. Myrdal A. Letters on disarmament. *Bull. Atomic Scientists,* 1979, **35,** March, 77
5. Sivard R. *World military and social expenditures 1979.* Leesburg, Virginia, World Priorities, Inc., 1979
6. Chichilnisky G. Development patterns and the international order. *J. Internat Affairs,* 1977, **31** (2)
7. Kaldor M. Arms and dependence. In Sharp J. (Ed), *Opportunities for disarmament,* Washington DC, Carnegie Endowment for International Peace, 1978

Bibliography on post military world

Piercy M. *Woman on the edge of time*
Huxley A. *Island*
Bahai and Sufi writings
Vacca R. *The coming dark age*
Pederson H. *et al, Revolt from the middle* (in Swedish)
Sivard R. *World military and social expenditures*
Johanson R. *Toward a dependable peace*
Sharp G. *Politics of non-violent action*
Boston Study Group. *The price of defense*
Mische G. and P. *Toward a human world order*
Boulding E. *Stable peace*
Mead M. *Cooperation and competition among primitive peoples*
Leguin U. *The word for world is forest*

2. Can we educate for disarmament in the present world order?

Robin Burns, *School of Education, La Trobe University, Melbourne*

On the long list of crucial factors facing the world today, that of survival is perhaps the most basic. And two aspects of that survival are development, as a positive process of change in both the material and non-material conditions of our existence as individuals in society, and power, which can be seen as the struggle to gain control of resources, human and non-human, to further the interests of individuals or groups against others. An important element in the exercise of power is thus control over the development process and direction of that control, dominant groups not only maintaining their own interests in it as foremost but both limiting the access of others to the means of development and determining the directions which others' development can and should take.

Three important aspects of power and development are the means by which dominant groups gain and maintain their power, the resources used for this and the effects on decreasing the alternatives available to the dominated for their own development. The first is largely a question of force. A breakthrough in thinking about this problem has been the recognition that it is not only direct but structural violence, exercised through the control of institutions from politics and economics to education and the media, which is used in the process of domination. The second then requires an examination of the ways in which these institutions are used, and the effects on development of the deployment of resources for the maintenance of control by and enhancement of, the dominant group(s). The third can be seen as on the one hand, the concrete withholding of possibilities, through direct or indirect means, and on the other the convincing of others that the dominant group's definitions and actions are the best, only feasible or most desirable for the maintenance of individual and social life.

A current target in the diagnosis of the world's ills and the analysis of the operation of power is the arms race. Thus disarmament is seen as a solution to war, the threat of war and all that that entails, providing not only a 'nicer' world but resources which could be better employed for improving the living conditions and material standards of humankind. And education is seen as an important means of spreading the message of disarmament, whether the content of the message is a decrease in inter- and even intra-individual aggressiveness or a universal casting aside of military weapons. As will be shown here, there is certainly a direct link between the use of resources for the arms race and a lack of resources for the solution of basic problems of human development. However, an adequate diagnosis of the problems and the proffering of solutions involves a significantly more far-reaching analysis of power, the industrial/military complex, and politics and economics on a national and international scale than is undertaken in discussions of disarmament, and a linking of psychological with social, cultural, economic and political factors. Further, the use of education as a tool for bringing about a more desirable world needs similar examination, to determine the extent to which existing educational institutions can be used to produce new outcomes in terms of human understanding and ability to act to bring about change, and the forms and processes which alternative educational means might take.

The task of diagnosing, let alone envisaging alternatives to the present ills, can either be oversimplified or made into such a complex exercise that it becomes overwhelming. Since the focus of this book is on education, I will start by outlining some dimensions of the current debate about the role of education in social change, and suggest some dimensions which an educational process, as distinct from an educational system, might have to increase people's power over their own development. As a backdrop against which the need for this reorientation of education can be seen, and as a suggestion for the dimensions over which the content needs to range, the second section presents a diagnosis of the state of thinking about development and its relationship to issues of arms and violence.

Education

Every society has established means for the socialization of new members into the norms and values of the group, and for transmitting accumulated knowledge from one generation to the next. Since the Industrial Revolution, formal schools have been established in the industrialized world, and translated elsewhere to varying degrees through colonialism, under the control of the State for the instruction of the young in various types and amounts of socially useful knowledge and skills. Sight should not be lost, however, of specialized institutions of much longer history for the inculcation of religious and military knowledge, values and skills, and centres of higher learning for the refinement and edification of the elite, both as individuals and as a class. A further development, particularly evident this century, which competes with the formal and informal channels of socialization for influence over the masses, is the media in various forms. The individual is thus subject to ever-increasing circles of influence, from the family to the owners of the satellite telecommunication systems. While it is a matter of examining concrete cases to see the extent to which the messages from each circle confirm or contradict each other, it is argued here that:

1. the direction of influence is in general greater from the more powerful to the less powerful circles, since greater resources are at their disposal, including the use or threat of use of violence to back up the messages;

2. an important implication of the existence of these multiple sources of influence is the fragmentation of individual and group life into public and private spheres, which may be held separate and, even where they overlap, the possibilities for the 'private' to influence the 'public' are far less than the reverse.

An example

To see some of the ways in which these influences operate, the case of a 14-year-old girl in 1980 in the city of Melbourne, Australia, can be elaborated. Her father is Australian born, of Irish Catholic background, and her mother is Italian born, having arrived in Australia at the age of 15 and worked in a small factory until the first child, a boy, was born. The father is a boiler maker, working for award wages in a small engineering firm, where he is also the union representative; the mother no longer works outside the home, although the family would be able to move to a 'better' suburb if she was earning an income. Her family considers that her marriage to a working-class Australian is responsible for the failure to live in the nice, outer-suburban bungalows to which most of her sisters and brothers have moved, even though they privately admit that they feel isolated and out of their depths away from the flats and tenements where most new immigrants begin their lives in Australia.

Maria, the 14-year-old, feels as if she lives at least three separate lives. At home, particularly with her mother and grandmother, she is expected to speak Italian and is constantly being told that she is in danger of becoming 'just like those rough Australian kids next door', so that no nice boy will ever want to marry her. With her friends, she has become 'Marie'; although they are a mixed group, Australians predominate and she tries hard to cover up when her family will not let her go out at night with the others, although the same restrictions do not apply to her brothers. At school she has given up trying to explain that she was born in Australia because in the eyes of the other kids, her complexion makes her forever a 'wog', and she sometimes becomes confused when the teachers call her 'Mary'. She tries hard at school, but is often told that her English expression is poor (Dad does not talk very much at home, and she knew very little English when she started school); she would like to learn Italian, like her cousins at the Convent school, but her father has insisted that she should go to the government school where the bright kids learn French and the others struggle with British history. She only becomes confused when as an effect of the new attention being given to migrants and multicultural education, her school decides to hold an ethnic week, where suddenly she is expected to take part in folk-dancing and projects about ancient Rome, which are as remote from her private world as the culture of the Aborigines (about which she is also expected to learn).

There are so many conflicting messages! Mum doesn't mind what she watches on television (three of the five channels are owned by huge private companies, with many national and international interests and the three daily newspapers are owned by two of the three companies controlling the television), even though most of the films are American and the advertisements scream at her every 10 minutes that to be one of the crowd, she should be out every night, and spending her (non-existent) pocket money on a variety of entertainments and products which certainly play little part in the life of her family. Still, it's better than the family fights when Dad has been on strike and tries to convince her mother that they would be a lot better off under a Labor government, while her brother unkindly reminds him of the strike which took place when Labor lifted restrictions on Third World imports and a lot of workers lost their jobs.

Although she is popular with her friends, she is running out of excuses for not going out at night, and she doesn't know what to think when they talk about leaving school to get jobs when they turn 15. She knows that most of her teachers expect that all the children will leave, and as she sits through the boring lessons, mechanically writing assignments on topics that have no interest for her, her ambitions to matriculate and perhaps go on to further study evaporate. She knows that her father is having a struggle to keep her brother at the university since his income is just over the limit for government support (the four younger children are not taken into account), while her mother is convinced that a secretary's job will enable her to meet the 'right' sort of young man. And her poor marks in English don't help: it had been different the year before when she overcame her fears of being labelled a *spazzo* and attended the rather muddled remedial and migrant English class, but the teacher who was so encouraging has gone (she was part-time, so was dismissed when the Education Department announced its new finance cuts for schools and no one else had the

training or interest to form a new programme for the school the following year).

With a sigh, she turns to her assignment — listing the causes of
World War II — but is ill-prepared for the family row when her confused question about Mussolini brings forth a string of anti-union,
anti-communist invective from her mother, who is beginning to sound
like a TV commercial for capitalism as she justifies her family's migrat-
ion and material ambitions, while her father, flicking through the
mounting bills, defends his decision not to be transferred into the new,
army contract job. The wages would have been higher, but the union
has banned it, and although he does not understand their analysis of
imperialism and the international arms trade as a reason for the ban,
he is determined that at least his increasingly alienated family will
understand that here he is the boss.

An analysis

Despite the rhetoric of many governments, international agencies and
reformers, the so-called 'accident of birth' still plays an important role
in determining the future life-chances of the greatest proportion of
people today. Race and gender are established, as well as a number of
secondary social characteristics, which from the moment of birth
become complexly interwoven. And both the existence of, as well as
the particular characteristics inherent in, formal educational systems,
play an important part in the formation of individuals and their operation in society. The increasingly recognized likelihood that the formal
educational system is a dependent institution can be seen to account
for both its function to reproduce the wider social order, and its failure
to do so perfectly: it is neither a leading institution for social change
nor does every individual receive the same messages and take the anti-
cipated future directions that in general could have been expected.
Thus, for some, upward mobility does become possible, while for
others, often designated the failures in the system, the very fact of their
failure may mean a resistance to the specific messages and hence
improper social reproduction which carries within it the possibility for
change. However, sight should not be lost of the fact that, while
educational rewards may diminish in significance the further one
moves from the academic apparatus, the coincidence between the culture of the dominant classes, the culture transmitted in formal
educational institutions and the system of economic rewards and power
in society is at a high level, at least within the industrialized capitalist
world[1].

It can therefore be maintained, as Bernstein states, that:

> How a society selects, classifies, distributes, transmits and evaluates the

education knowledge it considers to be public, reflects both the distribution of power and the principles of social control.[2]

Three 'message systems' can be distinguished, through which formal educational knowledge is realized: curriculum, pedagogy and evaluation. 'Curriculum defines what counts as valid knowledge, pedagogy defines what counts as a valid transmission of knowledge, and evaluation defines what counts as a valid realization of this knowledge on the part of the taught.'[3] Through the examination of these three message systems and their interrelationships, we discover the ways in which particular forms of knowledge are selected and transmitted and the model held out by society of what a successful product of the formal educational system should know, as well as how knowledge and behaviour associated with the manipulation of knowledge is rewarded or punished. Conversely, other types of knowledge and ways of knowing are learnt to be wrong, irrelevant or relegated to the private sphere. Although there is an increasing breakdown throughout the world between the amounts and types of knowledge consumed and later social rewards in terms of employment, the idea of a relationship between formal education, ability to participate in the labour force, and social rewards with their concomitants in the evaluation of individual worth, remains as a justification for certification-based employment and payment.

This approach to the social utility of a particular type of education has been labelled the 'banking concept'.[4] Insofar as the message systems have been selected by dominant groups in society in order to legitimize their positions of power in the current structure of society and to provide an ideological justification of that structure, they represent the reality of those groups. As a major way in which other groups can penetrate the 'mysteries' of the dominant groups, the acquisition of school knowledge can be represented as a process of demystification. The reality, however, is more likely to be that the knowledge imparted is further mystified by the frameworks and methods by which it is transmitted, aided by the incomplete transmission of the keys to the dominant structure, norms and values of society.

This process can be illustrated in the following example, which is quoted at length because it not only depicts a number of features of formal education, especially for members of subordinate groups, but also gives insight into the gaps in communication between teacher and learner and suggests aspects of the 'hidden curriculum' which will be discussed later.

> My second lesson is in social studies. The teacher is blandly standing at the front of the class, with the kids lounging around the separate tables which are scattered about the room. The theme is Government and Authority, which the boys carry through their first three years of humanities work. The

idea is to begin with studies of institutions like the family and lead out eventually to considerations of the United Nations, etc. Generally it's assumed that twelve-year-olds will be working at 'family' levels; by third year on issues in world government. Today the teacher is talking about local government and its similarity with authority patterns in the family. I mean, the teacher is talking. Behind him, a blackboard sketch of civil powers. Before him, about twenty boys who can hardly keep their eyes open. A few make an effort to look in the teacher's direction. Now and then the teacher pauses to ask a question which no one bothers to answer. There is no insolence in this class; no sign of that repressed resentment which prickles classes in military regimes. At the end of the lesson the boys simply leave the room as quickly as possible. The lesson is the stock tragedy of conventional schooling: a teacher begins with a good plan but there is a chasm between the plan and what is in a student's head.[5]

From this example it can be seen that another aspect of the schools' message systems needs to be taken into account in gaining a perspective on what they do both for society and for their pupils. The concept of the 'hidden curriculum' can be a shorthand way of expressing these functions. In terms of the message systems, it is not only what seems to be going on in classrooms and the intentions of the teachers, but the ways in which students perceive and react to the situation (even by 'switching off'), that determine the effects of formal schooling on pupils' lives. Holt has shown how a significant portion of learning is absorbed in finding strategies, including the use of behavioural cues from the teacher, to obtain 'right answers' and hence avoid punishment.[6] And even the most interesting and apparently relevant lesson, presented in a lively manner with participation and enjoyment goals, cannot be isolated from the total schooling experience and may be perceived as threatening by the students because it upsets the techniques they have evolved to cope with the whole situation in their education.

It is thus not only the content, process and assessment in formal education, but also the structures, which transmit social messages to participants. The structure of the learning process; the relations between teacher and pupils and between the pupils themselves, and the relations between the units of learning; the divisions in time (class periods, 'progress' through sequential stages based on chronological age), space (the physical arrangements in classrooms and the school as a whole, as well as the usual physical separation of school as an institution from the rest of society) and meaning (the division into subjects and units of work and their interrelations — or lack thereof — with each other or with anything else in the realities of students): all convey messages. To these should be added the overall structure of a school, including the ways in which decisions are made, the structure and functioning of the educational system as a whole and the relationships between each element as well as between the whole institution and the rest of society, if one is to see the messages about society, the role of education and the effects on individuals, which schools, as the interface between young people and society, propagate.

Overwhelmingly, formal educational systems reflect and reproduce social systems. Thus, an individual's social position will tend to be reinforced and he/she will be provided with a set of legitimations and self-evaluations for this in the process of schooling. It is this dual justification of the social *status quo* and of the individual's position and worth in it that is the hidden curriculum (hidden insofar as the range of aims and justifications given for the existence of schools usually refer to loftier goals, such as individual development and social progress, and thus attempt to mask the actual functions and effects). It is further argued here that, given the above, change in the message systems of content, pedagogy and assessment will singly, or even together, have little effect if the wider system is not also changed. The dissonance between message systems created by change in anything less than the whole package is unlikely to be resolved by individual learners in a way which enables them to change the underlying power system.

An alternative

It has been considered necessary to provide some analysis and a critique of formal educational systems — because it is maintained it is unlikely that attempts to change the content of formal education, with or without changes in the pedagogical processes for learning the new content, will bring about social change unless the educational system and the social system also come under scrutiny. Educational reforms in most countries in the past 20 years can be seen as reactions on the part of dominant groups to satisfy dissidents, in order to maintain the former's positions of power, and formal education now seems to be in a continual state of credibility crisis: on the one hand failing to fulfil the hopes held out to the consumers of education, and on the other providing a convenient scapegoat to governments and other interest groups for some of the economic and normative problems of society.

As an alternative to tinkering with the formal educational system while leaving the wider social context untouched, the following suggestions are put forward. Leaving aside for the time being the most appropriate locus in which the alternatives can best take place, it is asserted that first, education should be a process of leading out — of present realities to something new[7]. Thus, the starting point is consciousness of 'one's own situation as an individual in relation to the total situation in the past, present and future'[8]. Secondly, not only what is learned but the way it is learned is vital: the types of communication established between learner and environment (including the 'teacher'), between learners, and between components (ideas, feelings and actions) will determine the formation of the individual as individual and as social being, and the possibilities for generating knowledge and applying it to life in society. Using the foregoing framework of message systems, the following suggestions regarding their nature are made.

'Curriculum'/content. A characteristic of human beings is their ability to communicate not only directly but through the use of symbols. To a greater or lesser extent each individual gains knowledge deemed appropriate for his/her functioning in the social group of which he/she is a part. This knowledge concerns both practical techniques and skills as well as behaviour, attitudes and values related to the way the group works and the function of the individual in it. Groups vary in the extent to which the unique knowledge acquired by an individual, or his/her unique interpretation of or action in association with that knowledge is allowed expression, and may become incorporated into the stock of knowledge of the group; variation is also apparent in the extent to which the acquired knowledge relates only to the group in question or to the progressively wider circles which affect the lives of individuals. It can however be assumed that an overriding theme in the knowledge–transmission process is the subjugation of the individual to the group for the latter's survival, with individual survival in most situations only a subordinate theme.

In order to enable the individual to become self-determining (and it is assumed here that a healthy group or society incorporating principles of freedom and justice can only be built by self-determining individuals) awareness of the individual and his/her knowledge of past and present reality is the starting point for further learning. This awareness entails making conscious that knowledge so that reflection about it can take place — reflection with others so that the individual can develop and change his/her map of the world, understanding of the way that reality has come about, and his/her own and others' reactions to it, as a basis for pursuing the search for new knowledge. The content of the learning task before a group is thus not a predetermined set of facts and formulas, but emerges in the process of dialogue between learners. The ingredients in that dialogue should represent the range of human concerns and activities — feelings, values and actions, and cognitive processes — and not just abstract ideas or so-called objective facts.

If determining what we know and sharing that knowledge is the first step, the second is developing a critique of that knowledge, the way it has been acquired and its personal and social implications. At least two sources for such a critique can be distinguished, action and reflection, and their dialectical interrelationships must be affirmed as a basis for the knowledge-producing process. If the present definition of valid knowledge (which is Western in origin and an interest-based selection from all possible types of human knowledge, underpinned by a political and scientific ideology backed by superior power) is to be challenged, two points need to be considered. The first is that the perspectivist nature of knowledge must be recognized, so that the dangers of totalizing a single perspective and presenting it as the whole can be averted. The second is that the relationship between knowledge and interest or the socio-political aspect of knowledge also needs recognition:

> It is being realized that not taking a political position, not making a moral commitment, is not neutral: it is making a commitment — to the support and continuation of the system of which one is a part and within which one is working. . . . If one does not 'notice' oppression or injustice or exploitation because one is only a scientist and science does not concern itself with political issues, then one is being myopic and self-deluding about objectivity. Ultimately amorality is immorality.[9]

The third step in shaping the content of educational experiences is to ensure that they are participatory. While discussion of this will be considered in the next section, it is emphasised here that the conscious and critical participation of the individual in his/her own society's development is the aim of education. It therefore follows that: 'the processes of rapid change in which most communities and societies are involved at present, anywhere, can probably most fruitfully be studied and understood by participating in those change processes, *from within and from below*[10]. Thus 'gaining awareness of forces which to some extent determine one's fate is the initiation of a process of liberation.'[11] One way of conceiving this participatory approach to knowledge, learning and change is to see it as a problem of locating the individual between the intersecting dimensions of inner and outer space (i.e. from the individual-psychological to the social realms of reflection and action) and past and future time[12].

The content of education thus becomes a negotiation of starting points and a discovery through sharing. If that content is not related to the realities of the educands' lives, no matter how urgent that content appears to the educator, the temptation will be to impose knowledge without developing the critical tools of understanding for action and refinement of action through participation in and transformation of the present realities.

Pedagogy/process. It follows that there is an indissoluble link between what is learned and how it is learned. Freedom can be neither handed to the bewildered individual, who is then expected to practise it, nor imposed from above or outside. And while ideas and concepts provide part of the basis for action, learning also takes place through the social and emotional environment: the structures of knowledge transmitted and the structure in which it is transmitted constitute part of the learning experience.

An essential feature of education for conscious and critical participation in society is thus a conscious and critical participation in the learning process. This clearly implies the establishment of dialogues, or rather 'multilogues', between participants to enable horizontal communication to take place, and the establishment of agreement about the ways in which decisions are to be made. Such an approach is in direct contrast to the banking notion of education, since it implies that the learner is an active subject, who contributes to both transmitted and generated knowledge and to the learning process, and that learning results in individual and social change, i.e. the knowledge is used for social and not just individual/sectoral ends. This is so even if for immediate purposes it is the empowering of oppressed groups that is an explicit aim of education. This is an important contrast to most current formal education, where the outcome, if not the intention is the exclusion of many groups from full participation in society through the meting out of certain forms of preselected knowledge in specific ways. That process can even be seen in some recent educational reforms, where well-intentioned efforts to provide alternative experiences in formal education further preclude, or have little effect on, the life-chances of the educands, or where the learning process, regardless of the 'enlightened' content, reinforces individual feelings of helplessness and lack of social worth.

It follows that new approaches to the role of teacher and learner are required. This is perhaps best expressed through the concept of partnership, with equal participation. Perhaps the greatest problem in conceiving an alternative to present education is on the one hand in maintaining that everyone has some knowledge about a situation and that those most enmeshed in it know most about it, while on the other recognizing the limits of the knowledge and understandings of unreflected experience, and hence the role of particular people in assisting with the provision of resources, techniques and skills. It is argued therefore that it is not the presence of an outside facilitator, that poses problems of domination and manipulation, but the type of relationship established between that person and group members. If that relationship is open, enlightened by a readiness to learn as well as to give, and a willingness to take the group's perceptions of reality as a starting point, this can provide a model for desirable relationships on the wider social stage.

A third feature of new pedagogical processes is the need for active participation. If the idea of the individual as active subject is to be realized, and if the dialectic between action and reflection is to be practised, the involvement of the whole person and of all persons is required. The form that such action takes will vary according to issues being considered, and may range from the individual grasping knowledge in such a way that it becomes a reflected part of him or herself, to concrete actions in the environment to test ideas, obtain new information or demonstrate the practicality or otherwise of proposed changes. It also follows that there is a need for reflection on action in order to determine the results and to use these in the next stage of the learning process.

Evaluation. The two most important questions here are, who does the evaluating, and for what purpose? The whole notion of critical, reflective awareness implies evaluation, and it follows from the setting out of a participatory learning process that it is the participants who are the evaluators. Both self and group evaluation is implied, which, while not precluding outside evaluation, emphasises that decision-making in relation to evaluation is in the hands of the participants. It is suggested here that two important purposes of such evaluation are to establish what learning has taken place and to provide a basis for further learning-action-reflection. Such evaluation is not 'soft', as is often stated by its critics[13], but rather places the responsibility for developing effective skills, critical insights and appropriate action in the hands of the learning participants[14].

Structures and hierarchies. It will now be evident that an alternative education implies a structuring both of knowledge and of the learning process which reflects the types of social relationships considered desirable to attain certain individual and social goals. While those goals have not been explicitly defined, it should also be clear that this alternative education is based on a model of persons, society and social change which implies that people and their individual development are of central importance; that society should be built upon the principles of the recognition of the individual as a person, and basic human rights which constitute the framework for establishing society, free not just from overt violence but from structural violence, and that this is created by the maximum participation of individuals and groups.

Equal participation and dialogue thus form the bases for the structuring of education, both in the micro-situation of the small learning group and in the macro-situation of the relationships between groups. Because the formal educational systems in virtually every nation mirror the hierarchical and bureaucratic structures of the wider society, it is difficult to envisage a reorganization of existing educational systems which would enable an alternative learning to take place effectively

without reorganization of the societies of which they are a part. It has
not, of course, been definitely established that widespread social
change would or could not take place through change in present
education. It is however suggested that without change in the methods
of control over formal education, tinkering with present education will
have little effect on the lives and destinies of most educands. Therefore
it is to out-of-school groups that efforts can be more usefully directed
to try to realize education as the practice of freedom.

Whither disarmament education?

Given the foregoing analysis, it is appropriate to ask if disarmament
education, in terms of the teaching of certain facts about the world,
and attempting to convince individuals that they should not support
arms policies and should practise non-violence in their own lives, is
possible and desirable. The following points about disarmament as a
topic to be conveyed in education need consideration:

1. Who has taken the decision that disarmament is universally a
   good thing, and to what extent have the perceptions of learners
   been taken into account in that decision?
2. Has disarmament been considered in relation to the wider
   framework of power and violence? What are the implications of
   unilateral disarmament policies on national, regional and international politics?
3. To what extent is disarmament, especially without a range of
   positive policies in the fields of international relations, redistribution of power and resources within and between nations, etc.
   likely to change the present world for the better?
4. To what extent can disarmament education, especially in weak
   nations or amongst oppressed groups, be seen as yet another
   attempt to reduce the strivings of those groups and maintain
   them in a continuing position of dependency?
5. How can disarmament education, which does not recognize the
   micro-situation of the learners as a key to confirming present
   relations or presenting viable alternative modes of thought and
   action, produce changes in those thoughts and action to
   implement change?

The inevitable conclusion seems to be that disarmament is only a
special case of a much wider set of problems concerning the nature of
power and the mechanisms of domination and oppression. Disarmament education, especially within present educational systems, may
very easily become part of the maintenance of social control, either
through the limited consideration of disarmament and its implications,
the elimination of a means for liberation which, however undesirable,

may be the only way in which structural violence can be counteracted, or the communication of dual and conflicting messages, since the processes and situations used for disarmament education may be contrary to and more effective than the content intended to be apprehended.

It can be said of disarmament education: 'Utopias are perfect — be it perfectly agreeable or perfectly disagreeable — and consequently there is nothing to quarrel about'.[15] In contrast Freire maintains that: 'the fundamental role of those committed to cultural action for conscientization is not properly speaking to fabricate the liberating idea, but to invite the people to grasp with their minds the truth of their reality'.[16] In grasping this reality, education is challenged to become part of the quest for liberation, not for ideological conditioning of the perception of reality. To grasp reality, to act and to reflect on the dialectical relationships between humankind and world, is not utopian dreaming but the liberating vocation of those who consciously seek to build a better world.

Development and the arms race

An outstanding feature of today's reality is that the poor are still with us, and moreover, their numbers and the gaps between the rich and the poor continue to increase. While the fact of poverty can be treated as the basic problem to be solved, it is through understanding the reasons for poverty, and perceiving the mechanisms of domination and oppression, of which material deprivation is an important but not the only manifestation, that a picture of the reality which is to be changed begins to appear.

The development of development thought

The development debate, especially as it is presented for study in formal educational systems, can often be summarized around two basic issues:

1. The battle to win over the developing countries to either a capitalist or a socialist mode of production (both being seen as essentially unitary systems, their transportation outside the historical and cultural context in which they developed being largely ignored);

2. The argument over the finer details of how that mode of production can be brought about in order to lead to improved economic performance (according to indicators selected on the basis of the particular economic goals established by the purveyors of the development model under consideration).

Since development rather than civilization and progress became an internationally rehearsed problem, an economic growth model varying mainly in details between First- and Second-World versions has been advocated for the Third World.

Development or developmentalism?
While hard-line economic growth theories may still be propounded, many development theorists and practitioners have come to realize that development is a multifaceted problem. Even if economic growth remains the goal, non-economic factors have to be taken into account in order to achieve economic change. 'Economic growth implies changes in social structure, a redistribution of political power, and this is a dialectical process full of conflict.'[17]

Two broad approaches to the changes necessary in order to bring about development can be distinguished. The first consists of reforms ranging from change in the planning and administrative capacity of developing countries to certain changes in international economic activity. The most optimistic outcome of such change is an increased GNP without a change in its distribution, increased wealth for the developed trading partners, givers of aid and/or multinational enterprises being uncited consequences. The second approach is concerned with development as a socio-cultural and historical process which takes different forms and which is impeded by present structures of power within and between nations. There is an obvious and interesting parallel here between the two approaches and the approaches to education outlined earlier!

Reformist approaches. The UN development decades exemplify the development of liberal-humanitarian reformist thought. The first, launched in 1961, focused on economic growth, with aid as a key to its promotion. It was largely a failure and led to a 'crisis of aid', together with a recognition that there were political and social as well as economic factors in development. The second decade proposed a 'more just and rational economic and social order in which equality of opportunities should be more a prerogative of nations as of individuals within a nation', with 'qualitative and structural changes in the society' going 'hand in hand with rapid economic growth' together with 'reduction of existing disparities — regional, sectoral and social'[18] as the aims of development.

This has led to a second, more precisely defined approach, that of the New International Economic Order (NIEO). Adopted by the Sixth Special Session of the UN General Assembly in 1974, and based on growing concern at the trade barriers to developing countries and the unwillingness of the rich countries to make significant concessions to the poor, the NIEO is concerned with the question 'who shall control and who shall benefit from the world's natural resources?'[19] The drive for the NIEO came initially from the developing world. It recognizes two crucial aspects of development: the need for redistribution of wealth within the developing countries; and the redistribution of wealth between nations.

While the NIEO has been welcomed as a challenge which presents concrete proposals to be translated into action, the need for political changes if it is to become a reality has formed part of the criticism. Unless such changes take place, it could become 'at least in its current formulation . . . a rearrangement of the existing pattern, leading to a more thorough integration of minority elite and middle class groups in non-western countries into the existing international economic order'.[20] Changes in the international division of labour, the need for a more thorough-going ecological perspective and for maintaining a watch on the 'inner limits' of fundamental human rights are suggestions for making the NIEO a more workable concept.

Related to aspects of the contents of the call for a NIEO is another approach, espoused especially by the International Labour Organization, the basic human needs strategy[21]. This takes as the primary task of development the satisfaction of basic human needs such as food, shelter and medical care. While there are disagreements over what constitutes such needs and what are the minimal requirements for their satisfaction, this strategy focuses attention away from economic growth as such and, like the NIEO, attempts to face questions of the redistribution of resources. Its weakness lies in the absence of a firm political analysis of the reasons for the present maldistribution of resources and lack of change, and its espousal by reactionary governments in the Third World focuses attention on material needs without concomitants in the fields of justice, human rights and freedom.

An earlier approach, some elements of which can be seen in the previous two, is that of the limits to growth[22]. The first report of the Club of Rome bearing this title was widely criticized for its proposals regarding an equilibrium in the world, especially through policies of population control in developing countries, and for its failure to see the present crisis in global political terms. It was an essentially Western approach which largely regarded the problems of development to reside in the developing countries, ignoring the interaction between developed and developing. However, by introducing the concept of the finiteness of resources, and of the need to redistribute them and to alter present consumption patterns, it provided some basis for the further questioning of the growth model. It also raised the issue of global interdependence, although it did not translate this into just patterns for future development.

Structural change approaches. A problem in linking together the approaches outlined here is that there is a debate amongst theorists as to whether or not they contain a sufficiently radical analysis of the class structure of society, imperialism and the international political economy. At one level at least this is a debate between Marxists and neo-Marxists of varying degrees of 'orthodoxy', and Habermas argues that Marxist economic theory is undergoing a paradigm change as a result of changes in international capitalism. It is maintained here that a common thread in the approaches to be outlined, which owes its insight to early Marxists, is that the impoverishment of the peripheral nations is an outcome of the development of those at the centre. Thus, the continued dominance of the developed nations in the world economy is an expression of the dependency of the developing nations; this concept can be extended to peripheral groups within central nations, while 'centre representatives' can be discerned in the political and economic elites in peripheral nations.

Dependency theory has been articulated to depict this continued dominance. Its chief proponent, Andre Gunder Frank, focuses his analysis on the effects of Latin America's growing dependence on intensive capital and technology. This leads to the establishment of industrial enclaves by transnational corporations, at best benefiting already existing elites but mostly enhancing the wealth of the corporations. Dependency is not confined to the economic sphere, but spills over into all aspects of life including science, technology and culture.

Revolution has been seen as a way out of dependence, itself seen as a violent phenomenon. Fanon points out that, in the preindependence situation, both colonialism and decolonization were violent in the physical sense. The gap left behind by the departure of colonizers led to further possibilities for direct violence in the attempts to establish a new working order in society. This can be seen in its broadest in the international context and in the structurally violent relationships of imperialism, defined here not in strict Marxist terms but as continued economic, political and cultural domination, and hence being displayed in centre-periphery relations regardless of whether the centre has a capitalist or socialist mode of production.

Dependency theory has been attacked on all sides, for failing to take into account the class content of theories of imperialism, for its failure to elaborate the essential characteristic of dependency leading to confusion in the formulation of new policy[23]. However, its focus on the interplay between internal and international structures provides a starting point for understanding the processes of development and underdevelopment. And in looking beyond the economy to other aspects of dependence, the multifaceted nature of development and of the barriers to alternative development strategies are recognized.

A variant of dependency theory is liberation theology[24] which also originated in Latin America, although there is some continuity with earlier theologians from St Augustine to Teilhard de Chardin, with aspects of Jewish writers such as Martin Buber and trends in modern Islamic thought. It represents a concern for social and individual justice, with a stress on man in the context of history and the conditions which dehumanize him. It has been extended to a concern for and conceptual understanding of oppressed groups in a variety of situations, including racial minorities and women. Like dependency theory, liberation theology has focused on structural violence, and has been extended to the examination of and action about domination and repression as political, cultural and psychological mechanisms.

A further set of ideas about development alternatives can be summed up in the term 'another development'. The specific proposals of the Dag Hammarskjöld Foundation project bearing this title see another development to be based on the satisfaction of need, through endogenous and self-reliant strategies in harmony with the environment, and through structural transformation in and between rich and poor nations. 'Between the needs of the thousands of millions of human beings now alive or yet to be born and the ecological limits, there is a margin of freedom within which another development, aided by a new system of international relations, is organically linked.'[25]

The project groups represent a variety of standpoints, but there is an underlying assumption of both an optimistic outlook and an essentially harmonious model of society at the international level. As such, it will be challenged by those who hold that the necessary changes will only come about through conflict, although the possibility of conflict is at least implicit in the types of transformation which the approach is beginning to envisage. The proposals represent yet another attempt to see development in a broad perspective, and one which is man-centred and global, and to recognize the structural barriers to development in the present world order.

Hindrances to development

Just as development has many facets, so too do the barriers to development. And while it is maintained here that, at the broadest, it is the present structures of power and the ways in which they are perpetuated which constitute the basic causes of development, underdevelopment and overdevelopment, it is useful to look at some more specific factors. In particular, the ways in which power is exercised, as well as the interrelationships between them, can be seen in these factors. The five factors singled out are aid, the multinational corporations, the arms race, science and technology, and education.

R. Burns

Aid/development assistance. A paper presented some years ago had the provocative title 'Aid — or the golden fleece?' Despite the rhetoric and the often well-intentioned efforts of people and governments, it has become necessary to examine critically the nature, operation and effects of aid. Four types can be distinguished, loans, grants, technical assistance and investment, and all four may be transferred bilaterally or multilaterally through governmental or non-governmental agencies. In nearly all forms, motives for aid-giving are mixed, elements of that mixture including economic, political and psychological advantages to the donors and to the recipients. While it has become fashionable in some circles to criticize all aid without recognizing that under certain circumstances it may be the only way to solve development problems, it is important to recognize the negative effects. These include increased dependence, elite-enhancement in developing countries, profits to the donors which far outweigh minor advantages for recipients and ignore the effects on the physical and social environment in the latter countries, and the manipulation of the development process which the offer of, or withholding of aid often entails. Many case studies showing these effects can be cited[26], covering national aid programmes as well as critiques of the operation of international agencies such as the International Bank for Reconstruction and Development and the International Monetary Fund[27].

Multinational enterprises. The growth of these corporations can be seen as a new stage of capitalism which has implications for governments and people in developed as well as developing countries. These corporations penetrate into every sphere of life and play a significant role in bringing about a future which is primarily of benefit to their shareholders. Mattelart says:

> National differences seem to be most acute when the rate of economic development is low, but as people prosper, their spending patterns tend to parallel those of other affluent societies . . . This development, perhaps more than any other single factor, accounts for the success of the multinational company with its great potential for translating knowledge and experience from more sophisticated markets to those that are a phase behind them.[28]

The range of multinational enterprises is enormous and includes frightening effects in the area of agribusiness and the production of food[29], in advertising, the media, communication systems and armaments. Not only are they successful business enterprises and agents of change in the direction of a consumer society in the developing nations, but through the new partnerships which are being forged between governments and business they are bringing about at least the possibility of new political systems.

The arms race. The annual world expenditure on arms is estimated as between $300 and $350 billion, of which three-quarters is accounted for by the six leading military spenders, the USA, the USSR, China, France, the UK and the Federal Republic of Germany[30]. The world has several times the capacity to destroy itself, and while the concentration of this capacity is in the hands of a few nations, increase in military spending in developing countries in the past two decades is six times that of previous figures, compared to 1.7 for the world as a whole, and military spending is on average six times as high as development assistance[31].

It is important to reflect on the actual quantity of the world's resources devoted to military ends; it is however more relevant to consider the consequences of this spending. The most obvious is that the present distribution of armaments and of access to suppliers and allies maintains world dominance based not only on possession of the means of force but also on fear of the consequences of inadequate defence.

This follows from the position of the military/industrial complex as a dominant feature of national and international organization. Luckham suggests that there are four main aspects of the international arms economy:

1. The flow of armaments internationally is partly determined by the logic of accumulation and arms production in the major capitalist arms producing countries;
2. The arms trade is also sustained by its use as an instrument of the states and ruling classes in the struggle for hegemony within the international system;
3. There is competition in the world market for arms trade between societies based on antagonistic (socialist and capitalist) modes of production and this has a distinct impact on the economies and politics of the arms trade;
4. The expansion in the international market for arms is greatly accentuated by the presence in the Third World itself of nodal points of international political conflict, creating a demand for armaments[32].

Further connections between the arms trade and the international political economy can be discerned. These include the relationship between the arms industry and other forms of industrial development based on the importation of high-level science and technology, and the dual nature of the military both within nations and internationally where, despite its surface nature as an international profession, it is at best in an interstitial position between the nation state and the international system, and is thus critical in reproducing both[33]. Often specifically aided by developed nations (despite the fact that military aid is in fact mostly a hidden factor in aid plans and calculations) whose implicit aim at least is to secure further advantages and to provide a powerful modernizing force, the peace-time use of the military in development creates contradictions and divided loyalties. This is especially true for the non-commissioned officers whose loyalties may be split between the people with whom they are identified in class terms and the military hierarchy. When particular elements of the military elite are infiltrated or influenced by 'foreign powers', themselves not always under the full control of the governments of those countries (the CIA, KGB and multinational corporations can all be cited as examples), the complexity of the role of the military nationally and internationally is underlined, regardless of the types of weapons with which they are equipped.

Three 'myths' about the arms race itself that die hard are that military expenditure boosts economic growth, that the arms industry helps unemployment and the transfer of technology, and that military research is the major spur to technological progress[34]. Even if all three were true, both the economic and the political consequences of the arms race and militarization can be seen to be part of the structures of violence which distort the whole concept of development as a process of human liberation with justice.

Science and technology. These two are not only linked to the establishment of a basis on which a particular definition of development can proceed, but are interlinked in the three previous aspects of development. The transfer of science and technology to the Third World is perhaps the most common feature of the policies of First and Second World nations. The raising of science and technology as critical factors in development implies a definition of development as a particular type of industrialization. This on the whole ignores existing and traditional knowledge and skills and their appropriateness for the historical, cultural and social circumstances of the developing countries, and enhances the process of elite formation and dependence which is a common thread in many development efforts. Even the call for intermediate or appropriate technology can be interpreted as an attempt to maintain dependence through denying to developing countries access to knowledge which has certainly played an important role in creating the powerful position of the developed countries. There are several ways in which the role of science and technology in developments can be considered. Perhaps the most important questions centre around the fact that science and technology are not, as has been maintained in the whole logical positivist tradition, neutral. The development of science and its application through technology is another aspect of the selection of knowledge and its legitimation in the socio-cultural and political spheres, which may either enhance domination or be used for liberation depending on the way in which it is generated, owned and transmitted in society.

Education. It should be clear from what has been stated earlier that education as a dependent institution is, through the formalization of schooling, a part of the present world order. It is not just the numbers of graduates from various levels of that system, but what they have learned and the manner in which it has been learned, which determine the ways in which knowledge is put to use in society. Formal education, established during colonial times on colonial models and continuing its influence through foreign-educated elites, overseas experts, textbooks and indigenous systems modelled on industrialized countries, is overwhelmingly part of the system of national and international control for the maintenance of the political and economic *status quo*[35]. This will only change when the structures within education and the relationships between education and the wider context are no longer part of the exercise of domination in society.

Implications

The aim here has been to argue that it is necessary to see both education and disarmament within an analysis and critique of the present operation of power and domination, nationally and internationally. As Freire has said, 'There is no such thing as a *neutral* education process. Education either functions as an instrument which is used to facilitate the integration of the younger generation into the logic of the present system and bring about conformity with it. *or* it becomes the "practice of freedom", the means by which men and women deal critically and creatively with reality and discover how to participate in the transformation of their world.'[36]

The implications of the analysis of the ways in which formal education is an instrument of the present system (and disarmament in itself can be seen to contribute to the maintenance of that system are twofold. First, it is vital to understand, in ways which may lead to action for change, the use of education to maintain the *status quo*, and to seek alternatives which both allow for the generation and transmission of knowledge in non-oppressive ways and also lead to the development of a critical consciousness and an ability to act to change present realities. This implies finding new ways to communicate in dialogue and to ensure that participation forms the basis of the learning experiences.

Secondly, while each has his/her perception of the critical issues which should be transmitted to others, it is both pedagogically and morally undesirable to insist that these must take precedence over the

R. Burns

expressed concerns of learners. In seeking basically to add new material to the curricula of formal educational systems, even where new methods are also being advocated, efforts which avoid critical questions are but partial and limited. Perhaps the most fear-provoking aspect of 'cultural action for freedom' is that it is open-ended, and while it starts with the affirmation of the authenticity of the participants — both 'learners' and 'teachers' — it requires a trust in the capacity of humanity to develop a critical self and social awareness which will lead to action to bring about a more just society. Without that trust, and without a commitment to work with others to imagine a liberated world and to struggle critically and reflectively to bring it about, we are merely rearranging existing knowledge and structures, presenting partial solutions to partially conceived problems and hence, at least to some degree, falling prey to being co-opted into the dominant systems.

Notes and references

1. See, for example, Bourdieu P. Cultural reproduction and social reproduction. In Karabel J. and Halsey A.H. (Eds). *Power and ideology in education.* New York, Oxford University Press, 1977
2. Bernstein B. On the classification and framing of educational knowlege. In Young M.F.D. (Ed). *Knowledge and control,* p.47. London, Collier-Macmillan, 1971
3. *Loc.cit.*
4. See, for example, Freire P. (trans. M.B. Ramos). *Pedagogy of the oppressed,* chap. 2. Harmondsworth, Penguin Books, 1972
5. Hill B. *The schools,* p.129. Harmondsworth, Penguin Books, 1977
6. Hold J. *How children fail.* Harmondsworth, Penguin Books, 1969
7. CCPD. *Trends in development education:* introduction. Geneva, Documents 1, 1973
8. Haavelsrud M. Raising consciousness through a global community curriculum. *Bull. Peace Proposals,* 1974 (5) 277
9. Keesing R. *Cultural anthropology: a contemporary perspective,* p. 537. New York, Holt Rinehart and Winston, 1976
10. Huizer G. Anthropology and politics. Occasional Paper 2, Third World Centre, University of Nijmegen, 1978, 54
11. *Ibid,* 55
12. Haavelsrud, *op.cit.*
13. For some aspects of this debate see Tawney D. (Ed.). *Curriculum evaluation today: trends and implications.* London, Macmillan, 1976
14. This does not preclude the use of so-called empirical or quantitative techniques, but as contributors to Tawney show, outside evaluation so often serves the interests of evaluators and bears little relationship to the situation to be evaluated or the experiences and perceptions of the participants.
15. Dahrendorf R. *Essays in the theory of society,* p. 109. London, Routledge and Kegan Paul, 1968

16. Freire P. (trans. M.B. Ramos). *Cultural action for freedom,* p.76. Harmondsworth, Penguin Books, 1972
17. Sunkel O. The development of development thinking. *IDS Bulletin,* 1977, 8 (3) 11
18. International development strategy for the second UNDD. In *Partnership or privilege?* Geneva, SODEPAX, 1970, 4-6
19. GATT-Fly. *What is the NIEO?* Ottawa, 1976, p.2 (mimeo)
20. Eldridge P. How new is the 'New international economic order'? *ACFOA R & I Papers,* 14, 1977
21. ILO. *Meeting basic human needs.* Geneva, ILO, 1977
22. Meadows D.H., D.L., *et al. The limits to growth.* New York, Universe Books, 1972
23. O'Brien P.J. A critique of Latin American theories of dependency. In Oxaal T. *et al. Beyond the sociology of development.* London, Routledge and Kegan Paul, 1975
24. See, for example, Gutierrez G. (trans Inda and Eagleson). *A theology of liberation.* Maryknoll, Orbis Books, 1973
25. Nerfin M. (Ed.). *Another development: approaches and strategies.* Uppsala, Dag Hammarskjold Foundation, 1977
26. See for example, Bhattacharya D. Flow of resources between poor and rich countries. Paper presented to 48th ANZAAS Congress, Melbourne, 1977 (mimeo); Jalee P. (trans. Kopper). *The Third World in world economy.* New York, Monthly Review Press, 1969.; Pardy R. *et al. Purari: overpowering Papua New Guinea.* Melbourne, IDA, 1978: Singer H. and Ansari J. *Rich and poor countries,* 2nd edn. London, George Allen and Unwin, 1978; Weeramanty C.G. *Equality and freedom.* Colombo, Hansa Publishers, 1976
27. Hayter T. *Aid as imperialism.* Harmondsworth, Penguin Books, 1971
28. Mattelart A. (trans. Chanon). *Multinational corporations and the control of culture,* p.77. Sussex, Harvester Press, 1979
29. George S. *How the other half dies.* Harmondsworth, Penguin Books, 1978
30. The arms race. *UNESCO Courier,* April 1979, p.6
31. Barnaby F. Arms and the Third World: the background. *Development Dialogue,* 1977
32. Luckham R. Militarism: arms and the internationalization of capital. *IDS Bulletin,* **8** (3) 1977, 46-48
33. Luckham R. Militarism: force, class and international conflict. *IDS Bulletin,* **9** (1) 1928 19
34 Three myths that die hard. *UNESCO Courier,* April 1979, 26-7
35. See for example Branson J. and Miller D.B. *Class, sex and education in capitalist society.* Melbourne, Sorrett Publishing Company, 1979; Carnoy M. *Education as cultural imperialism.* New York, David McKay Co. Inc., 1974
36. Freire P. *op. cit.* ref. 16, p.76

Framingham State College
Framingham, Massachusetts

3. Education for disarmament: a Gandhian perspective*

Narayan Desai, *National Peace Committee, Varanasi*

An attempt is made here to present the subject of education for disarmament from the Gandhian point of view. In doing so I shall try to correlate the Gandhian idea of non-violent defence with his style of education. Gandhi held war to be an unmitigated evil, but would not consider disarmament in an isolated way. He considered disarmament to be one of the tools for a comprehensive strategy for creating a non-violent society. To Gandhi education was both for the individual and the society. I shall try to draw a picture wherein the Gandhian type of education at various levels is employed for the training of non-violent defence as he envisaged it.

Changing goals of education

One of the factors that has distinguished man from other animals is education. Although birds, beasts and insects also train their little ones, man has made education the tool not only to carry on the heritage of the past, but also to project the vision of the future. It is by the process of education that man has incorporated the knowledge, information and skills of thousands of years into the present. While the training methods of birds and beasts have remained stationary throughout history, man's methods of education have changed from generation to generation, along with the changing goals of education. Education today is no longer complete, with the elder generation handing over its knowledge to the younger. The goal of education today is to prepare the younger generation for an entirely new and better world. Modern technology has brought about tremendous changes in the world. On the one hand it has turned the earth into a bird's nest, on the other it has ushered in an age of extreme centralization of both economic and political power. The problems created by this over-concentration of power are manifold. It militates against the values of freedom and liberties, because centralized control induces the intervention of the state.

* Reproduced by permission of UNESCO. Document S-80 Conf. 401/16.UNESCO © 1980

Centralization of economic power breeds exploitation of the many by the few, and centralization of political power, which often is the corollary of centralization of economic power, begets proliferation of bureacracy and a consequent expropriation of freedom of the many by the few. The centralized structure of society also produces psychological and social problems such as alienation and loss of a sense of belonging. Pyarelal, Gandhi's secretary and biographer, has stated the problem aptly:

> We are living in an age of mounting tensions . . . Never before perhaps has the acceptance of the ideals of equality, brotherhood and world peace been so ubiquitous, and yet never has humanity or human values stood nearer to the brink of total destruction than they do today under the menace of the atomic bomb.[1]

One of the goals of education today has to be to resolve these contradictions.

Among Gandhi's great contribution to the modern world was his method of working. He introduced non-violence as an effective tool of social change. Gandhi called his new tool *Satyagraha,* which literally meant insistence on or adherance to truth. To Gandhi his own long and colourful life was an experiment in truth. Love of non-violence came to him as a corollary of that search. *Satyagraha* was practised by him for over half a century in two continents for the liberation of some of the most oppressed people. Gandhi's approach to the problem of armaments must be considered in this context.

Although Gandhi was very much for disarmament, he considered disarmament to be but an insufficient and partial goal. He went to the very root of the cause and wanted to plan for a society without wars. Thus his approach to this problem was holistic. He was concerned not only with the problem of some nations accumulating arms, but with the very causes of arms. He found that man's greed for wealth and lust for power were at the root of wars and therefore was in search of a new incentive for mankind. The new incentive that he found was, in his own works, as old as the hills. That was the incentive of love, or 'soul-force', as he often described *Satyagraha.* Love, Gandhi thought, should not be treated in isolation as an antidote to arms, but should pervade the whole spectrum of human life.

It was through this exploration for the working of the law of love that Gandhi hit upon the instrument of social change, *Satyagraha.* Taking his argument a step further he said:

> I claim that even now, though the social structure is not based on a conscious acceptance of non-violence, all the world over mankind lives and men retain their possessions on the sufference of one another. If they had not done so, only the fewest and the most ferocious would have survived. But such is not the case. Families are bound together by ties of love and so are groups in the

so-called civilized society called nations. Only they do not recognize the supremacy of the Law of Non-violence. It follows, therefore, that they have not investigated its vast possibilities.[2]

Thus we find Gandhi to be an experimenter of truth and non-violence. With the insight of a scientist he tried to discover the laws of love in nature and in the human society which he considered to be an indivisible part of nature. As a scientist he had his visions. But as a scientist again, he would not move an inch without testing his visions in the laboratory of practical life:

> The religion of non-violence is not meant merely for the Rishis and saints. It is meant for the common people as well. . . The Rishis, who discovered the law of non-violence in the midst of violence, were greater geniuses than Newton. They were themselves greater warriors than Wellington. Having themselves known the use of arms, they realized their uselessness and taught a weary world that its salvation lay not through violence but through non-violence.[3]

Gandhian concept of non-violent defence

Gandhi's plan of a non-violent defence has been explained by Pyarelal in a nutshell. His plan of action was in three parts: before the invasion, during the invasion and after the invasion. Before the invasion the technique consisted in prevention by a counter-invasion in advance of the aggressor nation by goodwill, friendliness, a spirit of reconciliation and selfless service.

> During the invasion the technique would consist in offering non-violent resistance unto death and to the last man to the invader and total non-cooperation with him, while not missing any opportunity of rendering humanitarian service to the individual members of the invading hosts in their personal capacity whenever they might be in distress . . . Should action outlined in the first two stages prove unsuccessful and the aggressor come to occupy the country, resistance would take the form of non-violent non-cooperation and all other forms of Satyagraha that were practised during India's non-violent freedom struggle against the British power.[4]

The first important step towards a world without war, according to Gandhi, would be to create an atmosphere of friendliness between neighbours. In fact, to carry on a cold war or a diplomatic war often bordering on the verge of actual war, and initiating talks on disarmament on the other side is self-contradictory. Gandhi therefore would have advised a free India to go in for a unilateral effort to generate an atmosphere of the brotherhood of nations: 'For me patriotism is the same as humanity. I am patriotic because I am human and humane. It is not exclusive.'[5]

Gandhi's plan of non-violent defence was not that of a cowardly submission to the invader, but of a courageous non-violent resistance even at the cost of risking one's life. Non-resistance never implies that a non-violent man should bend before the violent aggressor. While not returning the latter's violence by violence, he should refuse to submit to the latter's illegitimate demand even to the point of death[6].

In 1942 when the Japanese army had conquered Malaya and Burma and were marching towards India, Mirabehn (Miss Scade), a close associate of Gandhi, had gone to Orissa on the Eastern coast of India thinking that the Japanese army might land on that shore. She worked with the people of Orissa trying to discover how Gandhi's idea of a non-violent defence could be worked out in such a situation. She exchanged letters with Gandhi on the subject wherein she discussed the plan in some detail. According to her, the maximum sustainable stand expected from the average people would be:

1. To resist firmly, and mostly non-violently the commandeering by the Japanese of any land, houses, or movable property;
2. To render no forced labour to the Japanese;
3. Not to take up any sort of administrative service under the Japanese (this may be hard to control in connection with some types of city people, government opportunists and Indians brought in from other parts);
4. To buy nothing from the Japanese;
5. To refuse their currency and any effort on their part at setting up a Raj.[7]

This quotation will give some idea of the atmosphere that was prevalent in the circles around Gandhi at the time of the Japanese invasion of India. Non-violent defence was not a mere theoretical proposition to Gandhi and his colleagues. It was very much a practical proposition to be tried out by the millions.

The theory behind Gandhi's plan

The theory behind Gandhi's plan was basically the same as that behind all non-violent non-cooperation and civil disobedience. Sharp has explained the theory in his monumental book *The politics of non-violent action.* I borrow copiously from him in explaining this theory. Sharp begins his chapter on the nature and control of political power by defining social power as the capacity to control the behaviour of others, directly or indirectly through action by groups of people, which action impinges on other groups of people. Advocates of non-violent action, Sharp asserts, do not seek to 'control' power by rejecting it or abolishing it. Instead, they recognize that power is inherent in practically all social and political relationships and that its control is 'the basic problem of political theory and in political reality . . . Political power thus refers to the total authority, influence, pressure and coercion which may be applied to achieve or prevent the implementation of the wishes of the power-holder'.[8] Sharp maintains that all types of struggle, and all means to control governments or to defend them against attack, are based upon certain basic assumptions about the nature of power. Non-violent action is based upon the assumption that power in all governments continuously rises from many parts of the society. It depends for its strength and existence upon a replenishment of its sources by the cooperation of a multitude of institutions and people. Non-violent action, Sharp continues, is based on the view that political power can most efficiently be controlled at its sources. The sources, according to Sharp, are as follows:

1. authority or the right to command and direct, to be heard or obeyed by others;
2. human resources: both numbers and the extent and forms of their organizations;
3. skills and knowledge of those who are controlled by the power;
4. intangible factors such as habits and attitudes towards obedience and submission, etc;
5. material resources including natural, financial, economic resources and the means of communication and transformation;
6. sanctions at the disposal of the ruler.

Sharp infers from the above that the rulers' power depends ultimately upon the obedience and cooperation of the subjects. No matter how great their means of physical coercion, all rulers require an acceptance of their authority, their right to rule and to command. If a ruler's need for acceptance of his authority is basic, loss of authority will have serious consequences for his position and power. If the subjects deny the ruler's right to rule and to command, they are withdrawing the general agreement which makes possible the existing government. The ruler's power also depends on the continual availability of all the skill, knowledge, advice, labour, and administrative ability of a significant portion of his subjects. Sanctions are important in maintaining a ruler's political power. But the ability to impose sanctions itself derives from the obedience and cooperation of at least some subjects[9].

This theory has been proved a number of times in ancient and recent history. It is on this theory that Gandhi based his programme of civil disobedience and non-cooperation. It was because this theory was sound that the British government had to bow before the wishes of the Indian masses, and it was because of the soundness of this theory that even Hitler's forces had to yield before the non-cooperation of the striking Norwegian teachers.

Gandhi himself has explained the practicability of his non-violent defence thus:

The underlying belief in this philosophy of defence is that even a modern Nero is not devoid of a heart. The spectacle never seen before by him or his soldiers — of endless rows of men and women simply dying, without violent protest, must ultimately affect him. If it does not affect Nero himself, it will affect his soldiery. Men can slaughter one another for years in the heat of battle, for then it seems to be a case of kill or be killed. But if there is no danger of being killed yourself by those you slay, you cannot go on killing defenceless and unprotesting people endlessly. You must put down your gun in self-disgust.

Thus in the end the invader must be beaten by new weapons, peaceful weapons, the weapons of civil disobedience and non-violent resistance.

Practically speaking, there should be probably no greater loss in life than if forcible resistance were offered to the invader. How many men have been killed in Holland, Belgium and France? Hundreds of thousands? Would the invading armies have shot down hundreds of thousands of men in cold blood if they had simply stood passively before them? I do not think so.

I have drawn no impossible picture. History is replete with individual non-violent resistance of the type I have mentioned. There is no warrant for saying or thinking that a group of men and women cannot act as one in offering non-violent resistance.[10]

While Sharp has tried to give the rationale behind the theory of non-violent non-cooperation, Gandhi seems to have worked on it more intuitively and instinctively. 'How would you meet the atom-bomb . . . . with non-violence?' he was asked by an American journalist on the last day of his earthly sojourn. The reply he gave a few hours before the end is worth recording here:

I will not go underground. I will not go into shelter. I will come out in the open and let the pilot see I have not a trace of evil against him. The pilot will not see our faces from his great height, I know. But that longing in our hearts — that he will not come to harm — would reach up to him and his eyes would be opened. (Then guessing what was probably passing in the questioner's mind, he added) If those thousands who were done to death in Hiroshima, if they had died with that prayerful action — died openly with that prayer in their hearts — their sacrifice would not have gone in vain and the war would not have ended so disgracefully as it has'.[11]

Sharp's approach is rational, Gandhi's was moral and spiritual. Education must combine both these approaches, for neither is complete without the other and the role of education must be to tackle a problem from all angles.

Gandhian concept of education

Gandhi's ideas about education were revolutionary from the point of view both of its content and its methodology. It encompassed the whole spectrum of human life.

Man's progress so far has been in two directions. He has tried to develop his inner faculties through study, inner search, meditation, yoga, etc. This progress is concerned with the journey within. The other direction has been in the line of social change through reforms, the journey without. Gandhi's concept of education was to blend both these processes. Education for him was both for the development of the individual's personality as well as for the building of a non-exploitative and non-oppressive society. The secret consists in developing not only the intellectual but also the physical and spiritual faculties of the individual.

Gandhi's method was to make education life-centred. The three media that he suggested for imparting education were: (a) some productive and socially useful craft; (b) observation and living with nature; and (c) learning through the various activities of the society.

Dr Zakir Hussain, ex-President of India, who was a great champion of the Gandhian type of education, described the objectives of that education thus.

The objectives of basic education can be summarized as a two-fold aim, each part of which is integrally bound up with the other.

1. All boys and girls in India should grow up as citizens of a new social order, based on cooperative work as envisaged by Nai Talim (New Education) and with an understanding of their rights, responsibilities and obligations in such a society;
2. Every individual child should have full opportunity for balanced and harmonious development of all his faculties, and should acquire the capacity for self reliance in every aspect of a clean, healthy and cultural life together with an understanding of the social and moral implications of such a life[12].

The programme of work described by the committee presided over by Zakir Hussain was to be planned round the following practices: clean and healthy living; self-reliance; a productive basic craft; citizenship in a community and recreational and cultural activities[13].

According to Pyarelal, Gandhian education was based on the theory that the intellect and the whole personality of the child could be developed through intelligently directed activity of the 'thinking hand'.

The Gandhian system of basic education taught the children to solve by their own efforts the problems facing their families and their community in a non-violent and democratic way. By learning to tackle such problems as communal tension, religious toleration, self-government, food, its cultivation and processing, clothing and disposal of garbage etc., in a non-violent and democratic way and correlating it with the why and wherefore of it, they got not only the whole education for life but an education that also carried with it the guarantee that the knowledge thus gained shall be rightly used. Basic education was thus not merely a new technique of education but a technique for the realization of a specific ideal — the ideal of world peace and universal brotherhood[14].

Gandhi, the revolutionary, had completely discarded the old idea of education being a process of thrusting knowledge, or rather information, into the brain of the child. To him education was not a one-way traffic from the teacher to the taught. It was a process of total development, an 'all-round drawing out of the best in child and man — body, mind and spirit'.

> Man is neither mere intellect nor the gross animal body nor the heart or soul alone. A proper and harmonious combination of all three is required for the making of the whole man and constitutes the true economics of education . . .[15]

The all-round development of the child was but one goal of Gandhian education.

> My plan to impart primary education through the medium of village handicrafts . . . is . . . conceived as the spearhead of a silent social revolution fraught with the most far-reaching consequences . . . by obviating the necessity for highly specialized talent, it would place the destiny of the masses, as it were, in their own hands[16].

This, according to Gandhi, was the road to freedom:

> The ancient aphorism 'education is that which liberates' is as true today as it was before. Education here does not mean mere spiritual liberation after death. Knowledge includes all training that is useful for the service of mankind and liberation means freedom from all manner of servitude even in the present life. Servitude is of two kinds: slavery to domination from outside and to one's own artificial needs. The knowledge acquired in the pursuit of this ideal alone constitutes true study[17].

By having a socially useful productive activity as a medium of imparting education, Gandhi was not only giving an opportunity for the all-round development of the personality of the child, but was trying to bridge the gulf between the classes, as also between the working class and the intellectuals. By using nature as a medium of instruction he was giving the child an opportunity to observe nature, record his observances and analyse them as a scientist does, thereby developing the scientific faculties of the child. In doing so Gandhi also touched one of the most urgent problems of modern man. He gave the child basic education in the science of ecology.

Futility of negotiations and treaties on disarmament

Having discussed Gandhi's idea of a non-violent defence and his ideas about education, we may, for a while, turn our attention to man's modern efforts towards disarmament. By far the most significant that have been made so far have been at two different levels. On one side governments have tried to discuss the problem of disarmament bilaterally or multilaterally. On the other non-official individuals and organizations have tried to make an in-depth study of the various implications of disarmament and supplied their findings in the form of reports, resolutions or literature to governments and non-governmental agencies who may be interested in the study of disarmament. The first kind of effort, e.g. that by governments, has yet to record any significant success in spite of the time, money and energy spent on talks. It is through the studies made by the non-official agencies that we are able to draw the attention of the world towards the futility or the near-futility of these former efforts.

The introduction of one of the small books on nuclear disarmament published by SIPRI in 1975, begins thus:

> For more than a decade now, disarmament negotiations have been in the doldrums. The concept of General and Complete Disarmament, much alive during the 1950s, is still referred to in official statements and treaties but only in lip-service to an ideal of the past. Most people have even forgotten what the initials GCD stand for. Nor has there been any nuclear disarmament, the ostensible objective of negotiations during the 1960s and 1970s, in spite of the fact that most of the nuclear-weapons powers have legally committed themselves to it in a number of treaties. Quite the contrary. The nuclear arms race between the USA and the USSR has continued virtually unabated. And the world-wide spread of the most sophisticated conventional armaments — a result mainly of the international arms trade — has created grave new dangers for international peace and security[18].

A drastic and radically different approach is needed to deal with the problem of arms today. Both Gandhi's method of defence and his method of education offer such radically different approaches. It is true that Gandhi's method of defence was never tried by any country, although there have been thousands of successful applications of the non-violent approach, at levels lower than the national throughout history. Non-violent non-cooperation, civil disobedience and its thousand other variants were used in the Indian struggle for freedom. But non-violent resistance was not used by India or any other country to defend its national frontiers. But never before in the history of mankind has violence been proved to be more futile than today. That is the reason why there is so much talk about disarmament, and that is the reason why the UN had decided to treat the next decade as the Disarmament Decade. In that event, why not spare some time for a plan for non-violent defence?

Civilian defence

At this stage it must be made clear that Gandhi's plan was not what is generally described as 'civil defence' by some authors. Although many of the factors are common in both these plans, there are some distinguishing factors of the Gandhian plan for non-violent defence:

1. While civil defence is envisaged more as a strategy or a technique of defence, the Gandhian defence is based on a living faith in non-violence as a way of life.
2. Civil defence may not insist on having non-violence as the only means of defence; Gandhian defence would. Civil defence would welcome violent aid from allies, or would cooperate with violent efforts on other fronts; Gandhian defence would shun such action.
3. Civil defence would welcome sabotage as a non-violent means and may propagate maximum use of it; Gandhian defence would not consider sabotage as part of its programme.
4. Civil defence would not mind, or even be happy, if some damage is done to the enemy; Gandhian defence would not only not dream of it, but would go all out to find possible opportunities to help the adversary when in distress or difficulties.
5. In times of peace, civil defence would plan as if the country were surrounded by enemies; but the Gandhian defence would plan for a more and more friendly neighbourhood and consider that to be part of the defence programme.
6. Civil defence would begin functioning only after the invasion or attack of the enemy; the Gandhian defence would try many stages of unilateral acts of love before the invasion.

Before proceeding further some of the common features of civil defence and Gandhian defence should also be mentioned here. They are as follows:

1. Both are methods of defence that differ radically from traditional or conventional methods of military defence.
2. Both depend primarily upon non-violent means.
3. Both depend upon the theory that the sanction of the civilian population is necessary in order to gain power or control over a country.
4. Both try to express their opposition to the invasion by non-cooperation in day-to-day life, in the running of government machinery, the means of communication, etc.

For the past two decades there have been discussions about civil defence in peace-research circles, some criticisms of it being common to those of the Gandhian defence. The main criticisms are the following[19].

There are insufficient historical precedents. The non-violent defence of the Ruhr area of Germany in 1923, some incidents of non-violent defence in Norway, Denmark and France during World War II and the defence of Czechoslovakia in 1968, can be cited. Some of these methods were so non-violent that Gandhi would have been proud of them. But it must be conceded that the historical precedents are too few compared to the long history of violent and military defence. However, a method is not disqualified by the mere fact that it was never tried before.

It cannot face up to extreme repression. This seems to be only a hypothetical criticism. During the freedom struggle in India, under Gandhi's leadership, the world was witness to innumerable acts of extreme repression. It is true that the repressive measures of the British were not as brutal or fiendish as those of the Germans or Japanese during World War II, but even then what the experiment of non-violent non-cooperation proved is enough to give hope of surviving even the atrocities of the dictators. Gandhi argued that even an adversary who believes in violence cannot be as brutal towards non-violent defenders as he can be against violent ones.

It might not be a good deterrent to prevent foreign attack. This is more true of civil defence than the Gandhian defence. Gandhian defence provides an additional deterrent by using a unilateral invasion of love.

It requires an improbably homogeneous, impossibly disciplined, and perhaps dangerously nationalistic populace. All defence envisages some nationalistic populace. Whether non-violent defence needs it more is a debatable point. While military and violent defence is by its very nature bound to be restricted to a minority in the population, civil or non-violent defence gives a much larger part of the population the chance to involve itself in the process of defence. This is likely to help in building the will of the people.

Education for Gandhian defence

It must be understood that Gandhi did not expect everybody to be a *Mahatma*, or great soul, in order to be able to practise non-violence. The non-violence that he preached during his lifetime was followed by millions of people, including illiterate women and children. It is true that not all the non-violence that was practised by the Indian millions was the 'non-violence of the brave' as he put it. Even the Indian National Congress which was the backbone of many of the campaigns led by Gandhi, accepted non-violence only as a matter of policy and not as a creed. But one of the qualities of Gandhi's leadership was his ability to devise tools that could be used by a large number of people. Gandhi's technique of non-violent action was based on his discovery that seemingly insignificant things when performed by millions as a part of consciously directed effort, produce results far greater than the sum total of their individual efforts.

The education that Gandhi recommended and imparted to the volunteers of non-violence was of two types:

1. The training for the *Satyagrahis;*
2. The education for life that would ultimately produce non-violent citizens.

He described his ashrams (community centres) as training centres for the Satyagrahis. The eleven 'Ashram Observances' were the disciplines that he expected the inmates of his Ashram to observe as self-training for the non-violent struggle against the British. Several of these observances were a common heritage of all the religious and spiritual teachings of the world, while others had a special significance at the point of history at which Gandhi was teaching them. But whether universal or confined to the time and place of the practice, each of these observances had one quality in common; each was an effort to transform measures that were hitherto considered to be personal virtues into social values. The eleven Ashram observances or vows were: truth; *ahimsa* or love; *brahmacharya* or chastity; control of the palate; non-stealing; non-possession or voluntary poverty; fearlessness; removal of untouchability; bread labour; tolerance i.e. equality of religions; and *Swadeshi* or service of the neighbours. It was through these observances or disciplines of the Satyagrahi, that Gandhi tried to train his volunteers for non-violent action.

This is no place to go into the details of these observances. One of Gandhi's most important books[20] deals with them. Suffice it to mention here that Gandhi not only tried to practise these observances throughout his life, but also encouraged his colleagues to practise them. The observances were like a syllabus for the training of the volunteers, indeed a syllabus for the moral and spiritual development of the individuals concerned, but that is an essential factor in the education for a non-violent defence. As the eleven observances were not only personal virtues, but also social values, the syllabus had political, social and economic significance.

At the organizational level Gandhi proposed a programme which he termed the 'constructive programme'. This was a very important part of the overall plan of Satyagraha or non-violent action. Being a 'practical idealist' Gandhi's constructive programme was necessarily based on the Indian soil. In a nutshell it included:

1. economic revolution, 'constructing' the society on a decentralized pattern, making millions of people self-sufficient and 'self-reliant';

2. integration of the community by doing away with distinctions of religion, caste and class;
3. mass awakening and conscientization through basic education and allied activities;
4. cultural awakening through the service of the illiterate and the ignorant, the suffering and oppressed.

In short Gandhi's programme aimed to achieve liberation in the true sense of the term through economic, political, social and cultural revolution. Thus the constructive programme in its essence would be an inevitable factor in the preparation of a non-violent defence.

The second part of Gandhi's plan for education for non-violence concerns training for non-violent citizens. This may again be divided into general training for the citizens and the specialized training for the leadership. The following section is not based on the authority of Gandhi's writings. It is my own proposal based on my understanding of Gandhi's methods of training gained from my own training in Gandhi's ashrams as well as the study of Gandhi's writings on non-violence and education — and my own experience as an instructor of peace volunteers in post-Gandhian non-violent movements in India.

Education for non-violent defence

It is envisaged that although a considerable part of the population will have some kind of training for non-violent defence, a section of society will be specially committed to non-violence and trained in the organization and execution of non-violent defence. It may also be noted here that the word defence is being used in a very general sense. It includes conditions leading to non-violent defence, a government amenable to adopting such a policy of defence, a foreign policy of creating friendly neighbours and cooperation with agressors.

General education

This includes education at the prebasic level, or below 6 years of age, education at the basic, or 7 - 15 years stage and education at the post-basic 16-19 stage.

Education at the prebasic stage will be concerned chiefly with habit formation. It is at this age, even before this, that most of man's habits are formed and the foundations of the character of the individual are laid. Efforts will be made to form the habits of self-sufficiency, sharing, cooperation, courage and love of nature. This will be done by encouraging children to put on their clothes with their own hands (2 ½ – 4 years); cleaning their rooms; helping to serve food (4 – 5 years); sharing food and other things with other children; singing songs together; sharing small responsibilities, cooperating with other children in working on small projects; observation of plants, birds, pets, etc, caring for the garden, going out on excursions, listening to stories which would nourish the above values; taking part in dramatics which would reinforce the same. Care should be taken at this stage to introduce games that are cooperative and not competitive. Toys glorifying violence should be discouraged. Small and simple tools should be offered to the children to handle. Much can be said about the stories, children's plays and songs that should and should not be introduced at this stage. But suffice it to say that all these should be introduced very carefully and with a definite attitude for peace.

Education at the basic stage has a tremendous potential for training for non-violence and peace. Here I shall give only the barest outlines of some of the more important points connected with the course. At this stage the pupils should learn some craft of skill which would make them capable of being self-supporting citizens of a social system based on a decentralized economy. A country with a population capable of being self-supporting can be a good ground for non-violent defence. Mastery of a craft also builds self-confidence among the pupils: an essential quality of a non-violent defender. Maximum scope should be provided at this stage to the students' creativity. Creativity will not only facilitate artistic qualities in the pupils, but will also give them the training to deal with unknown or difficult situations.

In the school a number of opportunities must be provided for the pupils to manage their own affairs. One of the qualities that will inspire populations to sacrifice their lives for their country is love for the values that their country is supposed to stand for. Love for democracy, freedom and equality are qualities that could be developed in the students by providing opportunities for them to run their affairs without any hindrance from outside.

This is a stage where the love for nature, particularly love of Mother Earth, can best be given to the pupils. Unhappy is the lot of the millions of children who are imprisoned inside the four walls of the school buildings. It is these children who grow up to create societies which are inimical to nature. Many of our present day schools are the mirrors of our society; rigid, mechanical and stunted in growth. It is only the healing touch of nature that can cure mankind of this atrophying malady.

The years 6 - 15 are the period when the child can and should be made conscious of the fact that he or she is a singular member of the family of man. The subject of history must be taught anew in these schools: not stories of kings and warriors who fought wars for the protection of their territories, but of common man struggling in the course of civilization should be presented to the pupils. This is a stage at which a child can acquire qualities which will make him a fitting member of a non-violent society. Courage or fearlessness is one such quality. Opportunities will be provided at this stage to develop the quality of fearlessness in the children. The school can do so by:

1. Taking out children on excursions in the dark or in places which are supposed to be dangerous; the children may first be taken there accompanied by adults, but later they may be encouraged to proceed there by themselves;
2. Acquainting children with objects of fear; instead of making children scared, acquaintance with the objects of fear such as insects or snakes for example, will dispel all their fear;
3. fostering fearlessness by stories of bravery and courage;
4. giving opportunities to children to engage in work that will involve considerable risk;
5. giving them guard duties or duty to protect younger children;
6. observation of non-violent or courageous action, for example an act of civil disobedience or *Satyagraha,* may enhance the quality of fearlessness among children.

Even the games should be of a radically different character. They should not encourage cut-throat competition but support collective effort and improve individual records. The three values that are of the utmost importance at this stage of education are love, freedom and self-expression.

Education at the post-basic stage is a wide subject, but may be covered in part when discussing training for leadership. Here we can only indicate the direction in which the post-basic education will proceed.

If in basic education the training is to make the pupil self-supporting, in post-basic education the student must earn a substantial part of his livelihood while he learns. At this stage the student no longer remains a burden on society. This is especially important for Third World countries. The student furthers his studies, but he does so while he is producing something socially useful for the society.

At the post-basic stage efforts may be concentrated on what is described as appropriate or intermediate technology. The change from the violent to the non-violent society may necessitate a change from a highly centralized to a decentralized technology. Appropriate technology may be the logical step to bring this about. While simple and uncomplicated tools may be used at the basic education level, we may be able to introduce a technology which is higher than primitive, but simple enough to be creative and educative at the post-basic level.

A very important part of the syllabus at this stage may be to deal with the actual problems of the society. Village sanitation, management of the community dairy or library, construction of earthen dams, or managing part of the health problem of the neighbourhood are some examples. While the students at the post-basic stage may help in tackling some of the local problems, they may also further their studies in depth. Dealing with some social problems may give the students the sense of responsibility for the community which is essential for a society committed to non-violent defence.

Training for leadership
A plan for non-violent defence will certainly need leaders, though they may not follow the prototype of the leader needed for a violent defence. While a violent leadership tends to be centralized, non-violent leadership is likely to be more widespread and decentralized. The violent leader is also likely to be more authoritarian, while the non-violent leader has to be much more democratic in his approach. But they may have certain common qualities such as courage, farsightedness, the art of designing good strategy and tactics, influence over people, etc.

It is presumed that many leaders in a country that has accepted non-violent defence will have a background of the training described under basic and post-basic education. Here only the special training needed for leadership is discussed.

First of all the more the leader is trained and disciplined in the kind of qualities that make her or him fit to be a *Satyagrahi* (with the Ashram observances and constructive programme as part of his curriculum), the more she or he will be suited to be a non-violent leader, for the personal qualities of her/his character will be the most essential part of her/his personality as a leader.

The second quality that will be most needed, if it is not already included in the first, is a deep commitment to non-violence. A sound understanding of the working of non-violence should be one of the primary lessons in non-violent leadership.

Sound understanding of world politics with particular knowledge of the foreign policies of one's neighbours would be an important part of the syllabus. This should also include lectures, discussions and readings on the following topics:

1. the intensification of the arms race while talks on disarmament continue at the United Nations;
2. the possibility of nations curtailing part of their sovereignty and entrusting it to a world organization, without which disarmament will not succeed;
3. stopping expansionism in the political, economic and ideological sphere as a precondition for world peace;
4. the idea that nationhood is becoming more and more outdated with the advance of science and technology;

67

5. the evolution of the idea and philosophy of non-violence in the history of mankind;
6. the efforts and limitations of international organizations such as the League of Nations and United Nations.

An ability to deal with people and good understanding of their psychology would be another important part of this education. This would, of course, include the ability to deal with adversaries and to cope in unknown or extremely repressive situations.

Mastery over certain skills would be yet another essential part of the syllabus for the non-violent leaders. The skills would include:

1. first aid and principles of medicine and treatment
2. knowledge of languages, especially those of the neighbouring countries
3. methods of mass communication
4. management of decentralized institutions such as cooperatives, folk-schools, local governments etc.
5. the art of keeping the morale of the people high in adverse conditions, by composure and serenity, music and folk arts, dramatics, good humour and caring for others.

The non-violent leader must also be able to comprehend the niceties of the various implications of different methods of conflict resolution, such as persuasion, arbitration, adjudication etc.

Part of the training of the leaders should be the ability to organize non-violent struggles. Sharp mentions the following as essential for the organization of non-violent struggles: investigation of alleged grievances; negotiations with the adversary; sharpening the focus of attack; generating cause consciousness; organizing the public, the volunteers and the leadership.

Sharp suggested these measures with reference to struggles directed against some local injustice or for the freedom of the country. He was not referring to the larger problem of non-violent defence of a country. While all the measures that he has suggested might be helpful in one way or the other in non-violent defence too. I suggest below a few additional measures:

1. organization of information centres, particularly on the border areas, to inform the public about the movement of the invaders;
2. organization of a communication network, if possible with a number of radio transmission centres, that could keep the public informed and instruct them from time to time;
3. organization of a 'sacrificial squad' willing to act as 'cannon-fodder' of the invaders;

A Gandhian perspective

4. organization of a publicity cell which could inform the outside world about the happenings in the country;
5. organization of rations for possible refugees coming from the areas occupied by the invaders;
6. efforts to mobilize the opinion of conscientious people on the other side of the border to bring pressure against their government's unjust aggression and atrocities;
7. preparation of a system of communication to inform and influence the soldiers of the invading army regarding the unjust action of their government;
8. organization of supporting action on a mass scale in the country in connection with the non-violent action on the borders.

Need for training

Before closing I must confess that though based on the experience of non-violent action at local levels and training of a small number of peace-volunteers, most of my proposals are hypothetical. As there have been only a few instances of non-violent defence, efforts for training for such defence are bound to be few. Personally I am not aware of any effort in this direction. Inexperience is the lot of all pioneers, but that should not deter the pioneers from their efforts. Absence of experience cannot minimize the importance of training. I quote Gandhi at the end:

Just as one must learn the art of killing in the training for violence, so one must learn the art of dying in the training for non-violence. . . . There is no royal road [to train in this difficult art], except through living the creed in your life which must be living the sermon. Of course, the expressions in one's own life presupposes great study, tremendous perseverance, and thorough cleansing of one's self of all the impurities. If for mastering of the physical sciences you have to devote a whole life time, how many life-times may be needed for mastering the greatest spiritual force that mankind has known? But why worry even if it means several life-times? For, if this is the only permanent thing in life, if this is the only thing that counts, then whatever effort you bestow on mastering it is well spent. Seek ye first the kingdom of Heaven and everything else shall be added to you. The kingdom of Heaven is *ahimsa* (non-violence).[21]

References

1. Pyarelal. *Gandhian techniques in the modern world*. Ahmedabad, Navajivan p.3
2. Gandhi. *Harijan*, 22 Feb., 1942
3. Gandhi. *Young India*, 11 Aug. 1920. p.3
4. Pyarelal. *Op. cit*, ref. 1, pp.25-26
5. Gandhi. *Young India*, 16 Mar., 1921, p.81

6. Gandhi. *Harijan*, 30 Mar., 1947, pp. 85-86
7. Pyarelal. *Op. cit.*, ref. 1, pp.54-55
8. Sharp, G. *Politics of non-violent action*. Boston, Porter Sargent, pp. 7-00
9. *Ibid*, pp.8-16
10. Pyarelal. *Mahatma Gandhi, the last phase*, Vol.II. Ahmedabad, Navajivan, p.815
11. Pyarelal, *Op. cit.* ref. 1. pp.28-29
12. Hussain S. *Basic national education*, p.3. Wardha, Hindustani Talimi Sangh,
13. *Ibid*, p.6
14. Pyralal, *Op. cit.*, ref. 1, p.44
15. Gandhi. *Harijan*, 8 May, 1937, p.104
16. Gandhi. *Harijan*, 9 September, 1937, p.293
17. Gandhi. *Harijan*, 10 Mar., 1946, p.38
18. Barnaby F. *Nuclear disarmaments or nuclear war?* Stockholm, SIPRI, p.5
19. All four criticisms are drawn from Roberts A. Civilian defence twenty years on. *The Pacifist*, 1979, Sept., p.9
20. Gandhi. *Vervada Mandir. Selected works*, Vol.4. Ahmedabad, Navajivan, 1931
21. Gandhi. *Harijan*, 14 Mar., 1936, p.39

4. Two ways of linking the teaching of science to disarmament education

Antonino Drago, *Institute of Theoretical Physics, University of Naples*

The central point of this communication is the question: why are political science, social-economic theories and logic almost completely absent from the syllabus of secondary schools? I am referring to the syllabuses of Italian schools, but I think the question is valid for almost all the countries in the world.

It is held to be a fundamental duty of the citizen to interest himself in public affairs: but the school gives him no help at all in this direction, because it does not help him to acquire familiarity with the variety of theories of social organization; he will learn of them at his own cost from newspapers and TV debates after leaving school.

Economics is the basis of all social action, but the subject is taught only in technical schools and in such a way as to teach only banking techniques instead of the relevant theories of economics. Since students generally are supported by their families, they are completely isolated from economic processes and usually understand little of them; thus after finishing their studies they have no entrepreneurial skills and they will be destined to sell their intellectual labour to an economic enterprise which is foreign to them.

It can be objected that political and economic doctrines are too open to discussion and are not formative enough. Although I do not agree, I should like to ask: why then is the science of logic also excluded? Since the time of Aristotle it has clearly been a science and it has been formalized in a mathematical manner for more than a century: it is also one of the most important and formative sciences. In our maths courses we teach a great number of mathematical exercises which today can be done perfectly well just by pushing the buttons of a calculator, simply in order to teach our students how to reason. But why then do we not teach the rules by which we reason, namely logic? Why do we not inform the student of the aim of teaching, that is reasoning, by illustrating it appropriately in such a way that he can become conscious of it?

I think there is only one answer to these questions: all these subjects are conflictual, that is they would reveal different ways of practising science. In other words, it is not possible to teach these subjects in the classical manner, as truths which are indisputable and the same for everyone. Indeed, it is obvious that there is a wide range of political doctrines, from liberal, to socialist, to anarchist, to non-violent.

Economics too is clearly divided into two major theories, the classic or neo-classic and the Marxist. There is no way of reconciling these, they are totally opposed. The first attributes fundamental importance to the market and the market price of goods, the second to the factory and the exploitation of the worker by the owner; only the second theory explains how and why capital is formed.

Finally, logic, from its very beginning when it was mathematically formalized, has taken several forms. Classical logic gives rise to paradoxes which modal logic, for example, eliminates. And, for 70 years now there has been an intuitionistic logic which actually renounces the principle of the excluded third (statement A is either true or false)[1]. It would be a great advantage for the student's culture if he were able to link this logic with the schools of dialectical thought with which he becomes acquainted through the study of other subjects, such as history or philosophy.

What does present-day non-conflictual teaching involve?

It is not true that formal education deals with all these problems in the history of philosophy. After all, few students study philosophy. Furthermore the history of philosophy barely mentions the problems of science, and does so in an episodic manner, that is, without comparing one scientific theory with another. It immerses these problems within philosophic theories which are themselves very complicated and in such mutual disagreement that the student is unable to choose between them. Lastly, it is all confined to the intellectual plane, separated from active life. Thus philosphy teaches the student to know only how to contemplate these problems and not how to resolve them.

By avoiding any conflict, present-day teaching of science is repressive in that it ignores conflict except as something which is outside the school and scholastic knowledge, and it considers all students as children who cannot be allowed to know the real situation regarding the sciences they are studying. Thus, science is presented mythically, attracting students by its false splendours; and only when they are grown up do they possibly discover that there are conflicts involved,

Thus, present-day teaching regards the results of science as unquestionable and equal for all people. For this reason it always presents the same propositions and their inevitable results. It is repetitive, both for the teachers who teach those results and for the students who learn them; all the propaganda for creativity in the teaching of science has added only extravagant, though sometimes useful ways to present the final results; the results remain what they always were.

Present-day teaching is the imposition on the students of a scientific culture which is already definitely constructed; they have only to accept and repeat it, whatever may be their individual or group cultures. Those students who are not motivated towards this type of study are marked as lazy or incompetent, while those who succeed will all have a similar way of thinking.

It results in being partial and separated from the daily experience of life, isolated from personal and social values. Thus it does not lead to the formation of a unified and complete culture. Nevertheless, it claims to be the only complete, self-sufficient vision of the world able to throw light upon any cultural development.

This has profound consequences on professional life. It results in being abstract because it presents indisputable truths which are not linked to the uncertainties of professional life nor to the reality of conflict in social life. For example, anyone who has studied in this way will not link ethical problems with scientific problems. But has the scientist who invents a new weapon no responsibility for it? Has the technician who develops and builds it no responsibility? In fact they are not aware of their responsibilities because, from their youth, they have been accustomed to thinking of personal problems as separate from scientific ones. Teaching of science has taught them that when some problems arise one has to call in the scientific experts in that field, who will supply a rational and scientific solution which will avoid subjectivity and emotivity. And if by any chance this should not solve the problem, then there is a duty to obey one's superior; just as when one does not understand a scientific train of thought, one must repeat what the teacher says.

This abstract knowledge supports the concept of the neutrality of the professional stance in the face of social problems. Those problems would be resolved if everyone did his individual duty, and the various institutions dealt with the social problem for which they were scientifically planned. This results in directing professional activities first to the satisfaction of institutional aims, and subsequently to social problems. In particular, there is not supposed to be a collective responsibility — for example, of the scientists preparing genetic manipulations — because it is for the science of politics to regulate the problem with laws. Finally, the myth of scientific truth leads people to think that this type of social organization is inevitable.

What positive action can be taken?

According to what has been said above, it is necessary to teach

A. Drago

students all the knowledge that man has accumulated without the exclusions that hide the realities of science and human knowledge from them, that is, it is necessary to teach the history of political doctrines, the history of economic doctrines, and logic. This will serve to unveil the conflict which exists within social knowledge and within science itself. Furthermore it is necessary to demystify the present-day teaching of science by revealing those conflicts that are now concealed. Indeed all those subjects which today are taught in an abstract and neutral way have internal conflicts.

Even mathematics cannot claim to teach absolute and neutral truths. For more than 50 years now there have existed two profoundly different ways of practising mathematics: first of all the classical one, which, put briefly, attributes to mathematics the power to carry out an infinite number of operations and then more; while the other, which is called contructivistic, restricts itself only to a limited number of operations. This leads both to a restriction of classical mathematics and to more controlled results[2]. Thus, when irrational numbers and real numbers are introduced in the secondary school, it is necessary to be honest and declare to the students that there are various ways of defining and obtaining real numbers and the concepts which follow them (series, derivative, integral).

The 'new maths' emphasizes the abstract character of classical mathematics in order to achieve greater efficiency in learning and in managing mathematical techniques. In reality, when restricted, as is usual, to finite sets, set theory is equivalent to an important part of logic theory: the relevance of the new maths partly follows from the tacit introduction of the subject of logic during teaching.

It is also important to notice that even the most fascinating science, physics, conceals internal conflicts. In fact since the rise of thermodynamics there has been no single theory of the physical world: for 50 years there have been two, relativity theory and quantum mechanics, whose formulae and research programmes are incompatible. This may perhaps seem remote from the schoolboy studying mechanics, electromagnetism and thermodynamics, but in fact in this last study there exists a principle which is often left out but which is actually of the greatest cultural importance, as the present energy debate emphasizes: the second law of thermodynamics.

Normally it is expressed through the entropy function, which is defined in a very abstract way. In fact the second law (which strangely enough was discovered 20 years before the first law!) resulted from an enquiry into practical experience regarding the efficiency of real steam engines.

Its original formulation is that perpetual motion is impossible; that

74

expressed the century-old experience of mankind. This formulation makes clear what is usually obscure: that this law contradicts the other theory of physics usually taken as a model and which is studied first by students, namely mechanics[3]. Indeed, this latter study takes as the model of motion for its first principle, straight uniform movement; i.e. perpetual movement. In effect it can be held that mechanics is a special case of thermodynamics, to the extent that friction is considered to be negligible, or more precisely, when the phenomena which give rise to irreversible processes are so considered. Present-day teaching sacrifices the second law of thermodynamics by formulating it in an abstract manner, after presenting mechanics as the principal theory of physics; this leads to ignorance of the fact that time in physics is not a variable which can run either backwards or forwards indifferently; as established by thermodynamics, it has only one direction — ahead.

As a consequence, the second law is ignored or undervalued in day-to-day living, so much so that as the energy crisis has now revealed, we waste enormous amounts of energy by the unscientific way we build houses and produce energy[4].

Consequences of change

It is necessary to consider science with its internal conflicts and it is necessary that this consciousness should be shared by the students. They must understand the conflicts of opposing scientific theories in the same subject, the wider concepts to which these lead, and what is involved in choosing one rather than another.

This introduces science as an integral part of our culture, so that culture grows by developing a particular conception of science.

Then the science teacher will no longer be required merely to repeat immutable truths, surrounding them with various attractions to make the material more interesting, but will again be a man of culture who is able to help others to achieve their own culture; because he faces problems which are essentially cultural in nature, such as the internal conflicts within science. In this way he will become an educator, that is a person who is able to develop not simply the faculties of the students but their personalities.

From the students' point of view, study will not be simply the learning of more or less abstract mental techniques, but will consist of comparing what is studied with one's own experience of life so as to understand, study and choose a personal position in a scientific conflict. Study must lead him to a general synthesis between experience of life and the internal conflicts of the knowledge accumulated in the past centuries.

Even the motivations of students towards scientific studies will no longer be linked to emotional coldness (as shown by psychological tests), which leads in the profession to a search for power as compensation. They will be linked to interest in life as it is, i.e. in a life in which conflicting projects coexist and everyone chooses his own and learns to interact with others. In particular, the student will have the motivation to form a complete and adequate vision of the world, aimed at the complete development of his personality.

Resulting change in the search for peace

All this is also a different way of conceiving peace in society and in the world. Today's teaching implies the concept that science and education are peaceful activities, thus:

1. there are peaceful domains of social life and some people are living in peace (scientific researchers, teachers); even school life is peaceful in its nature; when this is not the case occasional conflicts are delegated to the specific authorities;
2. all social life would be peaceful if it were modelled on science and education; i.e. peace could be achieved and maintained if everybody entrusted the matter to competent persons who have the scientific knowledge to deal with it; if the people delegate the problems to the experts and leave them to act in accordance with their institutional rules — which means delegating to the scientific experts both the power to decide and the power to put their decisions into practice, with institutional violence if necessary.

This implies that disarmament can be achieved when everyone is armed as little as possible and the scientific and political experts have made an agreement on super bombs through technical discussion. The citizen has only to be sure that his own country has the political will to disarm and to hope that it be quickly achieved.

The other sort of teaching shows that seeking peace does not mean ignoring conflicts, or hiding them so that people regard them as a matter for experts. It holds that in the world nothing, not even science, exists without internal conflicts. Furthermore, it intends to face these conflicts in a way that involves each person taking part in the conflict, especially in the more historically important ones (for example those in science and technology), leading to a personal solution, with full responsibility towards one's neighbours without seeking suppression of others but looking for a solution useful for everybody. This exalts individuality, creativity and personality, pushing us to achieve a greater ability than we have at present to face social life with its problems. This increases the power of small groups in comparison with large institutions and leads to the resolution of violence on the same level as it is manifested, without the need to seek the intervention of large organizations involving institutional violence.

Formal education on conflict

Let us look at the whole of scholastic education. In comparison with the past, education is no longer military in type, exalting warlike values, such as blind obedience, fighting the enemy, destroying anyone who wishes us ill. Nevertheless it does not educate directly for peace. It has only eliminated war without inquiring whether the lack of a didactic organization itself inevitably leads people to clash with one another. Education in the resolution of conflicts which people receive is through repression (disciplinary sanctions) or the delegation of collective conflicts (election of representatives of the factions).

It is possible to reconstruct the history of how the school has conceived of conflicts through the following phases[5]:

1. Repression: exclusion of conflicts, seen as asocial or irrational incidents. The person who is the cause of the conflict must be found and his physical presence among the 'goodies' eliminated for fear that they may be contaminated.
2. Paternalism: conflicts are sometimes accepted, but only if they are limited and easily resolved, that is if they presuppose that one of the parties is an inferior (the child) and the other superior (the parent). This attitude supports repression because the parent is justified by the 'wickedness' of the child.
3. Democracy: all conflicts are accepted, among all people, but are channelled into preconstituted solutions by the existing institutions; the prerequisites for solving the conflict are delegation to the experts and faith in science. If we look closely, not all conflicts are really accepted, because those forming part of the social organization itself, mainly the conflicts within science and between different ways of establishing the rules for the resolution of conflicts, are still hidden.

Present-day teaching of science, holding that there are no conflicts in science, belongs to the first or third phase according to the degree of development of political democracy in a country. In an authoritarian regime it is repressive, except for some paternalism in the inter-personal relationships between teacher and pupils; it is democratic in a formal democracy.

The above phases are opposed by the socialisation of conflicts: the acceptance of all conflicts at all levels (even within the *sancta sanctorum* of this society, science) but giving people the means to resolve them, teaching each other the way to resolve them, apart from repression and delegation. Because education for resolution of conflicts is the heart of education for peace; and this is the new science, the science for peace.

Disarmament and international conflict

Let us look at a higher level, i.e. at world society. After World War II new political entities appeared on the international scene, the countries of the Third World. They expressed various cultures, traditions, religions and interests which were potentially in conflict among themselves and with other nations. A long period of world peace has been assured by a policy which integrates all the first three ways to control conflicts: repression — nuclear weapons possessed only by the superpowers; paternalism — aid to developing countries; and democracy — on the one hand faith in international institutions resolving international conflicts by means of discussions between representatives, and on the other science and technical progress considered as myths, as the unique social values superseding all cultures, religions and traditions. The promise of welfare for all peoples made everyone pursue the same objective. And schooling was modelled on the same policy about conflicts, the traditional way to teach science.

But this peace has been a false one: we are waking from a long sleep during which we did not notice that raw materials have been stupidly wasted, that the resources of the world are nearly exhausted, that pollution is perhaps irreversible, that now nuclear proliferation is unstoppable, that the arms race absorbs a great part of the resources of humanity and now gives the power to destroy mankind several times over. In reality, this peace has been attained by considering peoples and nations as minors, to whom the real nature of world problems could not be revealed, so they have been excluded from the solution of conflicts, asked only for irresponsible delegation of their power, pushed into belief in a mythified science and rewarded by munificent welfare, at the cost of consuming world resources.

This is why only now is it becoming clear that we have built an enormous war machine, not only the military machine itself but the whole social organization which is functional to it, starting with the school and ending with the whole political organization of society. Because of this, disarmament is not a point to be raised with a particular social sector, the military, considered separately from the rest of society which would be peaceful if it was left to itself; each of us must disarm himself at a personal level, and above all at the level of social organization, starting from the first social organization, the school.

Through the school the previous policies are perpetuated, when instead a real education for peace for the new generations should be begun. Moreover, we should disarm science and its teaching, which produces the most acute form of violence, ideological violence, which supports the arms race and the power of the military.

Disarmament and models of development

Moving to an even higher level, the two ways of teaching science are typical of the two opposing models of development, the hard and the soft, pointed out by Lovins in connection with the energy problem[6].

Lovins' study is of great importance because he was the first to show in a scientific way, by using the second law of thermodynamics, that it is possible to project a different progress from the present one; it was followed by many other studies. That of the IIED for the UK is particularly interesting since it actually forecast a general increase of individual consumption while diminishing the present production of energy! This shows that it is not true that there is only one sort of progress: it is possible to project a soft model of development, based on self-management and on productive and administrative decentralization.

For a long time people who were worried about the ever-increasing arms race have rejected the idea that national defence depends on scientific improvement of weapons and have looked for alternative solutions. They discovered the historical relevance of the liberation of India, the struggle of the Danish to defend Jews during Nazi persecution, the struggle of the Norwegian teachers against the Nazi regime of Hitler, the struggle of Czechoslovakia against the USSR. All these examples suggest that the alternative to the arms race is an unarmed defence where everyone is ready to sacrifice himself to resolve the conflict in the collective interest, there is a strong popular solidarity, decisions are decentralized, and small groups are self-managing[7].

To prepare this defence requires that the people follow a model of development resembling that indicated by Lovins, a soft model. The first to realize this was Gandhi who moreover deeply criticized formal education, Western science and technology; he proposed a general method for resolving conflicts, that of non-violence. He was the greatest teacher of this century on how conflicts may be resolved at all levels, without destroying the adversary, but with his rehabilitation.

So the two ways of teaching science are linked to two different ways to achieve disarmament: the first continues the delegation to experts, the centralization of decisions, nuclear proliferation, growth of multinational corporations, polluting technology; while the second

79

A. Drago

promotes the widening of the power of decision and involvement of the people in self-reliant defence, energy production, and scholastic education.

Notes and references

1. Several books illustrate these theories of logic; with few exceptions they do not present the conflict between the several logics because they maintain the hope of reconciling them in the future.
2. The best introduction is the dialogue in Heyting A. *Intuitionism: an introduction.* Elsevier, North Holland, 1966. A popular paper appeared in *Scientific American,* October 1979.
3. This was the point of view of Mach and the young Planck. The polemics are well presented in Rey A. *La théorie physique chez les physiciens.* Alcan, 1906.
4. See, for example, Commoner B. *The poverty of power,* 1974
5. These phases parallel the phases of the reconquest of science by the proletarian class as seen by Bogdanov A. *Nauka i roboti klass,* Moscow, 1920. (Italian translation: *La scienza e la classe operaia.* Bompiani, 1975).
6. Lovins A. *Soft energy paths.* New York, Ballinger 1977.
7. A classic book on the subject is Sharp G. *The political equivalent of war: civilian defence.* Carnegie, 1965.

5. The arms race and the role of education*

Jaime Diaz, *Corporation for Social and Cultural Development, Bogotá*

Research studies conducted over recent years have led to a distinction between physical or direct violence, and indirect or structural violence. Direct violence is usually considered first when talking about the need to stop the arms race. Nevertheless, structural violence is its fundamental cause: violence in an unjust economic and political system, be it within a country or at the international level, produces armed violence. Starving people are driven to despair and violence when they see no other way leading to a real change in their situation.

The former type of violence has — at least in Latin America — a fundamentally repressive character: arms become a necessity for weak governments, in order to suffocate protests, criticisms, and armed revolutionary endeavours or demonstrations by civil population: hence the violation of political and civil rights and the emergency situations by which legal guarantees are suspended. But the fundamental cause of the violation of civil and political rights is precisely the violation of the economic rights of the weak majorities. Therefore, the governments which should be protecting human rights are their main violators, acting jointly with those enforcing economic power, in spite of verbal declarations in favour of those rights.

All this results in a kind of state of war between governments and people, reflecting the whole problem of social and economic groups, also themselves in a chronic state of war.

Repression, nevertheless, does not eliminate the causes of that state of war; it merely suffocates its manifestations for an unknown period while, paradoxically, it aggravates the origins. Everything may blow up at any moment. Quite reasonably we speak of the 'spiral of violence', when we can see that one kind of violence leads to another. Even individual violence among citizens is tied to structural violence.

Violent protest by the people is particularly expressed by means of assault, guerrilla warfare and kidnapping of persons; repressive violence by unjustified imprisonment without trial or subsequent investigation, manipulation of justice and torture (which has attained remarkable

*Reproduced by permission of UNESCO.

81

technological advancements . . .) and is legitimized by emergency situations.

Worldwide violence between countries is closely bound to the desire to obtain or to maintain the domination of one country over another. Arms become necessary to attack, control and defend.

Injustice at all levels is the main context of all forms of violence and of the enormous sums of money spent on armies and military equipment. Consequently, we can never attack belligerence without, at the same time, remedying injustice.

Obstacles to peace

According to what has just been stated, the main and radical obstacle to firm peace is the poverty, and even misery, of a large part of the world's population, and the political limitations this produces. This situation should not be considered as affecting a large number of individuals, but as a poverty-generating system within countries and extending beyond national borders. It will be necessary to take advantage of the most recent social studies for establishment of a strategy aimed not to obtain economic profit, but to serve primarily the weak of the world.

Within this systematic context fall the economic relationships between rich and poor countries based on exploitation of raw materials to feed the great sophisticated industries whose products are exported to the poorer countries, at very high prices, resulting in the well known consequences of a growing imbalance of trade.

International military assistance agreements actually support technological dependence through the war system. This assistance is often the result of military complicity between assisting and assisted governments to stifle the needs of the people.

The arms-producing countries preach, on one side, peace, while on the other they furnish the tools for war, in which they are actually interested for economic reasons. They have already built up an economic system which must be fed by warfare in other countries, the buying countries. Therefore, it is necessary to push customers into war to obtain good sales. All this forms part of a system of hypocrisy which seems to be accepted in international relations. In order to discover the truth on the other side, spies are needed.

Technological competition between the great world powers has become an argument to dissuade one another from possible attack, and a permanent incentive for the progress of the war industry, always justifying the unimaginable amounts of direct or indirect military budgets.

Within our countries, low salaries, lack of fundamental services such as health and housing, as well as the constantly rising prices, have become the prime obstacles to peace. Sluggishness or inefficiency of governments, and the lack of resources to solve social problems foster despair, and confirm among many the conviction that only through violence can justice and peace be achieved.

It is necessary, on the other side, to point to the diffusion — it could be said organized and conscious diffusion — of violence and war, the export of an ideology of violence through literature and films, and the growing systematization of the structure of war, in which warfare specialization plays a very important part. To many people, military service has become the only means of serving their country in an organized way for a relatively long period of time. Military service is based on hypotheses, or rather dogmas, which should be revised in depth. It is wrong that the forces of youth should continue to be wasted in the name of the country, the nation, the blood of our forefathers, and in order to fortify the war system, rather than being able to devote their generosity, their capabilities and their country's resources to the solution of urgent and fundamental problems. Military service is a typical case of ideologization of practices born out of long surpassed historical circumstances. Religion has contributed, be it consciously or not, to this ideologization and justification of militarism. In South American countries, the armed forces often appoint the Virgin Mary as their 'General'. There are clergymen who also hold military rank. Even if these positions are not operational, but honorary, it is the significance of such a situation that is important. The way the church carries on its pastoral service to the armed forces, becoming itself, in a way, part of the army through its military chaplains, being subject accordingly to military discipline, creates serious ambiguities. The question may be raised whether in order to serve soldiers spiritually you must become a soldier yourself.

The school is child and mother of the warfare ideology. It reproduces the ideology that feeds it. The school structure is based on competition and struggle between individuals. And its organization has been inspired by military discipline for a long time. A real warfare ritual has evolved mainly around national festivities and symbols. The study of the history of one's own country or of one's neighbours' is centered on the wars and the victories which constitute the glory of citizens and an example to be followed. Every act of domination over another country is justified; injustices become, almost miraculously, heroic gestures to be celebrated. History is relative to the country that makes it. Also, as long as history is a tool for the justification of any event favourable to a country, and especially to a government, it will be impossible to recognize mistakes and look ahead with different eyes.

Citizens cannot continue to be absolute defenders of the past of their countries. There are other ways of loving one's country. This is closely bound to the unconscious meaning of what is called 'patriotism'. National anthems, marches, colours, flags, etc. are placed at the service of this patriotism. But would it not be worth examining in depth the implications of traditional patriotism in order to create another form, more in accordance with a world in which it would be possible to be citizens of the world, not just of one country, and in which co-operation could replace competition and domination? Mass media are a powerful instrument for ideological diffusion, especially concerning conflicts affecting one's own country *vis-à-vis* others.

In general, we may say that the agents of education, be it family, school, formal or non-formal, lack awareness of the problem; they often act unconsciously in a contradictory way, and need to be supported by instruments of action concerning education *against* warfare and *for* peace. All this, plus a more and more aggressive atmosphere, particularly in the larger cities, erects an obstacle to peace.

The place of education

It is necessary to become aware of the educational influence, not only of the school but also of the family and mass media, of political parties, unions and civic organizations, religious groups, etc.

It is not only a matter of changing thematic contexts, or of historical evaluation, but of creating or developing new attitudes consonant with the type of society we want. It will be necessary, as stated in the 1974 UNESCO Recommendation 'to stimulate the intellectual and affective development of the individual . . . by combining learning information and action. . . . to develop social responsibility, solidarity with the weakest groups . . . to attain a critical comprehension of national and international problems'. In order to achieve this, it will be necessary to face a critical analysis of 'present and historical economic and political factors which lie at the base of contradictions and tensions between countries, as well as the means to overcome them'. In fact, it is not just a matter of knowing, but of becoming able to participate 'eliminating situations which maintain and aggravate the fundamental problems conditioning the survival and welfare of humanity'.

In other words, it is a matter of forming a new type of citizen: not passive human beings who know merely how to discuss a matter, but individuals who exercise their responsibilities towards the functioning of society, through thinking and action; who are not content just to live themselves, but who think of others; who do not just conform to what has already been done, but who become progressively capable of transform-ing their society, starting with what lies closest to them.

Within the logical context of what has been stated, concerning the major obstacle to peace, we must assert that the role of education should be to contribute to changing the present war-generating system for another through which justice and, consequently, peace, are possible. It is a matter of, to quote UNESCO's recommendation, 'changing society in order to obtain the practical application of human rights'.

Social education, understood as concerned with the life of man in society, thus becomes the main task of any type of education. It will then be necessary to consider alternative societies and to have the possibility of choosing between them. Man has organized society: it is man's task, then, to change it, and it should be possible to do this lucidly. Technical education, ordained for economic profit and based on a man-nature rapport, has taken a foremost place. Technical education is necessary to transform nature. But it is, at the same time, blended with social education; it is, consciously or not, at the service of a society. Neutrality of science is a myth that should be revealed. All science is involved with the society it serves.

Such an education cannot ignore the overall dimensions of the world's problems. Nowadays, a merely national vision is insufficient. The internationality of our lives is a fact.

This new education — for justice and peace, not for war — demands a change of mentality, of values, of perceptions, of emotional milieu, of content, of methods; all of this in a context of the philosophy of a transforming action, which is not repressive nor military, but pacific. The task is enormous, and it will be necessary to work on a long-term basis. But the historical impetus for a different future is already present.

What can be done

I would like to stress the suggestions presented by Reardon[1] on behalf of IPRA's Commission of Education (to which I belong). I would like, however, to point out some things in particular.

If we are to get at the roots of the obstacles she refers to in her study, it will be necessary to work towards having governments fundamentally change their war policies, so that there is coherence between agreements, declarations, etc., and practice. The lack of coherence which is so evident today has already been pointed out. It is important to study, find and make known the means to apply more directly the recommendations, resolutions, etc., concerning disarmament, according to particular situations.

The 1974 UNESCO recommendation in particular is a document which should be known and applied by educators at all different levels. Up to the present, however, very little has been done about it. We could say here, once more, that governments very often lack coherence. What can be done about this? Different initiatives, already applied in a number of countries, could inspire realistic solutions.

It is important that people know about their own government's actions and decisions concerning military matters, expenses incurred for military purposes at national, continental or worldwide level, as well as the future consequences to be expected, should the present situation continue. At the same time, they must press the issue of disarmament through governmental or non-governmental channels. It is necessary to keep in mind that disarmament is not an isolated issue, and that it should be regarded within the whole of the present economic and political structure. It is therefore not merely a question of decreasing military expenses and alotting the savings to assist in the development of other areas of the world, but, at the same time, taking a step towards changing the present order of the world for a new international order. Otherwise things will get worse . . . The issue of human rights is inseparable from this problem.

It is necessary to take measures aimed at giving social education the place it deserves. Consequently, an element of critical analysis should be made available, not only to an elite group but to the common citizen, according to what is necessary today in order for him to truly participate in the life of society. It is particularly necessary to revise the field of social studies, especially history and civics, in order to turn them into a means of education for peace, not for war.

In order for experienced values and the explicit contents of education to be coherent, it is necessary to be aware of all the elements which, within the school, contribute to the diffusion of the warfare ideology, so that schools can be demilitarized schools.

The experience of non-violent transforming action (known in Brazil as *firmeza permanente* or permanent firmness) should be used and diffused as a significant contribution to transformation into an unarmed society, and as an awareness of the new possibilities offered to us. This experience has been mainly outside the school. For the cause of peace, there is a large human potential which, having never attended school, has not been the victim of the present school system.

6. Disarmament education: why and how?

Amalendu Guha, *Institute for Alternative Development Research, Oslo*

Education on armaments and diffusion of knowledge on armaments and their research and development, the arms race and its destructive effects, etc. have been so well publicized by mass communication media such as newspapers, special journals, television, radio and films, at military training centres, at higher military specialization centres, at military manoeuvre areas, etc. that interested people throughout the world can obtain the latest or almost latest knowledge on armaments. On the other hand, until now there have been few efforts on behalf of education on disarmament at either national or international level. While armaments education and preparation lead to the development and spread of the values of aggression, disarmament education, in contrast, can raise the consciousness of the people not only against arms and the armed forces, but also towards forming an alternative attitude, free from war-like preparation and expenditure, in which satisfaction of fundamental social and human needs at normal and subsistence level can be assured to every citizen, both at the periphery and at the centre, in the rural regions and urban settlements.

Mutual mistrust of opposing socio-political systems and military power blocs as well as of most of the neighbouring nations, has reached such an acute stage, particularly during the last 10 years, that an irrational arms race, modernization of existing armaments and means of armament production, diversification of production of strategic arms and arms-carriers, increased investment in military research and development etc. are taking place at an alarming rate. SALT I and II have given both time and space for the existing super-powers to proceed from the so-called stage of imbalance to the stage of balance. This is nothing but war-like preparation during peacetime. We cannot but term this a period of peacelessness or tension under the umbrella of peace.

The theory of balance is one of the most important guiding theories which has emerged during the last 10 years in disarmament. That might gives the right to talk on an equal footing with the opponent is the logic of this approach, and the arms race is accelerating to justify it.

Underestimation of one's own strength and overestimation of the opponent's gives rise to new preparations as well as overdevelopment of existing armaments. The untruths and half-truths of the propaganda war intensify the arms race and create confusion and misunderstanding between and among systems and nations.

To counteract the peaceful competition of the current arms build-up between the super powers, between systems and between and among nations, a climate of total and general disarmament and a moratorium on the use of nuclear arms has to be systematically created. Disarmament education is the most effective background for this. The measures for disarmament taken by governmental organizations, the UN agencies and other international government-sponsored and supported bodies have the characteristics of measures from above, of implementation from the top. But mobilization of the masses and equipping them with the ideology of disarmament is the prime function of non-governmental organizations or mass groups. Its nature is rather that of development from below. When the masses are educated in and convinced of the principles and ideology of disarmament they become a force, which in turn can enforce the political and administrative decision-makers to move actively and positively towards disarmament.

Therefore, 'why disarmament education' does not need clarification; 'how to achieve disarmament education' is the basic issue. Besides, giving arguments for 'why', it is hoped to contribute here some means as to 'how'.

Why disarmament education?

Only general and real disarmament can bring back the lost faith and feeling of safety and security in man as a true global citizen, the feeling of trust in and understanding of fellow citizens of neighbouring and far-distant nations, the rediscovery of self-identity and self-dignity with its contribution towards global understanding and the progress of humankind in general. The good human values have long been lost during the course of devastating wars and during the process of the arms race within and without wars. Winning a war, whether actual or forthcoming, requires an attitude of desiring supremacy over the enemy, a feeling of superiority over another nation or nations, a wish to subjugate others, etc. which give rise to extreme nationalism, irrespective of the system. This extreme nationalism, in the course of its development, destroys the power of judgement, and leads a nation in the irrational direction of chauvinistic, hegemonistic, arrogant, and dogmatic behaviour.

Superpowers, sub-superpowers or emerging superpowers, irrespective of the system, can be accused of this type of attitude. This extreme nationalism sows the misconception of 'might is the right way towards national dignity' and 'military might is the source of both national and international discipline'. The speeches of national political leaders, mass communication media, teaching curricula at primary, secondary and tertiary education levels, etc. in some countries are formulated and publicized in such a way as to influence and educate the respective nations to proceed in the single direction of so-called triumph. National history books are written, or better said, re-written, to glorify national wars and war-lords. It is a pity that, in the history books of most nations, man and his contribution towards the progress of civilization and human development has been replaced by the role of wars, war-lords and similar personalities. War has been glorified as the source of national progress, and some history writers of the dominant nations term the period of war and dominance the 'golden age' of their national history. I call them history-writers, rather than historians, as they are seldom objective in writing the history of their society. The political, educational and functional ideology of the dominant nations was always to spread a feeling of hatred or malicious kindness towards the dominated enemy or neighbour. This was true in the past and is true in this century also. The ultimate analytical result of this type of education and perception is armament education, processing the mind of the entire nation or society in the ideology of war and armament superiority.

The social elites of the dominant 'overdeveloped' nations, possibly in order to distract the attention of ordinary people from national socio-economic and cultural problems, have injected the narrow concepts of 'national identity' and 'national loyalty' into the mind of their societies, instead of the concept of positive human development. Therefore the display and conviction of national identity through military power and preparation, and national loyalty through compulsory and advanced military training and services, have become the logic and magic of the armaments education of today. Only effective disarmament education can neutralize the above misconception of national identity and national loyalty based on false, egocentric and subjective premises and principles.

It is not enough to talk of limitation of further development and research on armament technology, production of armaments and army personnel. There should be real alternative action on the conversion of armament technology and personnel into civil technology and personnel. Disarmament education and the mobilization of social forces in its favour can help in the implementation of this alternative.

Is disarmament possible and if so, how, is still the question for the majority of the common people all over the globe, whether in the West or the East, in the North or the South. And it is unanswered because

A. Guha

of ignorance on the aspects and prospects of disarmament. People still fear the consequences of disarmament such as unemployment, economic dislocation demanded by the restructuring of the entire national economy, fears of aggression from the enemy or unknown sources etc. This is because alternative socio-economic development models and actions cannot be presented to the common people, who might then see that

1. unemployment could be avoided if a rational and gradual conversion policy from armament technology and personnel to civil technology and personnel is adopted;
2. economic dislocation could and can be avoided through minimum restructuring of the national economies;
3. that bi- and multilateral and bi- and multinational non-aggression treaties can be adopted, with international and UN guarantees.

These actions could and can help in the removal of existing mistrust and misunderstandings between neighbouring countries, and between nations. But it is unfortunate that no country, whether big or small, wants to begin with charity at home. The small nations argue that they have to maintain sufficient security and defence measures against any unforeseen aggression while the big nations argue that they have to maintain the same in order not to be defeated by any small or big nations. The very basis of this logic is mutual mistrust. Disarmament education has to adopt very serious arguments to overcome this.

Ideological differences

The world armament-disarmament politics of today are divided into contrasting ideologies: the so-called free-world ideology promoted by capitalism, and the so-called mass ideology promoted by socialism in the name of Marxism-Leninism. Both are convinced of the virtue of their own ideology and afraid of being counteracted or counterpenetrated by the other. Monopoly, multinational and social democratic capitalism in the West thinks of 'freeing' the masses in the socialist countries. The nationally oriented and technologically dependent socialism of the East thinks and acts to 'liberate' the masses in the West and in the dependent Third World periphery. The East promotes the theory and activity of class struggle even under the cover of peaceful co-existence, and the West comes forward to protect the existing and traditional socio-economic interests and the reactionary regimes of other countries in its own interest under the pretext of saving them from a communist take-over. In a systemic struggle, each side considers its own system as paradise and that of the other as hell. The political decision-makers in both systems determine both the armament and disarmament policies, and so it is their political honesty and wishes which will constitute the fundamental determinants for disarmament policy. This very basic determinant is still lacking in the international arena.

The superpower system and bloc build-up has created an undignified dependency relationship between these powers and the sub-powers and in the bloc members. In the case of NATO, member nations tend to follow in the steps of the USA in political and military decisions, by sacrificing their national desires. The same is true of the Warsaw Treaty nations. Only France and Romania make some occasional gestures of disagreement with their big brothers. The opinion-building of uni- or bilateral disarmament at the level of military power blocs and between and among members, can create an atmosphere of lowered tension. The reduction of arms expenditure and diversion of the savings towards human and social development can become a strong objective for disarmament education.

Balance theory

The balance theory of armament development and competition, in essence, is that unless you are on an 'equal footing' or at equal strength with your counterpart, he will not pay attention to you, nor come to any understanding. Unfortunately, the present-day functional behaviour of the international system proves this. Either underestimation of one's strength and potential against those of the counterpart or opposing system, or the ambition to surpass the strength and potential of the rival or so-called enemy, constitute the very essence of this theory. The process of this competitive behaviour has the characteristic of a spiral. If the action is from one side, it is unilateral vertical, if it starts from both sides, as usually happens, the character of interaction becomes cross-vertical, and never-ending. An inferior imbalance of one nation is the result of underestimating its own strength and potential or overestimation that of the counterpart. This is the primary stage, from which both competing nations march forward to reach a state of balance as the secondary stage. Again, from this stage of presumed balance, they proceed to the next stage of surpassing each other, reaching the level of superior imbalance or overbalance. The distance between the sides increases to the point at which they began.

In the case of reserves of nuclear arms, armament-carriers, missiles, sophisticated offensive and defensive weapons, army strength, etc., both the USA and the USSR stay near to each other in some cases and far in others. The statistics released on the occasions of SALT I and SALT II prove the above behaviour, while the time-limit to SALT III and the forthcoming SALTs, enable both nations to reach a point of balance, by adding to the reserves of some items and subtracting through dismantling from others. This time-limit can be termed the limit for further development, under conditions of tension relief. There has not been any embargo on research, development and production of new armaments. Unless there is a total moratorium on production, research and development of any type of armament, whether nuclear or non-nuclear, on a global scale, the prospect of disarmament çan never be bright.

Who will monitor the armament producing, exporting, using and experimenting nations? The unity of peace-loving, non-nuclear, smaller nations can be binding on them, through both direct and indirect action, to proceed towards gradual armament reduction and disarmament. Among the direct measures which the non-nuclear and other smaller nations can adopt, are: (a) a total embargo on imports of armaments from armament exporting countries; (b) refusal to accept aid agreements of 'food with arms' from the super and sub-super powers; (c) refusal to export the raw materials which are used in armament production, specially nuclear arms, to armament producing and experimenting countries, etc. The most effective indirect measure will be to build up public opinion to provide a moral force in both these groups of nations in favour of disarmament. If Gandhi could succeed in the creation of a strong non-violent moral power against the then colonial giant of the UK for India's liberation, and ultimately could succeed in achieving India's independence three decades ago, why can this not be tried again now? Of course, structural aggression and hence violence have become more brutal and less logic-oriented now than they were three decades ago, but at the same time people's consciousness all over the world has also greatly improved.

Disarmament education: how?

A total ban on armament education and compulsory armament training and enrollment in the army must become the most fundamental principle and action for disarmament education. The right to national self-defence and hence the right to arms possession, armament research, development and experiment, etc. has become an internationally agreed and accepted principle which, in turn, paves the way to limitless armament preparation, arm race, aggression and armed interference. This right is, again, much misused when it is extended to either maintain or increase the political and economic interests of some countries in other countries. While the above is true at the international level, internal subversion and repression is practised at the intra-nation level, in most of the world's nation states. Armament education and preparation has created fear, agony and pathos among the common people all over the world and the use of armaments has not only resulted in the destruction of millions of human lives, invalidation of millions of human beings and destruction of nature, it has also destroyed human-social morality.

In order to stop further human and natural destruction and in order to revive human-social morality, disarmament education and action appear essential. Disarmament education should operate on two directions (a) activating the decision-makers or social elites at the top, and (b) mobilizing and educating the masses at the bottom, to create a positive and effective force for disarmament preparation and action.

The basic charcteristic and purpose of any type of education is that it should be easily communicated to the people and clearly understood by them. Therefore, disarmament education will not realize its objective — will indeed become meaningless — unless the *why and how* of disarmament are made clear to the common people. If the masses cannot perceive the objective, meaning and essence of disarmament the blame will fall on disarmament researchers and educators. Considering the widespread dimensions and bad effects of armament education and the arms race at the global level, one feels the urgent necessity of socialization of disarmament education. It should be introduced immediately at every level of education and at every social level and class. Disarmament education cannot be socially neutral, i.e., it should not impart or communicate neutral knowledge, but socially objective knowledge, i.e., the knowledge of how to change a society of armament into a society of disarmament. Disarmament education cannot negate the realities of the socio-economic nature of a society, and so cannot exclude its analysis. The ideology of disarmament includes the ideology of the development of a social system to be followed during and after disarmament. Therefore, disarmament education is the combination of both social and political choices.

About 50% of the population in the Third World and about 10% of the population in the developed and overdeveloped countries still live at below subsistence or sufficiency level, in terms of the satisfaction of urgent fundamental human needs such as food, fresh drinking water, housing, clothing, health amenities and basic education. Of the estimated total world population of 4.4 billion at the beginning of 1980, about 3 billion live below subsistence level. Why not bring them to subsistence or sufficiency in respect of satisfaction of basic needs, from their present sub-human standard?

The right to life is the most fundamental of all the principles of human rights. It is accepted, without any argument, by all nations, social classes and social strata of the world. But life and its continuity cannot be assured unless the basic needs of life are assured. Man cannot live in a normal way without satisfaction of basic needs. So, this most important human right can only be fulfilled under the condition of peace, which, again, can be produced through disarmament.

The right to life being the most essential problem and the premordial condition of life being the satisfaction of basic needs, disarmament education must include a clear understanding of basic needs. Galtung and Wirak[1] argue that needs are 'something located inside individual human beings', which in essence, attributes a personal character to needs. But something located inside a human being consists of both needs and desires. If desire has no objective limitation. it cannot be basic. Therefore, while suggesting that 'basic' can never be 'absolute', Galtung and Wirak contend that one's existence does not, essentially, depend on material objects. While physical needs are essential and fundamental for the existence and maintenance of human life, they first and foremost consist of material needs: and these are the very basics for mankind. Non-physical needs such as identity, freedom, security, etc. are not the immediate basics.

Moreover, basic needs for an individual have a ceiling or level. A man cannot eat more than his stomach needs and if he tries to eat even a little more, he will suffer from indigestion and diarrhoea. For sleeping and living purposes, a man needs room to lie down and sufficient space to breath, no more. In any climatic condition a man cannot put on more clothes at one time than he needs. He does not need more preventive and procurative health measures than his basic necessity.* Why mention these here? It is because the basic human and social needs can be measured and since they can be measured efforts can be made to satisfy them both at social and individual levels. Both the human and material resources released from and relieved of the process of armaments can easily be used to effect the production, in sufficient quantity, of the material goods and services to give relief to the poverty-stricken people of the world.

Disarmament education, therefore, at the preliminary stage, will suggest an alternative to armament education and the arms race, an alternative which will provide concrete plans for the creation and development of socio-economic activities to produce both the purchasing power and goods and services for all those people now living below sufficiency level throughout the world. Disarmament education, at an advanced stage, should study the causes and processes which hinder the fulfilment of the basic social needs for the global social majority. These investigations and researches and their diffusion will raise social consciousness by bringing out the causes and phenomena, and

---

*The concept of basic human needs is limited here to what is needed to maintain a man's normal healthy physical structure. If this norm is exceeded it enters into the area of desire. Desire includes elements of non-basic needs: comfort, greed and overindulgence.

society acting on that consciousness will move towards effecting the desired social change.

This desired social change can be achieved through real social process, by which is meant the proper functioning of equality of social rights and equality of social duties. Rights without duties or duties without rights are unthinkable in a society genuinely based on equity and equality. The excess of one over the other will generate social imbalance and unequal development. Social rights contain elements of equal power-sharing, and social duties require equal sharing of resources or created values. They, again, combine the functions of participation and mobilization.

The absence of war is not peace, because it does not eliminate peacelessness and tensions existing or appearing in a society. Social peacelessness is the result of the aggressiveness of certain social elements or classes. Such action generates structural inequality and structural violence. Disarmament education, therefore, must include the principles and aspects of non-violence as well as the means to solve problems, which can eliminate the aggressive behaviour and actions of such social elements. The absence of rights for the majority of a society gives rise to social discontent, and ultimately, to revolutionary violence. The absence of duties, on the other hand, makes difficult the implementation and sharing of rights. The possibility of social violence occurring cannot be ruled out unless and until the basic social needs of the majority are satisfied. Such violence may result in repressive measures by the minority to maintain its own interests. The curricula of disarmament education and action must take note of this.

Almost all present national economies are war-economies, as their national budgets reserve a good part for defence outlay, armament production, armament procurement or import, armament research and development, grants to civil industries which produce important and integral parts of armaments, etc. Only on the premise and promise of disarmament can these war-economies be converted into civil or peace economies. The world has never experienced so much misuse of material and human resources as it does today. Apart from overconsumption and wastage by some overdeveloped countries, most of this misuse is in the armament industries. National defence budgets and war industries also contribute much to the ever-increasing inflation in each of the national economies. Expenditure on armament production and the armed forces, in the sense of maintenance and promotion, are socially non-productive, because these goods and services do not have social use-value, or social utility function. Since they enter into social accounting without accruing any social benefit to the society, they can be termed the surplus burden on society. Therefore, armament products which are given monetary values cause additions to the prices of other national social products. As a result, they inflate the prices of socially

Table 1

Use of material and human resources under conditions of armament (1979 prices)*	Use of material and human resources under conditions of disarmament
Arms trade by super- and sub-military powers in 1979: $16 billion	Used for land reclamation and to bring uncultivated land under cultivation, this would add 5.3 million acres of new land (estimated cost $3000/acre)
Total 1979 military budget of 158 states of the world: $50 billion	Used for civil purposes this would provide 25 million water-pumping tube wells for drought zones (estimated cost $2000/tube well)
Total defence budget and defence production in state defence and private sector producing armament equipment and parts: $500 billion	A quarter of this amount would provide 125 big dams producing water for several million acres, energy supply for industry and houses, and aiding production of several million tons of food grains and cash crops (estimated cost of 1 dam: $1 billion)
World expenditure on military R & D in 1979: $65 billion (estimate)	Used for housing the homeless or those in overcrowded conditions, this would provide 3.25 million three-roomed houses (estimated cost of three room dweling: $20 000

* Calculations and estimates made by the author from data collected from different sources and for different projects by the Insitute for Alternative Development Research, Oslo

useful goods and services. So, why do ordinary peace-loving citizens bear this unnecessary and ever increasing burden of inflation, year after year?

It would be foolish to believe that the existing means of armament production and technology cannot gradually and systematically be converted into civil or social technology, and at the same time the armament personnel can be turned into civil or social personnel. If this

Table 1 continued

Use of material and human resources under conditions of armament (1979 prices)*	Use of material and human resources under conditions of disarmament
At beginning of 1980, the world's active military, paramilitary, security and police forces were estimated as 3% of world population of 4.2 billion, or 126 million (estimated on minimum scale). This is 9% of the economically active population (those engaged in armament production not included)	If these people, representing the most healthy and vigorous members of society, were used in civil life in production of food, housing, textile industries and farming, they could solve the basic problems of food, shelter and clothing for man in ten years.
Seven economically active civilians work for every soldier, and three for his arms equipment	If half this population used to support and maintain the army and armaments were transferred to teaching, global illiteracy could be eradicated and basic education could be provided for all. This basic education could be used for social and individual advancement.
Number of war scientists, war laboratory personnel and those engaged in auxiliary services for war R & D: 20 million (estimate)	20 million more doctors, nurses, midwives and sanitary assistants would provide better world health care and more preventative amenities, fewer diseases, lower infant mortality and better life-expectancy

conversion is gradual, at the rate of 10% per year, ten years would be quite sufficient to achieve this without dislocation or serious disturbance to the capital and technology market and without any serious unemployment problem on a global scale. Moreover, once conversion begins society will begin to feel three benefits: (a) further investment for armament will be stopped and the money utilised to increase production of goods and services for satisfying basic human material needs, (b) inflation will gradually be checked, because of reduction and finally stoppage of armament production, whose costs or burdens on the socially needed goods and services will consequently be removed, (c) a huge pool of active workers will systematically become available in the production and distribution of civil goods and services. But the most important gain will be the saving of a tremendous volume of natural resources. Some of these are already being depleted and the introduction of rational use is urgently needed. There are clear predictions that if the USA maintains its war production at the present level, by the year 2000 it will be dependent on imports for about 50% of the first twelve most important strategic minerals.

Disarmament education and alternative development action

The most important goal for disarmament education will be to produce alternative models, possibilities and actions for human development. Only in this way can disarmament education be strengthened. Theory becomes stronger through verification in practice and the principles of and education on disarmament will be more viable if strong and objective alternatives can be put against armaments and the arms race. There can be an alternative development model through disarmament for each nation-state of the world. Table 1 gives some alternative possibilities of using the material and human resources which are being wasted on armaments. It provides two distinctive pictures of (a) use of material and human resources under the conditions of armament, and (b) usable possibilities of the same or similar material and human resources under the conditions of disarmament, in order to show not only the contrast, but also objective aspects which can lead to development of social sufficiency.

Conclusion

Where and at which level can disarmament education be started? Like peace research, peace education and peace action, disarmament education and action must be interdisciplinary, i.e., it must be included in the core of all natural and social science disciplines. The educators and the researchers must themselves be convinced on disarmament, so that they in turn can convince their students, audiences and the masses with arguments and presentation of examples on disarmament. There are advanced and effective mass media in the East and the West of the northern parts of the world. These mass media should include regular programmes on and in favour of disarmament. Political mass meetings and personal contacts are the most effective contact media in the developing south. It will therefore be the prime duty of politicians, political parties and social workers to include the objectives and actions of disarmament in common and regular action-programmes. Without considering it as a prescription from above, social activists can try to translate them into social life. Society should regard disarmament education from both its preventive (in terms of eventual future war) and curative (in terms of tension due to preparation for war) aspects.

This is the age of nuclear mistrust and counter-preparation. Due to rivalry this preparation may proceed to infinity. If it is not to be too late to lament the consequences of an unlimited armament race, disarmament education and action must begin today.

If disarmament efforts cannot start on the mutual bloc or multilateral basis, they must be started on a unilateral basis. This is necessary in order to build confidence for the entire world. Some nations must take the initiative and this is an age when no nation can perish from the global scene. Therefore, disarmament education must start first with the objective of a less-violent world, and, finally, with the motive of a totally non-violent or peaceful world.

Reference

1. Galtung J. and Wirak A. Human needs and human rights. *Bull Peace Proposals* 1977, **8** (3)

7. On the substance of disarmament education*

Magnus Haavelsrud, *Institute of Social Science, University of Tromsö*

For every problem faced by humankind education is seen as an instrument for reducing or eliminating that problem. This applies to malnutrition, development, peace, ecology, minority problems, racism, sexism, fascism, etc. — and to the quest for disarmament[1]. This reference to and belief in education grows out of the frustration of those scientific researchers, politicians, bureaucrats and experts who attempt to diagnose the problems and outline alternative solutions for alleviating them on high, often international, decision-making levels. The gradual worsening of conditions since World War II justifies such feelings of inadequacy. In spite of at least rhetorical goodwill to do something constructive, destructive developments follow.

Educators respond to this challenge in different ways. Some believe that they are capable of changing the world for the better, and go about it in their daily work in more or less idealistic and romantic ways. A second type of response comes from those who believe in the dissemination of findings from peace research and other relevant sciences. Thirdly, some respond more cautiously to the challenge, on the theory that education is more determined by the society of which it is a part than a determinant of the development of that society.

Here I shall first examine some critical assumptions and limitations of these three approaches, which I have labelled the idealistic, the scientific and the ideological respectively. Then I shall outline my own proposal for disarmament education, *viz.* the politicization approach.

The idealistic approach

The UNESCO preamble is frequently referred to by the supporters of this approach, namely, that it is in the minds of men that war begins. This assumption, or as many believe, universal truth, leads to the logical consequence that the next generation needs peace education to

*Revised version of paper for *Research and teaching on disarmament in various disciplines of higher education.* Symposium, International Institute for Peace and Tampere Peace Research Institute, Vienna, 26-27 Jan. 1980. *Peace and Sciences, 1980,* **1** 27-32

counter man's tendencies towards the violence which has caused previous and present generations to wage war. The idea is that this rotten world can be saved by a more rational and good generation as opposed to the bad qualities of the present one. The proponents of this approach tend to base their analysis of the problem on an accepted universal truth concerning each and everyone without any reference to societal groups and their interactions. The solution, therefore, involves the 'conversion' of the new generation one by one so that the aggregated results emerge in positive future developments. Implied in this line of thought is of course that some of the adults today representing a war generation are capable of making the necessary steps towards inducing another set of moral values and standards in the new generation. The belief in this idealistic approach resembles the missionary zeal of some religions, e.g. Christianity, in that the peace educators will supposedly constitute the new priesthood and the uneducated and immature children and youth represent the unsaved souls.

Another trait in this approach is the ideal of pacification, i.e. that people should tolerate and accept each other. This means that the exposition of conflicts and contradictory interests becomes a secondary matter or wholly eliminated so that harmony can be achieved even between the oppressor and the oppressed. This type of programme is of interest to the oppressor, whose oppression depends upon docile and acquiescent victims.

A major criticism of this approach would be the lack of sociological analysis. I would argue that the famous sentence from the UNESCO preamble needs to be qualified in sociological terms. Although it might be true that a war, or any other phenomenon for that matter, including peace, begins in the minds of men, it is absurd to apply this to every man and woman. Hence, the question is: which men and women? It seems that any education for disarmament based on the idealistic approach would need to identify those whose minds are bent towards militarism and war and whose actions are conducive to this. This would involve a sociological and historical analysis of the actual political situation in a nation, with identification of the interests and power of the actors involved in the contradictions present.

The implications of an educational programme along such idealistic lines can be dangerous, in that the causal analysis of the problem of peace (and disarmament) is limited to the individual. The extent to which the individual is a product of the society in which he/she lives, determines the extent to which this educational approach can lead to pacification of the individual to the benefit of reinforcing the social order, which in itself can be a basic factor in creating the conditions for violence and war. Thus, this approach may turn out to be reactionary and contradictory to the liberation struggles necessary for societal change, in that it focuses upon the symptoms of violence and aggression without seeing these in relation to conflict analysis in a specific context.

The idealistic approach is exemplified through educational initiatives which (1) exclude action based on reflective processes about societal contradictions, (2) exclude local and national contradictory perspectives and focus on international or global aspects of a problem area and (3) isolate a certain theme (e.g. disarmament) as a distinct field of study so that the theme becomes separated from other themes from which it should not be separated (e.g. development).

Utilizing various isolation and exclusion techniques[2], the proponents of this approach seek to limit a highly controversial issue so that even the most hostile enemies can work together towards the same educational end. Recently, this approach has been best exemplified by Pikas[3].

> Introducing disarmament education into teacher training is dependent on symmetric and constructive interaction between professional teacher trainers of different power blocks who have the political confidence of their countries and/or blocks.

He makes it clear that disarmament education should be a distinct field in that its goal should be restricted to complete disarmament without comprising a complete peace system:

> In relation to peace education, it should be stated that disarmament education cannot bear the burden of all the values of 'positive peace' that peace education seems to try to fulfil.

This approach seems idealistic because a curriculum for use in teacher training produced by a committee with representation from hostile nations or blocs, would either be void of any political realism or at best contain the official views of the nations or blocs represented in the committee. The perspectives of sub-national groups (often in opposition to government views) would most probably be excluded, as well as the perspectives of other actors on the global arena such as Third World and non-aligned countries. The teaching of a conglomeration of views on disarmament from e.g. the Soviet Union and the USA without tackling the problem of 'positive peace' represents a simplification of the problem that is doomed to failure, not only because the very cause of the armament problem has to do with certain ideas about 'positive peace' on both sides, but also because opposition forces within the East and the West would neither be represented in the committee nor in the curriculum.

The scientific approach

Elsewhere in this volume, Wiberg discusses problems related to disarmament education as a transnational project[4]. He suggests two major criteria as necessary for the implementation of such a project: that it has to be scientifically defensible and politically acceptable. In his discussion of armaments dynamics, he presents three idealized and pure groups of theories related to what is seen as essential causal mechanisms, namely, internal factors in nations or international interaction. The conflicting and explanatory position between the three groups of theories is evident even within the scientific community[5].

It is characteristic of Wiberg's analysis that peace research findings concerning the arms race become a central focal point in the curriculum. This scientific approach to disarmament education is objective and neutral, in that contradictory and pluralistic views are represented — hence it also becomes more politically acceptable to governments. Wiberg's views are concerned with higher education in which these points are more relevant although there are limitations to this approach.

First, peace research in general and research on armaments in particular has to a large extent been marked by macro analysis at the international level. Hence, I fear that a curriculum based solely on this body of research may become too academic, abstract and far removed from the existential realities of most people. Another major limitation is belief in academic study of a problem void of the action component. This is further related to the lack of adequate guidelines on how understanding the present can produce transcending reflective processes in outlining alternative futures and strategies of change.

Lastly, it seems that even the diagnostic part of a curriculum built around these ideas might become too much restricted by the two criteria of scientific defensibility and political acceptability. In a world filled with a complex web of contradictions, there is a lack of agreement even on the definition of these two criteria. What is good science and politics to some represents the opposite to others. Thus, the role of subjectivity and political values seems to be underplayed in the scientific approach.

The ideological approach

In this approach the school system is seen as an ideological state apparatus serving to mediate the interests of the powerful as opposed to the interests of the weak[6]. The social and cultural reproduction role of the education system is emphasized, resulting in a more pessimistic view of the possibility that it can be an instrument for the production of a new society. Although a limited change potential might be acknowledged under certain conditions in micro-situations, the overall macro-sociological conclusion is that the educational system is a servant and not a master. This approach entails the educational system dealing with the question of disarmament in a way conducive to the government's policy on the problem. As most governments pay lip service to the idea and at the same instance find good reasons for doing the opposite, i.e. rearming, the proponents of this approach must expect the same practice in the schools: on the one hand adherence to the good idea and on the other the dissemination of official reasons legitimizing the opposite. In a society characterized by conflict of interests and oppression, opposing viewpoints concerning the matter would effectively be excluded from the curriculum. Even in liberal societies supposedly giving a voice to everyone, the proponents of the ideological approach would argue that disarmament education could not *systematically,* over time, be conducted within the school system in disagreement with that nation's official policy on the matter. Hence, if the nation, as is most often the case, is in a process of arming, education for 'disarmament' would have to be conducive to the armaments process.

An interesting version of the ideological approach to disarmament education is presented in several comments on the function of the educational system in the Soviet Union. Thus, Blishchenko and Ivanian view the school as a reproductive agency in a similar way as the theorists referred to above:

> Being a public institution, the school is a part of the society in which it functions and the overall environment, the social, spiritual, ideological and moral climate prevailing in that society accordingly determines the basic values imparted by the educational process and the moral and political upbringing of the young people. If society is based on social justice and if the nation's interests are inseparable from a peaceful way of life, this is inevitably reflected in the ethos of the school and has an influence on the outlook and the inner world of the individual?

Noteworthy in the above quotation is the small word 'if' opening the second sentence. Although this is a logical consequence of the first and in agreement with the general line of analysis in the reproduction theories originated in the West, the apparent harmony is in sharp contrast to the latter's conflict analysis of society at large and Blishchenko and Ivanian's lack of such as regards the Soviet Union, which in their view is a nation based on social justice and whose interests are inseparable from a peaceful way of life. Based on this assumption, a reproduction model of the school's function can successfully be applied also in the area of peace and disarmament.

The disarmament education philosophy described by Blishchenko and Ivanian deals with the causes of the arms race only in passing: 'So long as the forces of reaction and imperialism are at work fomenting wars of aggression and territorial aggrandizement, the people are compelled to defend their freedom and national independence[8]'.

Even though these 'forces' have not been specified, it seems clear that they are in agreement with the analysis given in a paper presented some months earlier by Professor Zasurski, Dean of the Faculty of Journalism, University of Moscow[9].

They continue Zasurski's legitimation rhetoric on Soviet society and its schooling system, although the repetitive criticism of Western powers has been almost excluded. The Zasurski paper, however, is a typical example of an analysis conforming to Wiberg's second model of the arms dynamics referred to above[10]. Zasurkis's one-sided treatment of the arms dynamics gives all the blame for the arms race to 'certain circles in Western powers', while 'an essential great contribution to the cause of peace has been made by the Soviet Union'. The bad guy–good guy mentality described in his paper is so consistent and repetitive that one must assume that years of school and mass media propaganda along the same lines would either make people apathetic about the whole issue or well-adjusted managers or mediators of the system. After a repetitive description of the fallacies of Western powers, the virtues of the Soviet Union are described:

> Peace and disarmament education is not only a basic subject in Soviet secondary and higher schools but also constitutes the foundation of the entire activities of Soviet society.
> An outstanding role in this respect is played by the media, Soviet press, television and radio, and all our mass media. The education of the people in the spirit of general and complete disarmament and peace stems from the principles of the Constitution of the Soviet Union and is implemented every day and in all spheres of life[11].

Professor Zasurski's view of disarmament education is in no way extraordinary, in that the same model is propagated by some in the West — only with the modification that the West is good and the East is bad. Wherever this model is the basis of disarmament education, however, it is designed to legitimize the arms race on the part of the 'good guy' and not to examine critically the role of all actors in the game.

In due course, it might be of interest to the peace research and education community to examine how the content of disarmament education has been defined in the school systems of the superpowers. The current international interest in the topic with the UNESCO sponsored World Congress on Disarmament Education in June 1980, will presumably have some consequence for the educational institutions in those countries at present showing keen interest in the matter. If not, there is reason to believe that the interest taken in disarmament education is not genuine, but a matter of convenience. In that case, 'the game of disarmament' will have been extended from the negotiating tables onto the rhetorical scene of international conferences, utilizing scientists and educators as hostages in playing the game.

Such types of academic and educational game are most safely played if the topic is restricted so that the relevant political, economic, cultural and social conflicts are excluded. Even without a conflict perspective, there are many facts that can be taught, for instance, about types of weapons, nuclear proliferation, military use of outer space, missile submarines and first-strike strategy, humanitarian rules of war and disarmament efforts. These and other topics may effectively be treated to the benefit of a specific ideological view by disseminating only that information which is positive to that view. Thus, disarmament efforts may be taught without exposing the disarmament game. For example, instead of saying that by the end of the 10 year term of SALT, each of the two superpowers 'will be capable of destroying the other, not 50 times over, as at present, but 100 times over' and that 'the numerical limits in the Vladivostok agreement allow each of the two superpowers to increase its arsenal by multiplying nuclear warheads into the tens of thousands, altogether representing more than a million Hiroshimas'[12], the curriculum can be filled with information about the disarmament proposals from the good side (own nation) and the negative reactions and lack of serious proposals from the bad side (other nation).

The politicization approach

A fourth type of response from educators to this appeal from well-meaning but frustrated researchers, politicians, bureaucrats and experts may be the admission that education has a constructive role to play in the solution of these problems, but only in conjunction with other efforts towards social change. This view is based on the idea that every societal subsystem should be an arena for the struggle to improve or completely change society, and that this struggle should be coordinated across subsystems to ensure greater impact on the change process. Such educators say: Yes, let us work within the educational system, but in conjunction with an overall process of social change in which many other categories of actors participate along with educators. These educators may attempt to cooperate with non-educators with the same interests, including some of the researchers, politicians, bureaucrats and experts. But their premises of cooperation grow out of an analysis of societal contradictions involving a choice as to how and in whose interests the contradictions ought to be solved.

As it is my assumption that society is characterized by contradictions between the dominators and the dominated, choice of partners is essential for the educational task to be performed. From a peace education point of view it is of course evident that the interests of the dominated groups should be the centre of concern, and that the usual educational task of mediating the interests of the powerful must be reduced, and ideally eliminated. This integration of social forces, including that of education, has a task of *conscientization* necessitating the building of bridges across the gaps which now exist in society between research, education and action. Such bold initiatives are characterized by 'profound interior liberty and liberation from fear of violence'[13].

The politicization approach represents my view of how the educational process can be of some significance in the quest for change. Although it recognizes the limited power of formal educational systems inducing change (in agreement with reproduction theories), this view implies that even formal educational systems constitute one of many arenas where efforts for change should take place. But as this view implies a close link between research, education and action in an overall process of social change, it emphasizes a concept of education which involves more than schooling. Schooling is, however, recognized as an important factor and its negative impact in the conscientization process must at least be reduced, so that its positive contribution can be made more possible.

The substance of education is defined in terms of educational form, content and organizational structure[14]. These three components are seen to be dependent and interacting, as opposed to the view that they are independent and isolated. Hence the substance of disarmament education cannot be determined solely on the basis of empirical and theoretical research in the field of disarmament. If this were the case, the task would simply be a technical problem of transmitting predetermined knowledge to those who do not posses it. This type of 'educational' effort is contrary to the philosophy of conscientization and has, moreover, proved a failure in that those who are directly responsible for the irrational arms race in the present world have a very good knowledge of this body of research. If disarmament education were to be targeted towards the managers of the military/industrial complex[15], the primary aim of such education would not be the imparting of the knowledge which they themselves to a large extent have produced and are in the midst of producing, but rather de-education and re-education involving a change in their analysis of present and desirable developments.

As I believe this group of people is largely made up of highly educated and successful middle-aged (and older), intelligent *men* with high salaries and status, it is reasonable to assume that they are not only capable of taking care of their own education in the field in which they are daily involved, but also that it would be a waste of time and resources to spend any educational effort on them due to their vested interests in the maintenance of the present order. If some of them want to use their high positions to challenge the *status quo,* they are free to do so if they are willing to take the risks (e.g. Ellsberg and Sakharov), but it is unthinkable that the managerial elite[16] as a group would challenge the present order.

Education for disarmament, therefore, should paradoxically not be directed towards those who need it most, i.e. those who are managing the arms race, but to those who are the victims of it and not the maintainers.

Acknowledging the role of subjective perceptions in the conscientization process, the question of approaching the topic of disarmament in education becomes rather difficult. Disarmament is usually seen as a global matter far removed from the local and experiental realities of ordinary people. Most people are confronted with problems closer to home, related to lack of food, adequate housing, water, work and human rights. Their concerns are centred around daily survival for themselves, the family and the community. Others who might live in abundance are confronted with all the problems of the consumer society — problems that tend to exhaust all energies. Others live in regimes denying their citizens any right to speak against the institutions, including the development of militarism and the accumulation of arms. Such existential problems account for the distance people feel from the disarmament question. If no regard is given to their priorities, disarmament education programmes are bound to fail.

This means that such programmes must start with the concerns of the people involved, in order to build bridges from the micro-level to global topics such as disarmament. This has many implications for the form, content and organizational structure surrounding the educational process. It means that disarmament content should not drop down from the sky from some educational expert, but be developed over time in a dialogue involving the people and what they are concerned about.

Research has shown that arms expenditure has an impact upon the development process as well as upon social life (militaristic attitudes, etc)[17]. The educational task of building bridges would thus have a large body of research to draw from.

Without action coupled with reflection, the bridge that is built would only be suitable for academics to walk on. The masses will remain without a chance to develop a process of social change and therefore be without impact. Action for such impact and change must deal with opposing forces within oneself, one's community, one's nation, and the world. At every level, ranging from the local to the global, opposing forces will show themselves if the bridge building is successful.

The organizational structure in which such two-way processes of conscientization take place must leave room for the people to participate actively as subjects of the process as opposed to passive objects. This will enable them to steer content-development in such a way that it is relevant for them. Unfortunately, most school systems, including universities, are characterized by a more hierarchical structure which is the base for their functions in society. Disarmament education programmes within formal educational institutions, therefore, are generally limited to academic understanding of the problem, devoid of the action component, and in many societies are limited in scope in such a way as to ensure the safety and legitimation of those in power.

In fact, 'disarmament education', I am afraid, would in some national contexts be overt propaganda by the *status quo* leaders to make the citizens believe that their government is working very hard for disarmament and peace, when, in fact, the opposite may be the case. This prostitution of a good idea is likely to happen in those countries heading the arms race, because they are in greater need of hiding the harsh realities from their own people in order to legitimize themselves. To use disarmament education for ideological purposes would in fact be a contribution towards the arms race and militarization process.

Conclusion

The four approaches to disarmament education outlined here have very different implications for what should be regarded as the substance of such education. The idealistic, scientific and ideological approaches are mainly concerned with the *content* of what should be taught, rather than the form of communication and the organizational structure surrounding the process. This similarity between the three approaches, however, stands in sharp contrast to the opposing principles of inclusion and exclusion as regards the content. These opposing principles are, as suggested, related to differing ideological interests, assumptions about what causes the arms race and views concerning the role of education in social change. The *politicization* approach, however, defines the substance of disarmament education not only in terms of content to be transmitted, but also in terms of the how's of educational interactions and desirable organizational frames surrounding the educational process.

If education is to become effective in the quest for disarmament, the game of disarmament must be made transparent, with an accurate picture of those who have been most responsible for this game since World War II, i.e. the two superpowers. This picture would have to include their political, economic, social and cultural characteristics and concrete actions in their relations to other countries such as Vietnam, the Dominican Republic, Czechoslovakia and Afghanistan. Their official arguments for participating in the arms race, for instance, the idea that the arms race leads to national security[19], should be examined critically. It should become known that all scenarios and present development of weapons are concentrated on offensive categories 'and that the ulterior aim of winning a world war is seemingly always present in the minds of the superpowers'[20].

With this perspective, the problem of disarmament is controversial because it is tied up with the most important contradictions in the present world. What are these contradictions? That is the topic of disarmament education. Disarmament education that isolates the theme so that it is not seen in relation to such contradictions will be in danger of furthering some ideology rather than investigating the causes. The choice is between indoctrination and politicization.

Important contradictions today are related to the global structures of imperialism and hegemony. Important operators are the West, the East, China in the North and various groups from the developing world in the South, more or less acting in the interests of the three major protagonists in the North.

Other contradictions are related to dominance structures within each country — these are certainly not independent of international imperialism and dominance. Such contradictions are again related to gender, race, ethnic group and class.

These contradictions are related to the everyday lives of people. People's subjective experience of imperialism, sexism, racism, and any kind of oppression depends upon their location in the oppressive structure. Such subjective experiences should be the starting point of any education, even disarmament education.

This approach coupled with an overall process of conscientization for the transformation of present-day reality would not be motivated by fear-creating doomsayers[21] but by 'profound interior liberty and liberation from the fear of violence'[22]. It might be that this type of disarmament education would be more difficult to implement in the two countries that are responsible for about 51% of the 1978 total world military expenditure and their military and political allies, than in the non-aligned part of the world. However, with the assumption that disarmament education should be relevant to the contexts in which people live, in terms of the problems they are confronted with in their everyday lives, it would be disastrous to treat this topic in a purely scholarly manner devoid of the action component involving those aspects of reality related to the political, economic, social and cultural realms on both micro- and macro-scales.

The importance of integrating the topic of disarmament with social justice and positive peace has been emphasized by many. Here I shall only refer to Diaz, who states:

Disarmament, as viewed from Latin America, would first of all involve eliminating the basic ills that lead to social violence and hence to the use of arms. Arms are not a cause but an effect; they are not the problem but the symptom of a deep-seated ill which must be tackled at its roots.[23]

Another essential in the politicization approach is the action component. In the words of Randle, militarism is challenged:

> by actions rather than by words alone and can break the spell exercised by the social and political reality as it currently exists and point to new possibilities. *In this process lies the most powerful aspect of popular action as an instrument of education, whether for disarmament or social change; at its most successful it can awaken the consciousness of whole communities or countries and convince the population that with their participation things can be radically changed.*[24]

The politicization approach to disarmament education would imply that the question of disarmament can be dealt with by everybody in all countries where it is ideologically and politically acceptable. This approach is based on the belief that the question of disarmament is not to be solved solely by anti arms race forces in the two superpowers, but by an alliance of these forces with forces of liberation from all kinds of oppression in those countries which are the victims of the economic, political and militaristic hegemony led by the two superpowers, with an emerging third one, i.e. China. The policing of the world through arms is not highly regarded by most people, as was demonstrated by the 104 votes cast in the UN against the Soviet invasion in Afghanistan and international reactions to the Carter doctrine to protect 'American interests' in the Persian Gulf if necessary by military means.

Against this background I am highly sceptical about the feasibility of introducing the politicization approach to disarmament education in the school systems of those countries which need to legitimize their role in the arms race. What they most probably will do is to show great interest in the disarmament education discussion on the international scene and then proceed to encourage programmes designed to further their own ideology in order to legitimize themselves.

The politicization approach would, however, be a viable solution in the formal educational systems of those countries whose interests are not too interwoven with those of one of the superpowers. In informal education the politicization approach is always a feasible solution even though it might be politically unacceptable to the government and hence would have to be implemented underground.

Notes and references

1. 'The arms race is irrational, and we are not permitted to let unreason stand unchallenged. Hope of reversing the trend must be built by untiring efforts to educate peoples and governments to recognize their true interests'

M. *Haavelsrud*

Myrdal A. The game of disarmament. In Jolly, R. (Ed): *Disarmament and world development,* Pergamon Press, Oxford, 1978, 88. In 'Ways and means to generate the political will' (also in Jolly *op.cit.,* p.99) Thorsson asserts that we 'must start by alerting every single man and woman, in particular, young people . . . to a sense of real participation in true life, instead of merely consuming one manufactured by industrial technology'.
2. See also, Haavelsrud M. On inclusion and exclusion. Paper presented at International Symposium on Peace Education, University of Utrecht and Vredesopbouw, May 1980.
3. Pikas A. Disarmament education through teacher training. World Congress on Disarmament Education, Conference document SS-80/CONF.401/8, UNESCO, Paris, June 1980
4. See Wiberg H. Dilemmas of disarmament education, pp129-144 of this volume.
5. The three types of theory are referred to as the action/reflection model; the military/industrial complex; and bilateral autism
6. Cf. the theory of Louis Althusser, as well as social and cultural reproduction theories such as those of Basil Bernstein and Pierre Bourdieu.
7. Blishchenko I.P. and Ivanian I.V. Disarmament research and education in the Soviet Union. Background paper 33-80/CONF. 401/28, World Congress on Disarmament Education, Paris, June 1980 p.6.
8. *Ibid.,* p.7.
9. Zasurski Y.N. Struggle for peace and disarmament and the role of training journalists, their instruction and education for peace and disarmament. Paper presented at the international symposium, Research and Teaching on Disarmament in Various Disciplines of Higher Education, Vienna, 26-27 January, 1980, published in *Peace and the Sciences,* 1980 (1) 18-26.
10. Paradoxically, both Wiberg and Zasurski gave key-note papers at the opening session of the same symposium. As Wiberg was the first speaker, the analysis by the second speaker served to exemplify the limited analysis suggested by Wiberg's second model.
11. Zasurski, *op.cit.,* p. 22.
12. Myrdal, *op. cit.,* p.89, 90.
13. Borelli M. Integration of peace research, peace education and peace action. *Bull. Peace Proposals,* Special issue on peace education, 392.
14. IPRA Newsletter, special issue on peace education, 1979.
15. The original concept of the military-industrial complex was introduced by President Eisenhower in the late 1950s.
16. An interesting analysis of the role of 'managers' is given by Reardon B. The knowledge industry: impediment to popular participation in education, Institute of Social Science, University of Tromsö, February 1980 (mimeo).
17. Cf., for instance, Jolly R. *op.cit,* 1978; the special issue on disarmament and development of the *Bulletin of Peace Proposals,* 1979 No 3, and *Disarmament, development and a just world order.* Centre for the Study of Developing Societies, New Delhi, 1978. The concept of militarism has been thoroughly treated in Eide A. and Thee M. (Eds). *Problems of contemporary militarism.* London, Croom Helm Ltd. 1980. There is a tradition of excluding questions of development, social justice and structural violence from the disarmament

112

issue. This same tendency is to be found in some of the research of the Stockholm Peace Research Inistitute, reflecting perhaps the views of its Director Dr F. Barnaby, that the concept of structural violence is a vague one, since a society may have a high level of social justice and still preserve much structural violence. (Peace research over two decades. *New Scientist,* 11 Nov. 1976. For an interesting counterargument see Borrelli, *op. cit.* p. 394).

18. For an interesting analysis of the relationship between reflection and action processes from local to higher levels and the dynamics between these processes on various levels, see Borrelli, *op.cit.* pp. 392-394.

19. The irrationality of this argument is analysed by Myrdal (*op. cit.* p.85) who asserts that 'all countries are now buying greater and greater insecurity at higher costs'.

20. *Ibid,* p.90.

21. Thorsson, *op. cit.,* p.99.

22. Borrelli, *op.cit.,* p. 392

23. Diaz J. Problems and outlook for disarmament education in Latin America. Background paper SS-80/CONF. 401/24, World Congress on Disarmament Education, Paris, June, 1980, p.2.

24. Randle M. Peace action as a form of disarmament education. Background paper SS-80/CONF. 401/20, World Congess on Disarmament Education, Paris, June, 1980, p.2.

8. The status of and recommendations for disarmament education*

Betty Reardon, *Programme coordinator, World Council for Curriculum and Instruction*

The research for this study was undertaken in 1977 and presented at a UNESCO experts meeting in April 1978. The meeting was one of the preparatory activities organized by UNESCO's Division of Human Rights and Peace prior to the 8th Special Session of the General Assembly on Disarmament, May-June, 1978. That experts meeting was one significant indication of the Division's commitment to bring to bear on the problem of disarmament the expertise of research and education.

The Director General of UNESCO articulated that commitment to the world community in his statement to the Special Session in which he called for the convening of a world congress on disarmament education. This congress provided a unique and unprecedented opportunity for educators and scientists from the UN member nations to set forth the directions and guidelines which will enable education to make its urgently needed contribution to the achievement of disarmament.

This study was intended as an early but limited beginning of significant efforts for disarmament education. The original report[1], of far greater length, carries an extensive analysis of obstacles to disarmament education and recommendations and suggestions for teaching about disarmament which have been deleted here. A more detailed paper ('A suggested sequence of learning objectives for education for peace and disarmament') has subsequently been prepared (see pp 238-252).

The portions of the report dealing with the status of disarmament education are still applicable some 3 years after the initial preliminary research. Little has changed except for the increased urgency of the need for disarmament education. Efforts to meet this need are growing very slowly in the formal system of education. Only the public education efforts of the non-governmental organizations (NGO's) have increased in volume and intensity, testifying to both the increased public concern over the issue and the failure even in this urgent crisis to overcome the traditional gap between social and political reality and

*Originally prepared for Network to Educate for World Society, NY, USA.

the content of formal curricula. Peace and disarmament educators have high hopes that the congress will offer a plan to bridge that gap in the field of disarmament.

While these extracts also comprise a preliminary study, the congress signifies that such research is but a limited preliminary step to what can be a major world-wide effort at disarmament education.

General status of disarmament education

The general state of education about the arms race, the war system, alternatives to the war system, the concepts and proposals for and potential consequences of disarmament is extremely limited. Even within the growing and highly professional field of peace education, there is still inadequate attention to the substance of questions on arms and alternative security systems. This circumstance was validated by a survey which produced something over 30 responses from eight different countries.* It showed that there is little or no material on the subject in use in the schools, and there is very limited material even available to schools should they intend to initiate programmes on education about disarmament. This is not to say that there is not a great volume of material on disarmament as such, but most of it is unsuitable for education of the general public, or use within school settings, and further educators, even those concerned with the area of peace, are not very familiar with even those materials which could be adapted for schools.

This lack of familiarity with sources and limited substantive knowledge on the part of peace educators is one of the most serious problems in the field, and is probably most responsible for the small volume of curriculum material and few teaching programmes on the subject. It is my opinion that this condition is due primarily to the over-emphasis on the technical aspects of disarmament on the part of both scholars and politicians, and also to the reluctance of politicians to state the political issues in simple, manageable terms, especially in general system terms or terms of alternatives and possibilities for change. Thus, the general status of disarmament education is to be diagnosed from the political as well as the pedagogical perspective. In dealing with any issues of social education or world politics, even within the supposedly objective environments of study and inquiry in schools and universities, we must acknowledge that the subjects are primarily political and, therefore, most subject to the constraints of the political climate. The subjects of peace and disarmament cannot be addressed in the same manner as other problems of education such as those of literacy

*A 1980 survey of curricula for secondary schools and teacher training institutions produced 1006 responses from 63 countries. It showed no change in curriculum development on disarmament.

or the sciences. Thus, the lack of widespread political support for programmes in peace education, as well as the lack of consciousness about peace education and disarmament education as essentially political education, have reinforced each other in a way which has served to impede the development of the field. There needs to be a systematic effort to raise consciousness among educators about these issues.

Yet, in spite of this extremely sensitive, political overtone to the field, and the many obstacles previously described, there is a good deal of educational development which forms a basis for and can be functionally related to disarmament education. There are currently under development many programmes in various parts of the world which deal particularly with the attitudinal and global systems obstacles to disarmament education which are closely related, but not synonymous fields.

Global education has as its general objective the achievement of what is now coming to be called 'global literacy'. Global literacy is a summary term to indicate awareness about the interdependent nature of the planet earth and the peoples of the planet and of global problems (see Hanvey[2]). Most widely attended to among these problems are population, ecology, poverty and conflict. It should be noted, however, that it is the phenomenon of conflict and not the war system nor the issue of arms policy which informs that study. In many cases, it is possible for such programmes to study conflict without ever addressing the questions of war and the arms race and the potential consequences of disarmament. Some global education still purports to be value free, in the sense that social education based on the social sciences has attempted in the past to be value free. Yet as social education in most countries inculcates a loyalty to the particular nation which plans and provides the education, there is an implicit loyalty to the human species and to the planet as the home of the species which underlies the global education movement.

Peace education[3], on the other hand, is for the most part an explicitly value oriented and normative form of study, in that peace is expressed as a value closely interrelated with the values of human rights. In most cases, the inquiries pursued by peace education acknowledge as their purpose the development of knowledge which will help to achieve peace and justice, moving beyond an awareness of global problems, at which most global education stops, toward the normative resolution of the problems. Thus peace education is distinct from global education in two ways. It examines values and explores global systems in terms of their relationship to the values of peace and justice; and it explores both the normative and the structural causes of the problems as well as a variety of alternative solutions. It is important to note that responsible peace education does not advocate specific modes for the achievement of peace or human rights, but inquires into them, leaving it to the students to decide for themselves which are most desirable and potentially effective. In spite of this normative orientation, the question of the arms system as such is not yet widely explored even within peace studies. However, many questions which relate to attitudes towards arms and the military are raised by most peace education programmes from early childhood through graduate school and continuing education. Thus peace education in its present status is a basis and a take-off point for education about disarmament and its potential consequences, but it is not yet synonymous with disarmament education.

Education for disarmament at the elementary level

If we assume a more critical attitude toward the necessity for force, and an inquisitive attitude toward alternatives to violence and arms, as prerequisites for effective learning about disarmament, then many of the present programmes in peace education provide just such a basis. At the elementary school level, much is now being done by way of attitude- and value-formation and the encouragement of cooperative, supportive behaviour which it is believed will create an open-mindedness to substantive study of the issues at more advanced levels of education.

For the most part, at least in the USA and some European countries, these programmes are conducted either in independent private schools, religious schools, or in public schools with the assistance of outside and/or private agencies, such as the World Studies Project in Britain. Another such example is the Quaker Conflict Project now operating in a number of cities in the USA. This particular project, through the use of stories, puppetry, role-playing and games, teaches children something about the nature of conflict and how it escalates. It teaches them about threat systems and the potential consequences of escalating conflict through the threat and use of force. From games which illustrate these phenomena, children are led to discuss their own behaviour and to observe the way in which conflict arises among and between themselves, and how those conflicts have the potential to avoid violence as well as to become violent.

Although most of this is done within the affective area of education, a good deal of cognitive learning also takes place in that children, although they are not given the explicit terminology, learn about the process of conflict and conflict resolution and the idea of alernatives to violence. By the time youngsters are 9 or 10 years old, such programmes have helped them to understand the desirability of having a number of options open when one is in conflict, and that the larger the repertoire of non-violent options and conflict management skills the less likely is the outbreak of violence — a most important lesson to learn for a generation we hope will be able to build a disarmed world political system. Programmes similar to this are also under development in western countries, most notably West Germany, where a transitional project for early childhood peace education is being developed under the auspices of the World Council for Curriculum and Instruction.

Another important aspect of peace education at the elementary level which can be a significant basis for the development of disarmament education is the emphasis on self value and a positive concept of self. Research has indicated that violent behaviour and aggression toward others is frequently the result of lack of satisfaction with or devaluing of self. Whether that self-devaluation comes from feedback from the society, the school, family or friends, or is self-generated, it has frequently been found to be the precursor to destructive behaviour, often self-destructive but equally as often aggressive toward and destructive of others and their rights. Thus in many parts of the world education in early childhood tries to help children to gain a sense of their own identity within their families, within their cultures and as members of the entire human family. The intention of such education is to create a sense of loyalty to and identification with the human species, so that the commonalities among and the common destiny of the earth's peoples can be better understood, forming a basis for programmes which attempt to analyse the common problems of humanity at later points in the educational scheme.

Disarmament education at the secondary level

When considered within the entire range of social education at the secondary level, peace education in general and disarmament education in particular is only a minuscule part of most programmes. Although in some systems there is an articulation of the desire and need for world peace evident throughout formal education, there is in most countries little or no substantive study of the issues and problems of peace and even less of disarmament. However, there is more being done in secondary education than at any other level of formal schooling, indeed more than the reviewer expected to find when undertaking the preliminary study.

Most of the education which relates to disarmament at the secondary level is done within the context of peace studies or what we have come to define as 'global community studies'. Global community studies differ somewhat from global education, in that they share with peace education a degree of normative explicitness. That is, they acknowledge that the problems to be overcome are war, poverty, injustice and ecological deterioration, and that the purpose of the study is to find solutions or alternatives to the present conditions, not simply to understand them. The 'community' aspect indicates that all actors have a responsibility to the system and to each other, as well as a right to share equally in the benefits of the system and a responsibility not to violate the rights of other actors. Thus, although global community studies are broader than peace studies and less explicitly concerned with war itself, they are, like peace education, based on certain value assumptions, one of which is that force and violence should be unacceptable in the world political system. One of the major purposes of these studies is to produce knowledge which will contribute to the elimination of violence.

There are also some courses at the secondary level called 'world order studies', following the definition of that discipline put forth by the Institute for World Order. It has developed a specific method of inquiry, based on the proposal and evaluation of a variety of alternatives to the present international system, designed to achieve a number of value goals including complete and general disarmament. Courses in this latter subject area were reported only from the USA.

One reason why activity at the secondary level may be more extensive than at others is that the pedagogical options are more varied, and the types of material and methods which can be adapted to the issues are of a much broader range than are used at either the elementary or university level — the elementary being limited by the lack of certain skills on the part of young children as well as by the level of their cognitive development, and the universities by a very traditional approach of readings and lectures, with only a few exceptions where some use is made of simulations. The range of materials and methods used in secondary schools to teach about arms policy and security extends from readings to films, sound-filmstrips, exercises in analysis, decision-making games, and full-scale simulation of armed conflict situations and disarmament systems. In some cases students are even invited to plan their own preferred system for a disarmed world based on a variety of criteria, including workability of the system itself and the possibilities of its being accepted by the various nations of the world. This technique is called model building.

There are, indeed, many possibilities for extensive and constructive education about the arms race at the secondary level. It should be noted, however, that the implementation of such possibilities is inhibited, probably by the same two obstacles which inhibit general discussion about disarmament, political inhibitions and psychological avoidance.

Schools are hesitant to take up politically sensitive issues. Indeed, the political sensitivity of the issue even affects certain international conferences which are supposedly intended to work on educational programmes for peace and disarmament, but wherein most of the time is spent on general discussion of the process of innovation, without specific reference to substance. At such conferences more attention is paid to cultural and attitudinal aspects of international understanding than to the education required to understand the structural and political questions related to the achievement of disarmament and the enforcement of human rights. Secondly, the technical nature of the problem makes even those teachers who have acquired some mastery of it themselves hesitant to raise it in their classrooms, because most materials available on the subjects of arms control and disarmament are so highly technical. It was for this latter reason that *World military and social expenditures*[4] was greeted with such enthusiasm by peace educators.

Disarmament education at the university level

At the university level, education about arms policy usually falls within three general spheres: strategic studies, international relations and/or world politics, and peace studies. In addition to these three general categories, there is a growing interest within departments of economics on the economic aspects and consequences of the arms race. An example is the course on the permanent war economy at Columbia University in New York City. This particular interest is expressed primarily by educators who have some personal, normative concern about social deterioration in the industrialized world resulting from excessive resource expenditure on arms, and from the limitations such expenditures place on the development of the poorer parts of the world. One of the important consequences of this concern is more economists moving into the general field of peace studies while maintaining their academic posts within departments of economics. We might also note that in the USA this has occurred in other disciplines such as philosophy, psychology and political science, as well as religion, particularly in religiously based schools. However, none of these aforementioned disciplines gives attention to the arms control/disarmament questions in standard courses.

Documented evidence on the extent of strategic studies, by which is meant study of and inquiry into problems of defence and security from a military perspective, was not available to me. But it is generally known that research in this area has been conducted in universities, at least in the USA, for the most part under government grants but sometimes with foundation support as well. This research penetrates the educational process by the involvement of graduate students and sometimes by the presentation of non-classified research findings or proposals within classes and seminars at the universities.

Such research seems to have two opposite purposes. One is the further development of expertise in weaponry and the technical efficiency of weaponry, along with strategic planning for the most effective use of these developments within world politics, and these inquiries are most widely understood as strategic studies. On the other hand, under the same title, there are some programmes directed specifically at strategies and techniques for arms limitation, and indeed sometimes at alternatives to arms for defence and conflict purposes. Most notable among the latter is not only the field of non-violent studies, which has given some highly technical and sophisticated attention to this issue, but also the field of 'transarmament', a concept defined by Sharp[5], which is gaining wider and wider acceptance within the peace studies field in the universities and has been considered by governments such as the Netherlands. Most notable among universities which carry out strategic studies are probably those in Britain such as Sussex, and the Institute for Strategic Studies in London, which has on its staff scholars from universities. Anecdotal evidence indicates that similar programmes also exist in Germany and in France. There is academic interest in the subject in other European countries, though whether or not this actually influences the educational programmes of the universities is uncertain.

It should further be noted that special institutes for research and investigation on arms subjects, while not necessarily within the structure of a given university, have a profound effect on what occurs in universities in two ways. Such institutes are largely staffed by academics, and the results of their research, when not classified for security reasons, often become the substance of seminars. Very notable among such institutes is the Swedish International Peace Research Institute (SIPRI), which has almost exclusively concentrated on the arms problem and contributed some of the most relevant data to understanding the true nature of the threat of arms production and the statistical likelihood of the use of nuclear weapons[6]. Such researchers form the second data base which is necessary for the development of responsible, effective curriculum materials for both the university and the secondary level, and which should be more widely used than they are in general public education endeavours at the adult level.

It is in the area of international relations and world politics that the greatest opportunity exists for university education on arms control and disarmament issues. From the perspective of those educators who believe that such education should be an inquiry into the openly acknowledged goal of achieving disarmament; this area is currently a disappointment, for it is even less normatively concerned than is global education at the secondary level. International relations as a discipline has for the most part perpetuated the ethic of power politics and the concept of the balance of power.

It has been pointed out by some scholars that this concept was a response to a 'naked power' approach to world politics, but nonetheless, this school of thought has not encouraged the search for alternatives, and has turned out a group of university educated people who assume that the power structure of competitive nation states is unchangeable, given world affairs. Nevertheless, there are in this field too a number of scholars and educators concerned about the dangers of the arms race, and studies about the history of the arms control and disarmament movement take place in a few international relations courses, as well as in history courses. Courses and seminars explicitly related to these subjects are infrequent. The subjects are in almost all cases likely to come up within the context of other subject areas or themes.

As with the other levels of education, it is in the field of peace studies that the most significant university work relating to arms control, disarmament and the consequence of the arms race and potential consequences of disarmament are to be found. Although peace research itself is at this point a discipline which exists throughout the world, probably more vigorous in Europe than in North America, and slowly but surely growing in the so-called Third World or developing countries, peace studies where the emphasis is as much on education as on research seem to be most highly developed in North America. The North American affiliate of the International Peace Research Association, the Consortium on Peace Research, Education and Development (COPRED), founded at the University of Colorado in 1972 with its Secretariat now at Bethel College, Kansas, has the largest percentage of its membership among university educators involved in peace studies, either within the traditional disciplines or in specific peace studies programmes.

Peace studies are rapidly growing in universities throughout the USA. This is made evident by the large number of inquiries that come to such organizations as COPRED, the Institute for World Order and the National Peace Academy Campaign, and by the excellent attendance at events organized by these agencies to present peace studies approaches and programmes to a university audience. This rapid growth is extremely significant, because it has not occurred without struggle. Peace studies have had two severe obstacles to overcome in order to establish themselves in the universities. Since it is a nontraditional discipline, it has been necessary for the advocates and practitioners of peace studies to establish to the satisfaction of their colleagues (most especially curriculum committees) that peace studies are a responsible academic pursuit, based on sound scientific research and study. Peace studies are taught not only through traditional pedagogic methods but also by a variety of widely admired, innovative learning techniques which are applicable in any area of the social sciences. It is important to take note of the pedagogical aspects of peace studies, because the willingness of peace studies educators to experiment with methods other than lectures were in large part responsible for the support which peace studies programmes received from students. Indeed, it might be noted that on a number of campuses such programmes were started by the insistence of students, who themselves undertook to research and plan curricula when this was not done by faculty. Such actions indicate the acute anxiety among young people about the arms race and the potential for war, and also their faith in the problem-solving capacity of the university. Some programmes, which were begun under student initiative, such as that at Colgate University in New York State, are now among the outstanding academic programmes of peace studies in the USA.

Further, peace studies have had to contend with some political resistance on the part of persons, even within so 'intellectual' an environment as universities, who believed that the study of peace was the advocacy of 'peace at any price' and, therefore, tantamount to disloyalty to the state and/or the defenders of the state. Although this form of resistance in the universities was not so basic and simple in its line of argument as that which the radical right put forth against peace and global studies in the public schools, the consequences were very much the same, and the requirements they imposed upon university peace educators were similar. The peace educators had to present evidence that these studies could be pursued in an objective responsible manner. They also had to explain clearly that 'objectivity' and 'neutrality' were not necessarily synonymous. This latter distinction is extremely important for the development of education for disarmament, and for the implementation of the 1974 UNESCO Recommendation. It is my opinion that if this distinction were clearly articulated, many of the political obstacles confronting the resolution of basic issues of peace and human rights in international educational conferences could be overcome.

Within the whole range of peace studies approaches, probably world order studies more than any other focus on the political and structural aspects of achieving general and complete disarmament. This undoubtedly is due to the origin of the discipline, which was an attempt to study the abolition of war as an institution and therefore carried a strong institutional bias which demanded exploration of the question of disarmament. For example, one of the key materials in world order courses has been proposals for disarmament, including general and complete disarmament such as the Clark-Sohn proposal. One of the exercises presented by world order studies is the analysis, or comparison and evaluation of these proposals (see McVitty[7]).

Since it is in the universities and colleges that teachers are trained and their professional formation determined, the lack of courses or even units within courses on any global matters or on cross-cultural studies is a shocking fact of the present status of disarmament education in teacher training. Most teachers go into teaching with little or no education in global affairs and none on disarmament. Teacher education in both the developed and developing world is constructed in far too narrow a context for the social responsibility it bears. The formation of teachers tends to be to prepare them to support and perpetuate the social order and in many cases to display virtually blind loyalty to the state which employs them. They are not trained to be reflective or critical, and are, therefore, unable to prepare students to explore and develop ideas on alternatives to the present war system. Without significant change in this area, the schools will never be effective in educating for a disarmed world.

Disarmament education in non-formal and adult education

Without doubt, the most extensive education to promote disarmament is being offered by NGOs, for the most part in Japan, Europe and the USA. It is understandable that these are the areas manifesting a great preoccupation with the arms race and the possible consequences of the use of nuclear arms, in that they represent the major producers as well as the one victim of the use of atomic weapons. If we accept that a major function of education is to encourage the acquisition of information, to facilitate reflection upon that information, and to capacitate action on conclusions drawn from the reflection, then clearly NGOs are the major educators in the disarmament field at the present moment. Local, national, and international NGOs in the areas previously mentioned have been for a number of years pursuing intensive programmes in discussion and education about arms issues, attempting to enlist the interest and concern of larger and larger numbers of the public.

Recommendations for education to promote disaramament

The following recommendations are made for the purpose of developing educational programmes that are likely

1. to promote support for general and complete disarmament;
2. to provide appropriate intellectual capacities for the planning and realization of a disarmed world;

3. to encourage attitudes of tolerance of ideological and political differences and appreciation of cultural and ethnic differences;
4. to develop skills of non-violent conflict resolution;
5. to build commitment to a value system based upon fundamental human rights and the acknowledgement of the dignity and worth of every human person.

In short, these recommendations are specific suggestions for carrying out the UNESCO recommendation concerning education for international understanding, cooperation and peace and education relating to human rights and fundamental freedoms through the substance of disarmament.

Programmes to be undertaken by UNESCO

Before specific recommendations are offered, I should like to acknowledge the significance and genius of the UNESCO recommendation. The significance is in its focus on two key concepts which are probably more crucial than any others to the survival of human society on this planet, namely, the assurance of fundamental human rights and the achievement of peace.

The genius of the recommendation is that it has been formulated and expressed in terms which permit the required basic political education to take place, without necessarily involving the possibility of political controversy. In the explanation of terms (section I, 1b), the recommendation, by subsuming the terms of international understanding, cooperation and peace, under the comprehensive term of international education, at once creates a buffer against the certainty of political controversy, and acknowledges the basic purpose of all such education, even though it goes under a variety of titles, the purpose being the achievement of peace and the assurance of human rights. Further, this definitional statement does not deny the differences among and between these approaches by claiming that they are synonymous. Thus the recommendation makes a clear statement of purposes but acknowledges that there are a variety of modes which can be used toward their fulfilment. In the context of the recommendation, therefore, UNESCO can play a most creative role in the further conceptualization and definition of areas of international education intended to achieve peace and assure human rights. It is toward the fulfilment of that that the following recommendations are made.

It is recommended that UNESCO commission an interdisciplinary transnational body to draft for circulation and review a statement defining the various approaches and current practices in international education, describing their methodology and putting forth the basic political and pedagogic assumptions which underlie their programmes.

B. Reardon

The purpose of such a statement would be to assess the variety of approaches and to investigate how this variety of resources might best be used by various educational actors committed to the purposes of the recommendation, especially to disarmament education. Further, these approaches should be assessed in terms of the possibility of their contributing to effective education for the promotion of disarmament and human rights and for understanding the relationship between human rights and peace. It should be emphasized, however, that the purpose of the definitional draft is not to make a statement of UNESCO's preference for one approach over others, or even several over others, nor is it to synthesize all approaches into one standard or orthodox procedure: rather, it is to fulfil the previous stated purpose, while attesting to the volume as well as to the variety of activity in the area of international education.

UNESCO should offer public recognition to the field of peace studies as a responsible discipline, of equal value with, although different from, other approaches to international education. This could be done by the organization of international symposia on peace studies, similar to those which UNESCO has supported in the area of peace research, and by assuring that actual practitioners of peace studies *per se* are represented in all working sessions dealing with the 1974 recommendation and with international education in general.

UNESCO should commission the development of a set of guidelines and criteria for education for the promotion of disarmament. These guidelines and criteria should be developed by a transnational group of educators, with particular expertise in peace studies and disarmament education.

UNESCO should prepare a handbook of teaching/learning practices on education for promotion of disarmament, with examples suitable to all educational levels and all learning environments, taken from a variety of cultures and political systems.

UNESCO should establish a programme of research on appropriate practices in teacher education designed to fulfil the 1974 recommendation VII.33 (a) through consideration of issues related to the promotion of disarmament. Such research should also explore ways in which recommendation 33 (b) on basic inter-disciplinary knowledge of world problems might be fulfilled in regard to the arms race, disarmament and human rights.

UNESCO should organize a series of international symposia on education for the promotion of disarmament, using as a basis for discussion the recommendations forthcoming from the research on teacher education and the exemplars presented in the handbook, as well as the criteria, guidelines and survey described in the first recommendation listed here.

126

UNESCO should publicize possibilities for disarmament education as widely as possible among educators through its publications and those of agencies and organizations with similar programmes.

UNESCO should follow its current research on violence with the development of similar projects on alternatives to violence, with reference to the achievement of disarmament and human rights. In this regard, commendation should be made of the research on violence and structural violence, on the seminars co-sponsored by UNESCO on non-violent strategies for social change and its general support of peace research.

UNESCO should organize a series of transnational workshops to develop skills and knowledge of education within the field of disarmament education.

Finally, and most strongly recommended, UNESCO should commission a broader and deeper study into the obstacles to and present practices in disarmament education, recognizing fully the limited nature of this present report, and acknowledging the need for a more thorough data base for the fulfilment of all prior recommendations discussed above. Such a study should be conducted by a transnational team with a research coordinator for each world region.

Recommendations for member states

Member states should allocate a percentage of the resources designated for research and education to the field of disarmament. This should establish within the government itself and promote in universities research into economic conversion from military to peaceful uses of technology and industry, the requirements of a political order based on non-violence and the public attitudinal changes necessary to achieve a disarmed world, and explore ways of teaching about obstacles to disarmament, and human rights and methods of developing the means for their achievement.

Member states should set up commissions on international education with special sub commissions on peace studies charged with developing programmes for the promotion of disarmament and human rights suitable to the educational system and needs for each member state.

In reporting to the UNESCO General Conference on activities to implement the 1974 recommendation member states should include specific reference to education for the promotion of disarmament and human rights.

General conclusions

At a time in human history when the nations of the world spend $450 billion/year on the military in the face of mass human suffering from unmet social and economic needs, knowing that such suffering could be relieved to a very large degree by the reallocation of such resources; when the human species is threatened with the very real possibility of nuclear annihilation, and daily endures increasing levels of 'conventional' violence, there is no more urgent or important area of education than that to promote disarmament. Although the present status of such education is lamentably limited and sadly scattered over the world, nonetheless the possibilities for a significant programme of education to promote disarmament exist. Further, in my opinion, a more extensive and thorough study would reveal many more educational resources which could be brought to bear on the development of such a programme. Clearly, there is growing public support throughout the world for such efforts. The opportunity should be seized to launch such a project on a global basis with full international participation.

UNESCO is to be commended for its efforts to bring about the 1974 recommendation and to initiate programmes and experiments for the implementation of that recommendation. A very special commendation is deserved for undertaking special efforts in the areas of disarmament and human rights — as previously stated, the key issues to the whole question of international understanding and peace.

References

1. Reardon B. A preliminary study of the obstacles to the status of and potential for education for the promotion of disarmament. UNESCO Experts Meeting on Obstacles to Disarmament and Means to Overcome them, 1978. UNESCO SS/78, Conf. 63; also *Bull. Peace Proposals*, **4**, 1979.
2. Hanvey R. *Toward an attainable global perspective*. New York, Center for Global Perspectives.
3. Carpenter S. *et al. Creating the future* (tape-slide presentation). North Newton, Kansas, COPRED.
4. Sivard R. *World military and social expenditures,* Leesburg, WMSE Publications, 1977, 1978, 1979.
5. Sharp G. *Social power and political freedom.* 1980
6. Stockholm International Peace Research Institute. *SIPRI Yearbook.* Stockholm, SIPRI, 1977.
7. McVitty M. *A comparison and evaluation of current disarmament proposals.* New York, World Law Fund, 1964.

9. Dilemmas of disarmament education

Haakan Wiberg, *Department of Sociology and Department of Peace and Conflict Research, Lund University*

The aim in this chapter is to formulate some of the problems that have to be solved in order to make disarmament education feasible as a transnational project. The underlying assumption is that since these problems must be tackled in order for any serious kind of transnational cooperation to succeed, there is no point in beating about the bush or staying suitably unaware of them: they should be formulated quite bluntly, if we are to have any hope of solving them. Hence, what I have to offer is problems, rather than ready-made solutions. In some cases I have more or less vague suggestions for how they might be solved; but these should be seen as outlines or hints, rather than as dogmatic assertions.

It should also be underlined that I deal with *transnational* disarmament education, where the idea is to use the same curriculum, the same textbooks and other teaching materials, and approximately the same methods of teaching in different countries. There is no assumption in this that *all* disarmament education has to be transnational: that would obviously be unrealistic on several counts. The point is rather that disarmament education carried out on a national basis only will tend to have some deficiencies, partly spelt out below, and that transnational cooperation would therefore by a valuable supplement.

Nor is it suggested that national and transnational disarmament education face the same problems: to some extent they certainly do, but in addition some problems are particular to the transnational side and therefore deserve special attention in the present context. For example, when it is stated that it has to be politically acceptable in the states in which it is undertaken, this by no means expresses a value judgement to the effect that all disarmament education ought to be politically palatable in its context — which I by no means maintain. It is merely a statement of the fact that if a proposed curriculum is politically unacceptable in some state or group of states, it is unlikely to be implemented there, as long as this requires the cooperation of some official authorities.

It should also be added that the following remarks are primarily

H. Wiberg

written with the northern hemisphere and the East-West armament dynamics in mind. Again, there is no assumption made to the effect that this has priority before other conflict axes: but when dealing with disarmament, we must face the fact that the problems of this world are mainly located there. Hence, we should give a brief overview of it as a background to these comments[1].

Armament dynamics and disarmament: present trends

Views may be more optimistic or more pessimistic as to the past development and the future prospects of armament dynamics and disarmament, and this very fact has to be taken into account when discussing the possibilities for transnational disarmament education.

Here comment is limited to different assessments of empirical facts, reserving theoretical disagreements for later discussion. Briefly summarized, the more optimistic view can summon the following arguments. Since the initiation of a long period of relative detente after the Cuban crisis in 1962, the average annual growth of military expenditures in the world has been much slower than it was before, in particular for the NATO-WTO part of the global armament dynamics[2]. It has been possible to conclude a long series of treaties and agreements restricting tests of nuclear weapons, banning biological weapons, stopping nuclear proliferation, keeping some parts of the globe and its surroundings non-militarized, limiting or stopping the development of some weapons systems, and providing for direct communication between leaderships in crisis situations so as to make wars by accident less likely[3]. Third, negotiations are still going on in a number of different international, regional or bilateral *fora* with a view to travelling further along this road.

A less optimistic view will contradict all these arguments. First, while the growth is admittedly slower during the second half of the post-war period then during the first, it is still there, and the latest decisions by NATO and WTO provide for an acceleration. Furthermore, while it has slowed down in East and West, it has speeded up in the rest of the world, partly due to the skyrocketing arms exports from the blocs[4]. The net result of this is that the stockpiled lethal capacity of the world is very much greater than it was in, say, 1962[5].

Second, with the possible exception of biological weapons, no single one of all the treaties and agreements has led to any disarmament. At best, they have lead to continuing non-armament, to rearmament at an agreed quantitative pace, or to the freezing of some kinds of armament. No effective slowdown has been achieved in the area of military research and development and the qualitative arms race engendered by it. Several near-nuclear states have not ratified, sometimes not even signed, the Non-Proliferation Treaty. The great powers have performed more nuclear bomb tests since than before the Partial Test Ban Treaty of 1963.

Third, no breakthrough seems to be imminent on any of these points. SALT II has not been ratified, and it is open to doubt whether it will be. After several years, the negotiations on reductions of forces in Europe have not led to any agreement. The philosophy of rearming to disarm has spread increasingly[6], and if the future of 'bargaining chips' bears any resemblance to the past, only the first part of the programme is likely to be the outcome of it. The hopeful signs in 1979, such as the initialling of the SALT treaty or Mr Brezhnev's announcement of unilateral withdrawals of troops, appear to have been washed away in a turmoil of actions, reactions and overreactions between East and West, with the NATO decision to deploy a new generation of nuclear missiles in Europe, the Soviet interference in Afghanistan, and the increase in the military budget in the USA as the latest and worst examples.

It is difficult to define a net balance of these and other arguments in both directions, but a pessimistic conclusion seems warranted. It should then immediately be added that this makes it much more important to search for what remain of grounds for hope and for possible alternative ways to halt and reverse the dynamics of increasing armament: continued contacts and negotiations, increased popular interest in peace and disarmament issues, possible confidence building measures, and disarmament education. Let us therefore look more closely at some of the problems that transnational efforts at disarmament education will have to tackle.

How to present the case for disarmament

The three main arguments for disarmament seem to be (1) that is would reduce the threat of war; (2) that it would reduce an unproductive drain of national and global resources that are needed for many other matters of high urgency, and (3) that it reduces trends towards militarization in the world. Yet all these arguments have been contested, and a curriculum for disarmament education would need to include some of that debate in order to see which counter-arguments are plainly unfounded, and which justify formulating the case for disarmament in a slightly more cautious way, in order to avoid inviting too easy accusations of naivity and wishful thinking.

As for war, while nobody denies that the destructive effects of the worst possible wars have increased with accelerating speed with the development of new and more sophisticated weapons systems, conventional as well as nuclear[7], balance-of-power theorists claim that, on the other hand and precisely because of this, the risks of war in general and continental and global wars in particular have decreased accordingly. They may also claim some support for this view, at least superficially, by referring to the fact that statistics of wars and statistics of armament and the arms trade have pointed in very different directions during the last decade[8]. They may add to this that Europe is at the same time the most heavily armed area in the world and the most peaceful — at least as long as argument is limited to wars inside Europe.

Precisely because the doctrine (or group of doctrines) of balance of power is so widespread and often manages to present itself as 'realistic', it is necessary for disarmament education to scrutinize it critically. This can be done in several different ways: by pointing out the ambiguities and contradictions that are often found in it[9], by pointing out how little solid empirical evidence there is for it, and by analysing its character as a legitimizing ideology for armament. For at first glance, a balance of power does not seem to preclude disarmament, as long as this takes place in a 'balanced' way. But since nobody has presented any agreed method for measuring 'balance' — and nobody is likely to — rigorous insistence on balance will in practice mean that the military establishment everywhere has something of a veto right against any disarmament proposal that is seen to threaten its interests, and most will. Furthermore, one may argue that even if there were some evidence that a mutual high armament level makes wars less likely, it is questionable whether this is enough to match the rapidly worsening effects of a war, if it should come about[10].

As for resources, it is a blatant fact that the postwar period has seen a greater part of the world's resources used for military preparations than ever before, from 8-9% in the early 1950s to 5-6% today. And there is no end to the comparisons that can, and should, be made between for example, the costs of a single bomber or nuclear submarine and the constructive uses to which such resources could have been put nationally or internationally[11]. Such comparisons, by being concrete and illustrative, will certainly be useful in disarmament education. Still, it may be dangerous and counter-productive to take them out of their moral context, and to imply that there is any automatic coupling between armament expenditures and more constructive expenditures. There is not; it has to be created, and this itself is an important challenge to disarmament education, e.g. by presenting the results of conversion research[12].

There is an even more important issue in this context, on which disarmament education has to take a stand. Both critics and protagonists of disarmament have often aired the idea that arms expenditure are in fact beneficial to the economies of at least some nations. This is a controversial question[13] and for precisely this reason, it is important that disarmament education should try to assess to what extent this type of argument can be scientifically discounted. It appears on empirical inspection that the employment argument at least is weak — military expenditure seems in fact to create fewer jobs than several other possible budgetary expenditures[14].

Militarization, finally, is also a moot point, both because the concept can be interpreted in different ways[15], and because most governments with high military expenditures tend to deny that they are militarized and emphatically maintain that their political leaderships have the military establishments under firm control. (This may or may not be true, but is beside the point in some interpretations of militarization.) Furthermore, disarmament education should take issue with the widespread notion of the military being a modernizing agent in many countries, even if and precisely because this now seems to have been revealed as a myth[16].

Thus, all three groups of arguments for disarmament carry some uncertainty, even if they are fundamentally sound, and this uncertainty is often exacerbated by political disagreements, within and between nations and blocs. When transnational cooperation in disarmament education is considered, one of the tasks that has to be taken up consists in finding some formulation of the arguments and their relative weight that is both scientifically defensible and politically acceptable in the participating states. I see no intrinsic reason why this should be impossible but it may not be simple.

How much analysis?

The discussion just presented may give the impression that disarmament education will have to deal to a large extent, or even predominantly, with analysis. This, however, is by no means self-evident, but rather presents an important dilemma in itself. To see that clearer, the two extreme positions that may be defined (without proposing that it is easy to find any important author that holds them in these pure forms) may be spelt out.

One extreme position would hold that since the moral and political case for disarmament is clear, the obvious thing to do is to work for it, using disarmament education as an instrument without getting bogged down in interminable theoretical disagreements on points of analysis or collection of ever more data. The primary role of disarmament education should be to create and reinforce positive attitudes to disarmament, and to do this in such a way as to engender commitments and the ability to work for it in such ways as are open to the participants.

H. Wiberg

In other words, disarmament education should be constructive and future-oriented rather than analytical and past-oriented.

The opposite position, formulated in equally extreme terms, would state that in order to change the world, we have to understand it. In order to work effectively for disarmament, we have to understand both the empirical characteristics of armament dynamics and the multifarious causes behind it, as well as the existing obstacles to disarmament and how to counteract them. Hence, the most fundamental part of disarmament education must be the analysis and explanation of armament dynamics. And since the scientific situation here is far from clarified, one of the most important tasks must be further scientific analysis of this kind, and for that matter also further studies of the mechanisms of opinion formation in these issues.

To resolve this dilemma means, among other things, striking a balance between utopianism (in the pejorative sense of that word) and paralysis, trying to avoid both. On the one hand, a commitment to disarmament that is not tempered by some understanding of mechanisms and legitimizations for armaments and of obstacles to disarmament and possible ways of overcoming them, is likely to be a shallow commitment, badly anchored in fundamental beliefs, and risks turning into disenchantment and cynical resignation after a few initial setbacks. On the other hand, the view that we have to understand everything before we start acting at all tends to engender paralysis covered up as prudent caution.

Where this balance is to be struck depends strongly on what level of education we think of: primary, secondary, university, vocational etc. No simple recipe can be valid for all levels, and it appears reasonable to assume that the higher the level, the more room there is for factual presentations and, to an even greater extent, for analysis. We shall return to the pedagogical implications of this.

As a concrete example, let us hint at what might be a reasonable balance at the middle level, say, somewhere around the ninth school year or corresponding levels. In that case, there should definitely be some presentation of basic facts on world armaments, as well as some outline of causal analysis. It would also be useful to include a record of cases where popular pressure or political negotiations or a combination of these have managed to bring about some amount of disarmament, or at least some halt in armament dynamics[17]. This does not mean that analysis and history should play a major role at this level — that would risk making disarmament education one more item in the curriculum fed to unwilling pupils unable to see its relevance to them and their lives.

Since we are discussing transnational cooperation and common curricula, some attention has to be given to the fact that there exist considerable disagreements as to what are the basic facts on world armament, and even more disagreement about what are the most adequate kinds of analysis of it. These disagreements become crucial to the extent that they correlate rather highly with bloc membership (or non-membership) in both cases. There is therefore another dilemma to be faced.

What kinds of analysis?

There may be branches of natural science in which a high degree of intradisciplinary consensus exists throughout the global scientific community on theoretical models as well as on methodology, and where there are few vested interests of a political or economic nature tied to different kinds of beliefs. This is certainly not true of armament dynamics. There are many different competing theories, some making irreconcilable claims that they provide the most important account of the subject, some irrelevant to one another, and sometimes flatly contradicting each other[18]. Furthermore, some of these theories carry political weight by having more or less 'official' status in different states and by serving in some cases as a part of the legitimization of current levels and trends in armament expenditure.

Clearly, an important problem in the creation of a transnational curriculum of disarmament education is to find some way of presenting the current trends in research on the forces behind armament dynamics that is at the same time scientifically defensible and politically acceptable in all the states under consideration for the joint programme. Let us once more use the technique of presenting the extreme possibilities in order to indicate the kind of balance that has to be struck between them.

One extreme possibility is, of course, to remain completely uncontroversial by abstaining entirely from analysis, merely presenting those facts that are not controversial (which would exclude some of the most important), and limiting the curriculum to general moral exhortations about the joint benefits to be reaped by disarmament, if it can be agreed upon. The other extreme would consist of selecting one single type of analysis on the basis of theoretical, empirical or political criteria, and making that type the basis of the whole curriculum.

The arguments against both extremes are obvious. Against the first, facts neither select themselves nor interpret themselves — both these activities normally take place on the basis of dominating theoretical or 'common sense' notions, explicit or hidden. Therefore, this approach would in fact mean the abandonment of transnationality. Furthermore, such a curriculum would in all probability be extremely dull, and might even be counter-productive, both in the sense of increasing rather than bridging international differences in percpetion of armament dynamics and the underlying forces, and in producing boredom in the pupils.

In the second case, the main problem is that there is no single model or theory that enjoys the required consensus, even if we limit ourselves to the scientific community. Joint research over several decades might eventually lead to one (although I doubt it), and to wait for that before doing anything about disarmament education would spell out the kind of paralysis indicated earlier.

The balance that might be struck would consist in agreeing to present in the curriculum both different existing views as to the basic facts (e.g. by each participating nation being invited to present its version of them), and an overview of different theories and models. This would present some of the controversies round them, pointing out that different schools at least disagree about their relative explanatory force and sometimes also about their content, leaving the rest of the presentation to the teachers in different nations. The following section attempts to outline what might be the skeleton of such an overview.

Models of armament dynamics

Many different theories exist about what causes nations to arm themselves, and they differ along several different dimensions. The following might be considered the most important:

1. *Scope:* some theories claim universal validity, whereas others limit themselves to industrial nations, great powers, or some other group;

2. *Complexity:* some theories see armament dynamics as a more or less self-contained process, whereas others attempt to explain it in terms of other phenomena (mechanisms and institutions inside states, processes and conflicts in the international system, etc);

3. *Formalization:* some theories are formulated in a highly precise mathematical language, whereas others are formulated verbally, and often vaguely;

4. *Empirical support:* some theories have been systematically tested, and some among them at least to some extent confirmed; others have not been tested, but rather draw their support from selective examples; others have been tested and received no support; many are purely theoretical in the sense that they have been subjected to no empirical confrontation whatsoever;

5. *Theoretical status:* some theories are independent in the sense that they deal solely with armament dynamics, whereas others are parts of or derivations from more encompassing theoretical frameworks;

6. *Social standing:* some theories enjoy widespread belief among the decision-makers in certain states or groups of states, and in fact serve as a part of the legitimization of their armament policies, whereas others have no such social standing or are even explicitly rejected at official levels;
7. *Precision:* some theories only claim to explain why nations tend to have armed forces or why they tend to increase, whereas others attempt to explain finer variations in space and time.

Some of the properties of these theories are evaluated differently by different epistemological schools; others are more consensual. If we limit ourselves to the latter, it may be said that an ideal theory would have a wide scope of validity, probably considerable complexity, good empirical support from systematic testing and high precision. It should be integrated into wider social theory. Apart from its scientific properties, it would naturally be a good thing if such a theory carried conviction with decision-makers everywhere, and were accordingly taken into account in armament policies and disarmament negotiations.

All this is, of course, too good to be true, and it must be said quite bluntly that no such theory currently exists, nor are we likely to arrive at one within the foreseeable future. This is not only a matter of scientific imperfection: some of the properties are hardly, or only partly achievable at the same time, and therefore have to be traded-off against each other, until, perhaps, we eventually arrive at a theory that enjoys a reasonable high degree of consensus in the scientific community. We are not there today and, as has been mentioned, the candidates are many. They may also be ordered in many different ways. Here they are ordered by what are seen as essential causal mechanisms: internal factors in nations or international interaction. It must be said in advance that the three types presented below are idealized pure cases, and that the theories are more or less close to them, or to some combination of them.

Model I

The first group of theories is often referred to as the action/reaction model[19]. In more or less mathematical ways such a model assumes that armament dynamics is a matter of interaction; each nation (the simplest versions only deal with two nations or coalitions) changes its level of armament in a way that is determined by what the other one has and/or how quickly it alters its level. Scarcity of economic resources may slow down armament, and it may be speeded up or slowed down by traditional relations between the two sides. Under certain circumstances this will lead to an arms race, which will end either in economic exhaustion or war, 'unless somebody stops to think', as the pioneer theorist, Richardson, put it.

Such a process may come about through many different causes or motives. It can be the result of purely defensive concerns, where both states try to stay superior in order to have some margin of safety; where both opt for parity but have different perceptions of what constitutes parity and exaggerated perceptions of each other's capabilities; or in other ways. Thus no assumption *needs* to be made that either side has any aggressive or illegitimate intentions — nor is such an assumption excluded. The motivating factors may also be attempts to achieve freedom of action elsewhere; to make political gains, political prestige or other ends that are believed, correctly or mistakenly, to depend on the military balance, real or perceived; for that matter to be superior enough to be able to launch a successful attack.

Model II
The second group of theories is often referred to by some variation of the term 'military/industrial complex'[20]. In their most simplified form, such theories hold that the armament behaviour on one side is determined by its internal phenomena and processes, whereas the behaviour of the other side is merely a reaction to what the first side is doing.

Again, there is a rich variety of different motives and mechanisms that may lead to this behaviour. Among possible internal forces are a military profession trained to perceive threats everywhere and hence easily finding arguments for its own expansion; economic interests in the armament industry, whether tied to dividends or profit or to bonuses for fulfilling or overfulfilling the norm; decision mechanisms in the large bureaucracies dealing with armament and military preparations; interests in employment, or particularly favoured employment for scientists and technicians in the arms industry; bargaining procedures between different political groups with varying ideological commitment to military means of national security; and so on. Likewise, as reaction mechanisms can operate in any of these situations, they may be more 'offensive' or 'defensive'.

Model III
The third group of theories may be referred to as bilateral autism[21]. In its pure or idealized form, such a theory maintains that armament dynamics really do not constitute an arms race at all. The armament behaviour on either side is determined by any of the internal forces listed above, and these forces need not necessarily be the same on both sides. Hence, no assumption has to be made about the two sides being essentially similar in their internal structure.

So much for the main types of theory. I must repeat that the summaries above are highly idealized, and hence cannot do justice to the more elaborate theories found in the literature. Whereas some theories lie close to the first type, and some close to the second, there is hardly any theory that proposes the extreme form of the third type. In addition, many theories combine elements from different types, for example by assuming that armament dynamics is determined by interaction as well as by internal forces on both sides; that interaction affects the extent to which such forces are able to operate; that internal balance of forces offsets the patterns of international interaction; and so on.

Which, if any, of these different theories is true? The simple answer would be none, at least as long as a high level of precision and empirical testing and verification are demanded. Several seem to contain some important leads for further research, and it may perhaps be stated that any adequate account of armament dynamics will have to take into account both interactive mechanisms and internal mechanisms on both sides. But there is little agreement in the scientific community on the relative role of interactive and internal mechanisms, and even less on the possibility of locating and identifying internal mechanisms.

Armament dynamics and disarmament education

Let us now try to draw some conclusions from these arguments on the creation of transnational disarmament education. First, as indicated, this presentation is only intended as a skeleton. When it comes to making curricula and preparing teaching materials, one obviously has to become more concrete, by adding a number of texts describing specific theories, and analysing specific mechanisms. The main point remains, however: the materials and curricula will have to present a diversity of theories and approaches, and will have to abstain from taking any explicit stand between them, at least in cases where this would be highly controversial. Since causal mechanisms are easily translated into distributing blame — or distribution of blame into causal mechanisms — it can hardly be expected that the authorities in any country will accept a curriculum which lays the blame for the arms race heavily at the door of that nation or the alliance to which it belongs. Therefore, the presentation of several theories without giving priority to any of them might be a way of combining scientific defensibility with political acceptability (and it should be noted that it is hardly possible to draw any clear and simple boundary between these two criteria). It is not intended to try to present a readymade proposal here: that will obviously be a problem for the groups engaged in the concrete work of defining curricula.

Second, there is one thing common to several of the theories which deserves to be strongly underlined. Many of the mechanisms involved are essentially social mechanisms, not dependent on various individual decision-makers. To put it pointedly, disarmament is more a matter of correcting harmful social mechanisms within and among nations than of reforming or ousting wicked people. Several of the effects pointed out above do not presuppose a conspiracy, or evil individual or collective intentions. They rather depend on professional socialisation, bureaucratic inertia, bargaining procedures, perception mechanisms explained by social psychology, collective historical experience, market mechanisms, etc.

This, of course, does not mean that individual decision-makers are always insignificant, or that conspiracies, manipulations etc. do not occur — the world is not populated by angels. The point is rather that these phenomena are not essential. They occur on top of, or as a part of social mechanisms, but they do not constitute them. There is probably more explanatory power in the assumption that people tend to define reality in such a way as to make their roles maximally relevant than in the naive idea of psychological egotism stating that people always try to maximize their own benefits.

Nor should it be taken as a dogmatic expression of social determinism, which would make any attempt at disarmament education pointless. At least some of the social and perceptual mechanisms hinted at are to some extent open to correction, and it may be assumed that many of them work with less power the more they are commonly understood. And this is precisely where disarmament education may come in.

Finally, the remarks made should not be taken to imply that disarmament education should avoid touching upon moral commitments or stands. The thrust of the argument is rather that moral commitment has a more constructive role to play in strengthening attitudes *for* disarmament than in distributing blame among present actors: after all, that is what much of traditional legitimization of increasing armament rests on.

To get a wider perspective on this, and to see the potential role of disarmament education more clearly, let us speculate briefly on the implications for action that the different types of theories have, and on the likely effects of these theories being generally believed.

Let us start with implications for action. If armament dynamics is essentially interactive (model I), that is, there is an arms race in the strict sense, then halting the arms race becomes very much a matter of international interaction, of evolving negotiations and treaties that may enhance the security of both sides by increasing mutual predictability, thus counteracting at least those mechanisms for armament that depend on uncertainty. In addition, unilateral initiatives may serve to slow down the race, and perhaps also to change some of the perceptions that tend to spur it on. The role of citizens and organizations inside the nations then mainly becomes that of supporting the negotiating efforts of their government, perhaps also urging it to unilateral initiatives to the extent that these are politically feasible, and counteracting exaggerated perceptions on both sides, internally by striving for more accurate views of the other side, and transnationally by engaging in various kinds of interchange that may serve to reduce the enemy image and the exaggerated perceptions on the other side.

The implications of model II are somewhat different. Here, the role for citizens and organizations on the side of internal armament dynamics would be to try to counteract it in various ways, whereas those on the other side would have something of the same role as in model I: supporting attempts at negotiated reductions, and counteracting over-reaction in their own country.

Model III, finally, is the one that allots the most important roles to citizens and organizations in counteracting increasing armaments. In this model, it is essentially a matter of revealing and attempting to weaken the forces encouraging armament in one's own country. This does not necessarily mean that international interaction, negotiations and agreements become completely irrelevant: they may well be seen as a joint effort of governments to get more control over their own armed forces.

One consequence of the arguments about the theories presented above is that a considerable amount of diversity will also be needed on the action-oriented side of disarmament education, no single model having clear and unambiguous priority over the others. Again, the transnational curriculum will have to contain some form of largest common denominator of what is politically feasible, and attention must be paid to symmetry. But that is also a matter for the elaboration of curricula and materials, rather than something to be presented as a ready-made solution.

In this context, it may also be illustrative to speculate over the probable effects of different combinations of beliefs in different nations. Obviously, some combinations are more conducive to disarmament than others. Whereas it may be difficult to rank-order several of the intermediate cases, the two extremes appear clear enough. If both sides believe in model III, then the prospects for disarmament appear brightest, whereas they appear most dismal where each side believes in model II, with the other side as the one with the internal forces making for increasing armament and one's own side merely reacting. The latter combination appears to describe rather well current dominating beliefs, and hence it becomes an important task for disarmament education to try to move away from this view.

Disarmament research and pedagogics

The relationship between research and pedagogics to some extent falls outside the scope of this presentation which deals with the content of disarmament education rather than with pedagogical methods. Let us, however, underline what appears to be one main problem in this area. If learning about armament dynamics and the possibilities for disarmament is not to consist only of learning by heart the results of research in this field (and this alternative has already been rejected) there is something of a pedagogical dilemma when trying to make it relevant for the students. Common sense understanding of social processes tends to perceive them in psychological terms by ascribing beliefs and intentions to individual actors, and by treating collective actors as if they were individuals or governed by leading individuals. But it has been argued above that it is precisely this type of understanding that disarmament education should try to counteract or at least supplement, by presenting a more genuinely social understanding of the phenomena.

Here, then, there is a certain amount of contradiction between creating relevance and giving an adequate presentation. For the former, disarmament will have to work with and present analogies on individual and small group levels, in order to make the research results understandable and relevant. The latter purpose, however, requires constant warnings concerning the validity of analogies between levels: nations are not small groups and do not have the same social dynamics, nor does the international system. There is no reason to assume that this problem is insoluble — the point is rather that it defines an important challenge to the development of disarmament education. One way of doing this might be to include in the teaching materials small group experiments, laboratory games, etc., that illustrate the point that the outcome of social interaction is often more a matter of the interaction process and how it is set up than about the personalities and intentions of the individual participants[22]. Similar materials could also be used to illustrate the point that when individuals appear as representatives of their groups, their behaviour is often more strongly coloured by the explicit or implicit expectations of the group than by their own intentions and personalities. But once more I limit myself to drawing attention to an important problem rather than trying to present any ready-made solution.

Notes and references

1.   For a more detailed view, see Wiberg H. Detente in Europe? *Current Research on Peace and Violence, 1979, 3-4*

2. SIPRI gives the following picture of development if we collate several year-books:

Period	Average annual growth in military expenditure			
	NATO states	WTO states	Others	Total
1949-63	7.9	4.1	5.8	6.3
1963-78	0.4	2.7	7.5	2.3
Whole period	3.9	3.4	6.7	4.2

3. See Sims N.A. *Approaches to disarmament.* London, 1979; *International detente and disarmament: contributions by Finnish and Soviet scholars.* Helsinki, 1977; and SIPRI *Yearbooks.* A more critical assessment is given in Myrdal A. *The disarmament game.* New York, 1976

4. The standard sources for data are the publications by SIPRI in Stockholm, the International Institute for Strategic Studies in London and the Arms Control and Disarmament Agency in Washington. For a critical assessment of their methods, see Albrecht U. *et al. A short research guide on arms and armed forces.* London, 1978. For an analysis of the trade patterns, see Öberg J. Arms trade with the Third World as an aspect of imperialism. *J. Peace Research*, 1975, **3**. A more journalistic view is given in Sampson A. *The arms bazaar.* London, 1977

5. Robinson J.D. The neutron bomb and mass-destruction conventional weapons. *Bull. Peace Proposals,* 1977, **4**

6. Westmoreland W.C. Reject SALT-2, seek a real disarmament. *International Herald Tribune,* 3 Oct., 1979

7. Lumsden M. *Anti-personnel weapons.* London, 1978; cf also Robinson, *op. cit.;* also von Weizsacker C.F. (Ed.) *Kriegsfolgen and Kriegsverhütung.* Munich, 1971 and Bellany I. Doomsday In Bidwell S. (Ed.) *World War 3.* London, 1978

8. Kende I. Dynamics of wars and of arms and military expenditure in the third world. *Instant Research on Peace and Violence, 1977,* **2**.

9. Galtung J. Balance of power and the problem of perception: a logical analysis. *Inquiry,* 1967 64

10. This argument is further developed in Niezing J. *Strategy and structure,* Chap. 2. Amsterdam, 1978

11. See especially, Sivard R.L. *World military and social expenditures,* 1977, *et seq.;* and *Economic and social consequences of the armament race and its extremely harmful effects on world peace.* United Nations, 1972

12. Albrecht U. *et al. Rüstugskonversionsforschung: eine Literaturstudie mit Forschungsempfehlungen.* Berlin, 1978. *Experiences in disarmament: on conversion of military industry and closing of military bases.* Uppsala, Dept. of Peace Research, 1978. *Sense about defence.* London, Labour Party Study Group, 1977

13. Wängborg M. *Disarmament and development: a guide to literature relevant to the Nordic proposal.* Stockholm, Swedish Defence Research Institute, 1979, and von Bredow W. (Ed). *Ökonomische and soziale Folgen der Abrüstung,* Cologne, 1974

14. It has been estimated that in the USA an additional billion dollars spent by the Department of Defense creates 73 000 new jobs, whereas the same amount spent on health, education and welfare creates 115 000 jobs.

15. Skjaelsbaek K. Militarism, its dimensions and corollaries: an attempt at conceptual clarification. *J. Peace Research,* 1979, **3,** Öberg, J. *The new international military order.* Oslo, Dept of Peace Research, 1978

16. Perlmutter A. *The military and politics in modern times.* London, 1977

17. Noel-Baker P. *The arms race.* London, 1958

18. For competing theories, see Brauch H.G. *Entwicklungen und Ergebnisse der Friedensforschung, 1969-1978.* Frankfurt M., 1979. Krell G. *Rüstungsdynamik and Rüstungskontrolle.* Frankfurt a.M., 1977. Senghaas D. *Rüstung und Militarismus.* Frankfurt a.M., 1972

19. The classic study is Richardson L.F. *Arms and insecurity.* Chicago, 1960. For a systematic survey, see Rattinger, J.R. *Rüstungsdynamik im internationalen System: mathematische Reaktionsmodelle für Rüstungswettäüfe und Probleme ihrer Anwendung.* Vienna, 1975

20. Senghaas D. *Op.cit.;* Barnet R. *The economy of death.* New York, 1969, and Melman S. *The permanent war economy,* 1977. Marxist discussions of the necessity of armaments for capitalism are found in Baran and Sweezy. *Monopoly capitalism.* New York, 1973; Mandel E. *Spätkapitalismus.* Frankfurt, 1973; Kidron, M. *Capitalism and theory.* 1974; Vilmar F. *Rüstung und Abrüstung.* Frankfurt, 1973; *Beitrage zur Militärökonomie.* Friederich-Engels-Militärakademie. There are also studies investigating the existence of A Soviet military/industrial complex, e.g. in Rosen S. (Ed). *Testing the theory of the military/industrial complex.* 1975; Holloway D. Technology and political decisions in Soviet armaments policy. *J. Peace Research,* 1974, **4.**

21. Whereas hardly any author proposes this model in its pure form, the notion that armament dynamics contain strong internal mechanisms on both sides is found in Senghaas, *op.cit.;* Gantzel K.J. Armament dynamics in the East-West conflict: an arms race? *Peace Science Society Papers,* 1973, **20.** Lambelet J.C. *et al. Dynamics of Arms Races: mutual stimulation versus self-stimulation.* Geneva, Graduate Insitute of International Studies, 1978.

22. Inbar M. and Stall C.S. *Simulation and gaming in social science.* New York, 1972; Wrightsman L.S. *et al. Cooperation and competition: readings on mixed motive games.* Belmont, California, 1972

II. CASE STUDIES IN INFORMAL EDUCATION

10. Disarmament education and peace action: report on a campaign for unilateral initiatives towards disarmament in the Netherlands*

Philip P. Everts *Institute for International Studies, Leiden University*

Ben J. Th. ter Veer, *Polemological Institute, University of Groningen*

We shall discuss the origins, aims and methods of the campaign which an organization of the churches in the Netherlands, the Interchurch Peace Council (IKV), has been conducting since 1977 to obtain the removal of nuclear weapons from the Netherlands, in order to initiate and help to bring about a process of disarmament. We shall try to analyse why, apparently quite suddenly, there is a revival of interest in matters of nuclear strategy and disarmament and to answer the question of the ways the campaign could affect public opinion and, through this, might have an impact on the foreign policy behaviour of the Dutch government as well as on that of its allies in NATO and the countries of the Warsaw Pact.

We shall describe briefly the changes in public opinion in the Netherlands with respect to (nuclear) disarmament and the backgrounds and character of the campaign. Then we shall turn to the criticisms levelled against the campaign and discuss its prospects in terms of political support and as a contribution to consciousness raising and peace education. In the last part we shall present some views on the institutionalization and contents of peace and disarmament education and its relation to political action.

It seems useful to state at the outset that our interest in this topic stems from two sources. One is a scientific interest in the role played by domestic factors in the making of foreign policy and in peace education in general. The second reason — though part of this more general concern about the conditions under which democracy can be made to

---

*A revised and integrated version of two earlier papers: Everts, P.P. Reviving unilateralism. *Bull. Peace Proposals,* 1980, 1, 40-56 and ter Veer, B.J.Th. Peace education and peace action. Conference of Arbeitsgemeinschaft für Friedens - und Konfliktforschung. Königstein, 24-26 August, 1979.

work in the field of foreign policy and the promotion of peaceful relations between nations — stems from personal involvement in the activities described here. Personal involvement in the subject of one's research can be both an asset and a liability: an asset insofar as it provides knowledge 'from within', which is not so easily available to the outside observer, and a liability to the degree that it tends to blur the objectivity of one's observations. One guarantee against possible bias can be sought in making one's position relative to the object of research as clear as possible and in trying to remain conscious of the fact that observations and inferences are always filtered not only through explicit theoretical lenses, but also through one's attitudes, values and experiences.

General approach

The role of peace research

Peace research as an academic movement has from its beginning been characterized by the desire to provide empirically verified knowledge, which could be applied to the promotion of a particular goal: peace, or to be somewhat more modest, the reduction of violence in the relations between nations and other large groups. It is therefore not unexpected that debates have centered not only on the scientific relevance of particular theories and findings, but also — and perhaps more so — on the problems of application[1].

The whole concept of an applied science assumes the existence of at least three elements:

1. the availability of empirically verified theories, which involve variables which can be manipulated and allow us to make predictions concerning the consequences of these manipulations;
2. the existence of political actors or institutions which are, in principle, prepared to make use of such insights and theories;
3. the relevance of the available insights and theories to the concrete situation in which those who should apply these results find themselves.

Peace research has therefore always been forced to wage a war on two fronts. On the one hand there were, and are, those in the academic community who question both its claims to be a new departure in scientific research and the validity of its results (often considered as 'politics in disguise') who tends to reject its *scientific* relevance. On the other side those who would or should be willing to apply the newly gathered insights, be they governments or political groups such as parties, often express the view that peace research does not provide answers to the most important questions that are occupying them: its *political and social* relevance is questioned.

More particularly the criticism is voiced that, while peace research may be relatively good at describing and giving reasons why the world situation is not as it should be and in arguing persuasively that with escalating armaments the world is set on a collision course, analysis has, by and large, stopped at this point. Peace research has not delivered the goods it promised, i.e. to provide alternatives which are feasible and applicable in that they are likely to generate political support. This observation seems to be correct. Peace research has contributed little applicable knowledge, let alone results which can in fact be applied (which is something else). In this connection the whole idea that the social role of peace research can be compared to that of the applied natural sciences has been questioned, because social institutions, unlike engineering offices and hospitals, do not exist. Those who could apply the results, i.e. the established powers and governments, are unlikely to do so, since they give (or are forced to give) priority to the more immediate protection of perceived 'national interests', while those who would be prepared to do so (pressure groups, such as the peace movement) lack the necessary power to challenge the war system. Thus Rapoport has claimed that 'peace research has no audience'[2].

The question how the power necessary for the implementation of the ideas which peace-researchers could offer can be generated, has been largely neglected either because it was, rather naively, assumed that increased rational insights in and by themselves would be sufficient to obtain more 'rational' policies, or because this was considered to be not the task of the researcher, but of the activist or the politician.

The need for alternatives

The degree to which people can be made receptive to the findings of peace research does seem to depend to a large extent on the feasibility of the alternatives which are offered. In this connection a distinction should be made between alternatives in the sense of alternative security *systems* which do not rely on the use or threat of physical violence in political struggles, and in the sense of alternative *policies*, which eventually could generate such systems.

The present system of security and its pseudo-intellectual basis or legitimization have evolved over a long period. How this evolution would take place could not be predicted at the start although its present contours were forecast by many observers. In the same way it is not reasonable to request that a complete detailed alternative security system should be drawn up now: it will have to evolve over time. It seems justified, however, to ask what the first steps toward such a system should be and what an alternative security policy should consist of.

Any security policy in essence is based on calculations or estimates and the weighing of risks. Nuclear deterrence deals with the incalculable chance of a unique event: nuclear war. All that can be said is that this chance by definition is larger than zero (otherwise the system would not work) and will be greater the longer the period under consideration. Although the consequences of a war with nuclear weapons can be envisaged, this danger remains abstract to a large extent: 'thinking about the unthinkable' remains difficult. This danger has to be compared with and weighed against the dangers which might arise from the adoption of security policies which would not rely on this ultimate deterrent.

Rationality of the elites

Although, therefore, this rational calculation of odds should be the basis of any sensible policy, we are faced with the fact that in practice behaviour, even that of the most sophisticated politician, is influenced so much by the uncertainties under which we have to operate and by the personal experiences, attitudes and value judgements of the decision makers, that this ideal can only be roughly approximated. Furthermore, of course, the influence of pressure groups and other interests may simply prevent the adoption of 'rational' solutions. If this is true, science can play at best a critical role; it can bring to light and question implicit assumptions and values underlying political judgements, it can criticize acccepted 'wisdoms' and 'common-sense' judgements. But its role is limited.

If this is true, it implies that the value of the claim to special authority on the part of those experts is greatly reduced. The lack of democratic control over foreign policy and the traditional treatment of foreign policy as a *domaine reservé* of the executive power are usually not only defended by the vital nature of foreign policy problems (the survival of the nation) and the need of secrecy in negotiations and other forms of power struggle, but also by the complexity of the matters involved. Leaving aside the fact that such opinions are often self-fulfilling prophecies, they do not take into account the degree to which decisions by the experts are subjected to considerations and values in which the interested citizen is, in principle, no less qualified than they.

The campaign described later aimed to break through the alienation from the way in which security is organized to enable people to gain control over this area, which so vitally affects them. The question must be asked whether it is possible to raise sufficient support for an alternative security policy and the criticisms which have been voiced against such an approach must be considered. Some of these cannot be easily discounted. If peace research is to be relevant, it should address itself to the kind of questions raised by the campaign we describe.

Efficacy of peace research and peace education

It has been argued that peace researchers should be interested in the societal conditions which prevent or further acceptance of their findings. What we in fact would like to argue is that both peace researchers and peace educators should have a strong concern for the effectiveness of their work. Why is it necessary to work for the involvement of as many people as possible in matters of peace and disarmament? 'Because it is such an urgent matter' does not seem to be sufficient answer.

An answer may first be sought in the processes of mutual interaction, by which the defence and foreign affairs elites of the large and middle-sized countries are controlled. It should be made clear that these elites are to some degree living in a sort of collective isolation in which they are tempted time and again to give priority to power political goals over the adoption of measures which contribute to safety through arms control and disarmament. At the negotiations conducted between East and West all kinds of interests are represented: political, economic, industrial and military. Yet the disarmament interest as such is not represented. It can be proven, sadly, that at crucial moments that interest has to give way to the others. Disarmament education is, we conclude, an absolute necessity for disarmament. The present elites as they operate at the moment, cannot be expected to put an end to the arms race on their own. They need to be supported or pushed forward by public opinion.

But it is not only the question *why* involvement is necessary that must be answered; there is also the question *how* it can be effected. Disarmament will have to be fought for, against all sorts of other interests and also against fierce competition from the major powers. This requires not only a well-informed public but also the development of proposals for alternative policies which can really lead the way towards disarmament. Such proposals can then be grasped by a determined minority of people who will then try to mobilize by a common strategy all the support they can get for the proposal and gather this into a power factor.

The contributions to be made to this objective by peace researchers and peace educators will depend greatly on their own attributes towards their work and the limits to which they think their work will be subject. Peace educators may consider it their task only to put peace research findings before pupils and adults within and outside the system of education. If this is all they do, this is not enough to be effective. In our opinion the peace researcher must devote more time in his studies to questions of whether and how the process of power creation and aggregation from the grass roots upwards can take place, centering round alternative policies put forward by peace research. They should study the questions which face people who are in the middle of those developments and processes. What there should be is analysis and research 'on demand'.

We do not believe that any researcher who chooses the task briefly described above should by definition be at odds with scientific standards. He is not concerned with 'scientific' legitimization in the strict sense of a direction once taken. What he is concerned with is the development of answers to questions which are essential, as they stem from a concrete social experiment. The same applies to a greater or lesser extent to peace education. Peace educators, too, will have to make themselves useful particularly to the groups of people who, from their own backgrounds, engage in resistance to nuclear arms.

From this, two more points arise: peace research and peace education in the Netherlands (and, we think, in other countries) have not always escaped one of the main dangers of professionalization and institutionalization, namely the danger of too much 'self-programming' and a lack of availability to people and developments in society. We think this should be guarded against.

Peace education and peace action

Secondly, we regard peace education, or its offshoot, disarmament or survival education, to be effective mainly if it takes place within the context of peace action. The unfortunate thing about this term is that many people think of it only in terms of demonstrations. Demonstrations may be a sound instrument at certain stages of the development of a protest movement, but the term peace action should be taken to have a much wider meaning. It largely concerns educational activities by groups and institutions which have explicitly opted for the realization of a certain political goal, and which subsequently try to win other people, groups and institutions over to that policy by a collective strategy and various methods of action. Peace education will occur most intensively when people, having opted for a certain standpoint, become engaged in the 'education' of themselves and others. It is most effective in a process featuring the alternation of action and reflection.

Recent development in the Netherlands

In 1976 Everts wrote an article which started from the observation that 'the protest against the bomb' had evaporated[3]. Apart from a small group of professionals and the remnants from the once-active movement against nuclear armaments no one seemed to worry about the nuclear weapons issue anymore. Several (potential) reasons were given why the movement, which was relatively widespread and active in the 1950s and early 1960s in countries such as the USA, UK and the FRG, and also in the Netherlands, had dwindled and almost disappeared.

First of all there was the 'abstract' character of the nuclear threat. The longer nuclear weapons were not used and the more people got used to their existence, the more difficult it became to keep the issue alive. The lack of success and the seemingly intractable nature of the problem also did little to attract new followers, especially since it seemed more worthwhile to use one's energy on other, seemingly more profitable or pressing problems. Thus a shift in attention occurred, away from the problems of nuclear armament and towards issues such as underdevelopment, exploitation and imperialism, both at home and abroad, and problems of pollution and environmental decay. This shift, in some instances, was the consequence of new analysis as well as a stimulus to this analysis. Thus in peace research the discussion of concepts such as negative and positive peace both reflected and stimulated a change in focus and choice of subjects for research away from the issues surrounding nuclear weapons, East-West relations and disarmament and toward problems such as dominance, imperialism and structural violence[7]. If the world images and priorities of the early peace researchers were shaped by the cold war and the advent of nuclear weapons, the new generation took the Vietnam war as its point of reference and departure.

Another explanation, in contrast to the previous one, points to the initial successes of the protest movement and the changing political climate: the Test Ban Treaty of 1963, the gradual demise of the cold war and the onset of political detente in Europe. The admittedly few agreements on arms control further contributed to relieving some of the pressure toward further steps. The feeling of urgency and the immediacy of the dangers were replaced by the idea that, though the problems were serious, we were on the right road.

In the Christian churches the idea that, although the use of nuclear weapons should be condemned, their existence provided what the German physicist von Weizsäcker called a *Gnadenfrist* or stay of execution, which could be used to reach more acceptable security arrangements, was widely acclaimed as the basis of a valid 'interim ethic'. But in fact, those who argued in this way were lulled by a false feeling of security, as is shown by steadily growing armaments and the change in strategic doctrines toward 'warfighting', rather than pure deterrence, and toward the acquisition of first-strike capabilities.

With regard to peace education we can conclude that from the middle of the 1960s a substantial movement arose for the introduction of development education into education programmes, both within and outside schools. They included problems like the North-South conflict, imperialism and structural violence. But education for survival or disarmament education failed to obtain a similar position. In the article referred to earlier, it was concluded that while the new concepts and the extension of concern to include new problems had provided gains, hard-core security problems, symbolized by nuclear armaments, should remain at the centre. They would not disappear merely by not thinking about them, but it was estimated that it would be difficult to focus interest again on this topic. It was all the more amazing therefore to see this analysis — which was shared, it appeared, by many — proved wrong in such a short time.

Recent events

Events since 1977 have provided ample evidence of the existence of widespread and strong popular concern in the Netherlands about the nuclear arms race, especially in its most recent manifestations. This concern has also drawn attention again to security concepts and policies of which the possession and continuous build-up of nuclear arsenals are a consequence.

Revelations in the USA concerning the proposed introduction into the NATO forces of a new generation of nuclear weapons based on enhanced radiation, popularly called the neutron bomb, gave rise to a storm of protest, extending beyond the traditional circles on the left of the political spectrum[5]. In the Netherlands a mass signature campaign sponsored by the 'Stop the N-Bomb' movement resulted in 1.2 million signatures. In 1978 resistance increased: the National Council of Churches came out against the introduction of the neutron bomb 'and every other further extension of nuclear armaments'; synods and bishops of a number of the member churches added their support to this statement. Due to these and other pressures, opposition arose also in parliament: to the surprise of some, the Christian Democrats were the first to reject the new weapon, followed shortly afterwards by the Social Democrats. Notwithstanding the fact that the parliamentary groups of both parties have consistently supported NATO membership by the Netherlands, statements were now made that the introduction of the neutron bomb would force the Netherlands to reconsider their membership. But despite three major debates in parliament no clear-cut motion to express the majority view was accepted, mainly for reasons of domestic and coalition politics. The government was left with room for manoeuvre to allow for the inclusion of this modernization in future negotiations with the Warsaw Pact. A sudden decision by the government to assign a 'nuclear role' to the new Lance missile (for which the new warheads were developed) was approved with Christian Democrat support. One year later their leader would say that he 'regretted' the way this had come about.

At the same time (1977) the Interchurch Peace Council (IKV), — of which more will be said later — started its campaign to obtain the removal of nuclear weapons from Dutch territory. The campaign met with much opposition, but also with remarkable shows of support and sympathy, from within and outside the churches. Thus an opinion poll held in April 1978 showed 54% of the adult population to be in favour of the IKV campaign slogan 'Free the world of nuclear weapons and begin with the Netherlands': in October 1978, this had increased to 58%[6].

Probably due to these and other pressures, in 1978 the government was forced to produce a policy paper giving for the first time a precise outline of the various 'nuclear tasks' of the Dutch armed forces and spelling out what it intended to do to implement its announced goal of reducing the role of nuclear weapons. The paper, according to its many critics, did not do this, but in fact implied an extension of this task. It was heavily criticized, even by the Christian Democratic Defence Minister's own party, which felt it necessary to give an indication that it took the criticism from the churches seriously. But again, the opposition to the government's policies did not result in a clear parliamentary vote. The only concrete outcome was a motion against the envisaged 'nuclearization' of the 155 mm howitzers, which Defence Minister Scholten accepted as support for his policy 'to study' this matter.

If the change in climate is to be characterized in one sentence, it could perhaps be said that there is now a reversal of roles, with the majority, which until now accepted a security system based on nuclear weapons as self-evident, being forced onto the defensive. This became clear as international pressure increased, to counter the introduction of a new generation of Soviet intermediate range missiles (the SS-20) by introducing in Western Europe new weapon systems with similar functions. Due to the impact of the previous debates and the pressure from the peace movement the nuclear arms race became one, if not *the* major topic of political debate in the Netherlands. Although these pressures have not yet resulted in real reductions in Dutch participation in defence with nuclear weapons, there is now unmistakably a political necessity to accommodate public pressures in this direction. The first real result of this was the parliamentary stand against the proposed 'modernization' of 'long range theatre nuclear forces' in December 1979.

Possible explanations

These developments raise the question whether the changes described are apparent or real. Do they contradict the validity of earlier analysis? And if so, why did the changes occur?

It has been suggested that the success of the campaign against the neutron bomb was due to skilful manipulation of people's emotional fears of this new weapon, which kills primarily through its radiation effects, producing horrible forms of sickness and ensuing death. But poll data seem to rule out this explanation: 61% of all respondents stated that they considered the neutron bomb to be as bad as the existing nuclear weapons, 28% considered it to be worse, 7% declared the opposite and 4% did not know[7]. But the campaign slogan 'Stop the neutron bomb' was apparently vague enough to attract also the support of those who thought that the USA's decision not to produce the neutron bomb should depend on a show of restraint on the part of the Soviet Union; 60% of all respondents supported the slogan, only 48% thought that the decision should be taken in any case and 34% shared the view that the Soviet Union should also show restraint[8]. In this connection commentators have stated that the campaign was under communist control and have tried to explain its success by the financial and organizational support which it received from outside (i.e. the Soviet Union)[9]. Whether or not this claim was justified, on balance it could hardly have contributed to the success, being more a liability than an asset given the general anticommunist climate. Indeed this communist influence was widely known and the campaign was for this reason hardly mentioned in the press until the later stages, when it could no longer be discounted or neglected.

It seems therefore necessary to look to other factors in the question of public acceptance of new nuclear weapons:

1. accommodation to the *status quo*: once weapons are introduced, they acquire, like everything else, their own legitimation; it is, on the other hand, less difficult to prevent new developments;
2. the generally accepted idea that increasing armaments to maintain or reestablish an equilibrium is justified and necessary;
3. once people realize what the actual use of nuclear weapons entails, this creates emotional boundaries, which work against the introduction of new weapon systems;
4. increasing popular involvement in matters of foreign and defence policy tends to strengthen the opposition against the continuation of the arms race;
5. increasing popular fears of the use of nuclear energy for civilian purposes strengthens the opposition to 'all things nuclear' and

broadens the potential scope of actions against nuclear armaments.

In the case of the neutron bomb the last three factors appear to have prevailed over the 'conservative' impact of the first two. We contend that, whereas the concrete and limited nature of the issues (to stop one particular weapon, to obtain one concrete step by the Netherlands) undoubtedly played an essential role in overcoming persistent feelings of impotence concerning foreign affairs in general and the arms race in particular, the introduction of these issues catalysed the manifestation of feelings and attitudes which had been latent over a considerable period of time.

Background of IKV and its campaign

The Interchurch Peace Council (IKV) was established in 1966 by the Roman Catholic Church in the Netherlands and the two major Protestant churches. Shortly afterward six smaller denominations joined in this effort[10] to further ecumenical reflection on the problems of war and peace, to promote the interest, awareness and involvement of the church members in these matters and to propose forms for suitable political action. The IKV was not integrated in the official ecumenical structure of the Council of Churches in the Netherlands. While it cannot be said that the statements of the IKV can be identified with those of the churches themselves (though both sympathizers and critics often try to do this) its status as an institutionalized pressure group or vanguard within the churches is firmly established. Its influence is determined by a combination of formal authority, the quality of its ideas and the degree of support it is able to generate among its constituents. Its political composition ranges from left-wing Social and Christian Democrats to Pacifist Socialists. Its members have included church officials, academic peace researchers, and a few officials from the Foreign Office and professional military men.

It has no formal membership, but a body of some 19 000 registered sympathizers, many of whom hold important positions as transmitters of information and opinion leaders. Its strategy of action has always included both information and consciousness-raising at the grass-roots level of the local parish as well as (though to a lesser extent) direct pressure at the level of government and parliament. The two are not always compatible, but in general each activity has reinforced the effectiveness of the other. During the first 10 years of its existence the IKV engaged in providing schooling and information primarily to members of the churches, by organizing once a year a so-called 'peace week'. Every year a special theme was chosen and materials were prepared around that theme. Gradually local groups working with these materials came into being in many places. The themes derived from three main areas: war and peace, development problems, and human rights. Methodological questions, such as how to work through existing societal institutions, were also taken up from time to time. The themes were usually kept rather general and rarely contained hard, political messages or action models intended to shock. During the annual peace week the Council sometimes provided opportunities for various other groups, whether based on the churches or not, to present their action models in the yearly 'peace paper', which was distributed on a large scale. These models sometimes included fairly hardcore models, such as boycotts of companies trading with South Africa as well as support for radical groups in the Third World. Others also profited from this opportunity, such as the Dutch self-tax movement 'X-Y'. Thus the IKV indirectly promoted the activities of these often more radical groups, without explicitly sharing their aims.

Attitudes toward nuclear weapons

Ideologically the IKV based itself originally on both the important statements of the Vatican (the encyclical *Pacem in terris* of 1963, the constitution *Gaudium et spes* of the Second Vatican Council and similar statements) and the 1962 Pastoral Letter of the Dutch Reformed Church, in which it was stated that Christians could never in conscience participate in the use of nuclear weapons. While naturally the possession of nuclear weapons cannot be separated from the prospect of their actual use, the statements referred to do not explicitly condemn this possession.

While it cannot be denied that there is a probable connection between the existence of nuclear weapons and the non-occurrence of a major war between East and West, there is no reason to assume that this will remain true. Indeed many observers assume that recent developments in the sphere of weapon systems and strategic doctrines (especially the possibility of a strategic first-strike capability and the development of strategic doctrines which stress the desirability of a 'warfighting capability' and the possibility of 'limited nuclear wars') have all contributed to the increased likelihood of a nuclear war in Europe.

The gap between nuclear and conventional weapons is gradually being closed by the development of smaller, more precise and more 'manageable' nuclear weapons on the one hand, and more destructive conventional weapons on the other. Thus the natural watershed between nuclear and conventional war and between those doctrines which stress deterrence and those which stress defence, is disappearing. Nuclear war is made conceivable again.

Technological developments are regularly causing very unstable phases in the security system. These developments are only subject to a small degree to deliberate political decisions and control. Insight into the dominant influences of military, industrial, bureaucratic and scientific interests on armaments processes is growing.

The process of proliferation of nuclear weapons is not being stopped. At best the Non-proliferation Treaty has somewhat retarded this process. It seems that as long as those who rely for their security on the possession of nuclear weapons or an alliance with nuclear weapon states are not prepared to get rid of them, any non-proliferation policy will retain strong elements of hypocrisy and for that reason will remain unconvincing and ineffective.

Countries tend to use their armament policies and their resistance to disarmament as psycho-political means in the international power struggle. In their view the most satisfactory armaments situation is not minimal armaments on all sides, but a situation in which the other side can be kept under politically offensive pressure and one's own side cannot be forced into concessions. In trying to reach or maintain such a situation security notions play a far smaller role than is usually assumed. On the contrary, growing international insecurity is taken into the bargain.

Finally, there is the virtually complete alienation and apathy of people as far as nuclear arms are concerned. The elites in all countries, in whose hands the arms problem has gradually come to lie, have demonstrably failed to bring the problem of nuclear armament any closer to solution or to safeguard the survival of our societies. Politicians, despite their well-meaning intentions, are apparently unable to extricate themselves from the arms race, unless the existing alienation is overcome and domestic pressures force or help them to overcome the pressures and vested interests behind established policies.

Character of the disarmament campaign

By these and other arguments the IKV in 1977 concluded that the balance of deterrence, instead of creating opportunities for steps toward disarmament and a continuation of the arms race, implies all kinds of processes by which the balance is sustained. For that reason it expressed the opinion that not only the use, but also the possession of nuclear weapons had to be rejected by Christian conscience. But the IKV did not wish to restrict itself merely to expressing its changed moral judgement and political assessment of the nuclear arms situation: it also proposed to contribute to a solution of the problems.

A proposal for disarmament

The proposal had to meet three criteria. First, it should express the IKV's moral standpoint concerning nuclear weapons as unambiguously as possible. Secondly, it should be a concrete political proposal, able to compete with other political proposals on the matter; specifically, by its radical nature the least it could do was to make other, less radical proposals appear more legitimate and acceptable. Thirdly, the proposal should be such that it could gain the support of large groups of people from as many political parties as possible. In order to meet the third criterion the proposal should be able to induce in a very large number of small groups (so-called 'cores') a feeling that they could work in a concrete manner to try to influence the views of the people around them in a positive way. In other words, the proposal should restore the feeling in people that security was actually their own concern and that they really could do something about the arms threat.

If negotiations on disarmament fail for any reason, and complete unilateral disarmament is neither advisable nor politically feasible for lack of support, an effort should be made to steer a middle course containing both elements of unilateralism (independently decided and executed steps, which can be characterized as self-obligation and a move towards disarmament) and multilateralism (both within and between the blocs) in later stages. Such unilateral steps will probably only be taken if sufficient domestic support for them is organized. It will not be possible to do so and to break through existing apathy and feelings of impotence unless concrete steps are proposed which reduce the problem to manageable proportions, small enough to overcome hesitations about 'disturbing the balance' and yet sufficiently large to stir the imagination and produce an international impact.

Furthermore the step to be taken should be one which shows a clear commitment to swim against the stream of constant 'improvement' in the system of deterrence. It should not be possible to interpret it as a step to improve military security, to alleviate financial burdens, or as an effort to loosen ties to an alliance. Indeed, the continued membership of a military alliance (NATO in the case of the Netherlands) has always been discounted as a subject for debate within the campaign.

Neutralism is not considered to be a feasible option for the Netherlands. The IKV recognized that it is essential to win over the allies in NATO, which means a long-term process, taking time to evolve. It is not necessary now to have a blueprint of an *alternative security system*. It is necessary, however, to work out a more detailed *alternative strategy*, consisting of a series of unilateral steps at the level of individual countries and alliances, preventing new and dangerous steps in the arms race, and preparing negotiated disarmament steps.

The IKV maintains that the process of learning from previous failures, the gradual gaining of democratic control over foreign policy, the rising awareness of the increasing dangers, the general concern about both civilian and military use of nuclear power, and the elaboration of concrete and manageable steps will combine to make the success of its campaign a serious possibility. How well founded this claim is will be discussed later.

Features of the proposal

The IKV summarized its proposal in the motto 'Free the world from nuclear weapons and begin with the Netherlands'. Besides meeting the above criteria, the proposal also has the following features:

1. It is a proposal for disarmament, not for arms control. It clearly tries to break away from the system of deterrence through weapons capable of destroying large masses of people and is not intended to modify that system or make it less dangerous.

2. The proposal is intended to get a process under way. In the field of armaments there is no scope for abrupt changes, so destabilizing reactions need not be expected.

3. The proposal implies that the Netherlands should commit itself to making a first move on the road to total disarmament, irrespective of whether other countries join in. This has the political significance of inducing other countries to take similar meaningful first steps. Such steps can concern both conventional and nuclear armaments.

4. The proposal will have to be carried out in stages and is directed towards both East and West. Its intention therefore is not total unilateral disarmament by the West, but initiation of a process of disarmament in both blocs by moves in various countries. The first stage must certainly feature a collection of first moves made independently in various countries on both sides. In subsequent moves the element of coming into step already taken by other countries will become stronger, once again in both East West. After the first stage this will entail intensification of talks within the alliance about further unilateral moves, but this will also hold for deliberations between East and West about bilateral disarmament moves. Thus in answer to steps in the nuclear field by the Western countries, the Eastern countries could respond by reducing their tanks. The steps could follow the GRIT pattern (policy of mutual example) elaborated by Osgood and others[11]. Gradually the unilateral element would be replaced by negotiations both within and between the blocs, while the improved climate would be strengthened by further confidence-building measures.

5. As far as the Netherlands is concerned, the removal of nuclear arms from Dutch territory and the Dutch armed forces would be a suitable first step.

6. The proposal is also intended as a contribution to a global policy against proliferation of nuclear weapons. The IKV is of the opinion that the only non-proliferation policy which is not hypocritical must be one which starts with removing from one's own house what one so urgently wishes to dissuade others from keeping. It should, the IKV estimates, be politically feasible to raise sufficient support for such a step to get a parliamentary majority by a campaign lasting several years, if this were well planned and organized.

The international effect of the campaign, if it were successful in the Netherlands, would not primarily take place via the direct influence which the Netherlands government could exercise within the NATO council. After all, the Netherlands forms a small country which is heavily dependent, economically and politically, on its larger European neighbours. Its direct influence might well decrease, for example in NATO's Nuclear Planning Group, if it decided in favour of nuclear abstentionism and opted for a dissident role rather than that of the 'loyal ally' which it has played for so long. The effects, in the eyes of the IKV, would be rather different and more indirect. It is expected that the action could serve as an example for groups in other countries to organize similar pressure on their own governments, to commit themselves to similar forms of self-obligation suited to the particular position of each country. If the Netherlands government made the decision called for, it would also have to commit itself to an intensive information campaign and a diplomatic offensive, explaining how the process leading up to the decision had taken place.

Strategy

Launching its proposal and supporting it with sound arguments has not been the only concern of the IKV. Its representatives are developing a strategy to get the proposal accepted, to persuade parliament and finally get it carried out by the government.

First of all, the IKV is of the opinion that for the campaign to succeed it will be necessary to persuade large groups of people inside the Netherlands to accept the views of the IKV as their own and to express these views politically and otherwise. Secondly, the campaign must succeed in persuading all kinds of institutions from a wide range of sectors in society to declare themselves openly, as institutions, in favour of the objectives of the campaign. While national institutions are important, they could well be pushed into the desired direction by their local branches. Among these institutions are the churches, women's organizations, the trade unions, health care and welfare organizations, and, last but not least, the political parties.

Whereas in the second year of the campaign activities were mainly directed towards local and national churches, in the third year attention turned to the local branches of the political parties. At the moment of writing the party programmes for the 1981 parliamentary elections are being drawn up and discussed in their local chapters. In this connection polls were conducted in 1979 in villages and towns all over the country, to find out people's opinions about the IKV proposal. These polls served a dual purpose. They brought out people's views and brought people into contact with the campaign and its advocates. Secondly, the polls were undertaken to establish how many people wished the party they were going to vote for to include in their 1981 election programmes the removal of nuclear arms from Dutch territory. If the polls yielded positive results, the local cores would be able to use these to persuade local branches of the political parties to include the IKV proposal in their programmes.

We now come to the third factor on which the campaign is based: a sustained effort to make visible everything that is going on in the country on nuclear armament: the weapon systems which have nuclear tasks themselves, the storage and transport of nuclear weapons, civil defence shelter programmes, decisions about nuclear arms (national as well as international), and so on. This involves also the effects of nuclear weapons, the consequences for the survivors of a nuclear attack, the sufferings of the victims, and the threat which nuclear armaments imply for democracy. Only when nuclear armament is made to strike the eye and mind of the people all the time, can the campaign reach its goal. In that sense the neutron bomb appeared a godsend 2 years ago. The madness, the threat experienced by the people, and the opposition to nuclear armament as a whole could be demonstrated as it had not been possible for 15 or 20 years, as a result of that particular weapon.

A final point concerns the people carrying out the campaign. The work is done by 300-400 'cores' — local groups which have formed in towns and villages all over the country since 1977. It is these groups which at the local level are carrying out the first two elements of the strategy. In 1977 they helped to collect the 1.2 million signatures against the neutron bomb. They are actively engaged in church communities and parishes. In 1978 they conducted talks with local and national authorities and with politicians about the government paper on nuclear armament. They conducted polls among the population to establish people's opinions on the IKV proposal. They intend to try to win the support of local institutions on the basis of the views expressed by the local populations.

Criticism of IKV proposal

As could be expected, the IKV proposal and its action have met with strong criticisms. Some clearly give evidence of deliberate or unintentional misunderstanding or even bad faith and can be discounted; others deserve serious consideration and point to problems to which a satisfactory answer has yet to be found.

The first category of criticism comes from within the churches: that the churches should not be engaged in 'technical political questions', which create polarization and internal divisions; they should address themselves to the roots of the (ideological) conflicts or give only general moral judgements. Others criticise the theological assumptions underlying the campaign as the form chosen to implement the Christian calling to promote peace. Others reject the concentration on nuclear weapons, either because as pacifists they do not accept this distinction or because they argue that the problem is attacked at the wrong end, that of the symptoms and not the cause.

Then there is a category of criticism which is directed at the unilateral character of the proposed step, both *vis-à-vis* allies in NATO and opponents in the Warsaw Pact. With respect to the former, arguments often heard are that: it is disloyal towards our allies, 'you cannot wash your hands of collective responsibility'; one cannot unilaterally improve one's security position; it would isolate the Netherlands in NATO and rob us of our influence, which has been beneficial in the past and which is needed to prevent further unnecessary continuation of the arms race.

To this IKV would answer that the aim is not to improve the particular security situation of the Netherlands or to divest oneself from a common responsibility. To undertake an effort which is aimed at facilitating a process towards disarmament which would involve the other countries cannot be seen as disloyal; it is an answer to a danger threatening all alike. With respect to the Warsaw Pact the critics stress the need not to make sacrifices in the field of force relationships without receiving something in return. The proposed step would weaken the position of the West; steps from the other side will not be forthcoming. If carried further, the process would lead to what is called 'self-finlandization'. The IKV would answer that its reading of the chances of reciprocation are cautiously more optimistic, in that it is counting on the fact that governments in Eastern Europe have long stressed the need for and their willingness to work for disarmament. This may make it easier for domestic pressure comparable to that expected in the Netherlands and other Western countries to arise in the Eastern countries too. Also the IKV stresses that the link between military power and political influence is more tenuous than many suppose; it would take really drastic changes in the power balance before the dreaded loss of independence would occur. In any case, the process which the IKV envisages would take shape over a long period during which its impact would make itself felt gradually and adjustments would be possible. If no or only negative reactions followed, it would have failed and could be stopped without serious harm. Other strategies should then be devised.

A third category of comments goes beyond arguing that no results would be forthcoming. It contains that criticism which stresses that the results would be negative and counterproductive to the desired goal. The following arguments are heard. If nuclear weapons were removed from the Netherlands and the Dutch armed forces, they would go elsewhere and the Germans (or other allies) would fill the gap, which would be destabilizing indeed. On the other hand, if the idea of nuclear disengagements caught on, it would increase German fears in particular, undermine the position of the SPD and strengthen the arguments for a German *Alleingang* and in general the position of those who favour an independent West European nuclear force of the major powers (Britain and France + German capital and technology); we would thus be farther from the goal of disarmament than before. Finally, nuclear disarmament would remove the decisive factor of the system of deterrence, for which at present no alternative is available; conventional relations of forces are incalculable and inherently unstable; nuclear disarmament would reintroduce the danger of terrible conventional wars in Europe.

To this the IKV answers that it recognizes the dangers referred to and the pivotal role of future developments in the Federal Republic of Germany. But it sees no reason why the coming into being of a popular movement, which would enforce a change of direction in security policies, should remain restricted to the Netherlands only. German fears need to be taken seriously, but need not remain permanent. With respect to the argument that conventional war would become an apparently attractive proposition again, it is argued that wars in general come about much less as a consequence of deliberate decisions after calculation of costs and gains, than out of conflict situations which are not under complete control and get out of hand. If a war should arise — the political situation in Europe being full of potential conflicts — the aim should not be to reach a military victory, but to control escalation and prevent *faits accomplis*, in order to gain time for negotiations. Both sides will recognize that even a conventional war would lead to senseless destruction, far outweighing any political gains. Finally it should be repeated that the IKV proposal does not aim at nuclear disarmament only, although it seems both reasonable and necessary to start there.

165

One point deserves some detailed comment. Some commentators have tried to take away the sting from the IKV proposal by arguing that the IKV is not taking its own proposal seriously. In interviews its spokesmen have agreed that it would be more important for nuclear weapons to be withdrawn, for instance, from the Federal Republic of Germany, in the case of an agreement to establish nuclear free zones. This perhaps implies that the Netherlands would retain nuclear weapons on its territory for the time being or even receive more of them. This has been picked up with a certain avidity by opponents of the second part of the slogan '. . . and begin with the Netherlands'. This interpretation fails to see an essential element in the campaign strategy. The IKV does not believe in the traditional approach of international negotiations among allies and from bloc to bloc, unless these are preceded by the building up of domestic pressures in each country toward the acceptance of the idea of self-obligation and the willingness to take independently first steps towards disarmament. Pressure from government to government will, in this view, only succeed if parallel movements are built up in individual countries. Thus the Dutch government should not concentrate on bringing about changes in the Federal Republic of Germany first, however desirable these would be in themselves. If the outcome of the domestic pressure generated in individual countries mutually reinforcing one another were to be some form of nuclear disengagement in Central Europe, it would indeed be strange for the IKV to oppose them.

Prospects of success: public opinion

The IKV campaign has now been going on for more than three years. Although IKV itself has estimated that a period of up to 10 years might be necessary to obtain its goal, it may be useful here to try to evaluate the results obtained so far. In terms of mass media coverage and the intensity of public debate the results have exceeded expectations. Certainly the response has not been entirely positive. Especially in its second year when the campaign gathered momentum, counterpressures both within the churches and in the mass media were very much in evidence. Yet a notable degree of support by the various elements of public opinion seems unmistakable.

On the basis of data concerning public preferences on membership of NATO, one would have to conclude that there is an overwhelming and stable majority in favour of this membership and the policies it entails, which has remained practically unchanged over time. The number in favour of withdrawal has never exceeded 20%. But a few surveys, which probed a little deeper, brought to light a more widespread dissatisfaction with present security policies and the existence of a strong degree of neutralist sentiments and rejection of the use of nuclear weapons.

A general conviction that the use of nuclear weapons cannot be justified, is shown by data from the National Election Survey of 1977, in which 79% said they shared this view. Similarly, in a general mass survey undertaken in 1978 by NOS (the Dutch Broadcasting Authority), 81% rejected nuclear weapons. In answering the question: 'Do you think that our security should be guaranteed by nuclear weapons or in other ways?' only 12% answered affirmatively. The same survey brought to light that the belief in the detente-promoting function of NATO is diminishing rapidly. In 1968, 65% still believed that NATO promoted detente in Europe; in 1974 this had decreased to 47% and in 1978 to 39%[12].

But a general reluctance to base security on nuclear weapons need not necessarily lead to the conclusion that a majority feels that the Netherlands should leave NATO. A majority, however, if confronted with the arguments for doing so, seems to support unilateral measures of the Netherlands undertaken with the intention to promote another system of security and bring about a process which could lead to disarmament. There is still a strong discrepancy on this point between public attitudes and the present parliamentary majority, let alone government policies.

IKV polls

We already referred to the fact that in a nationwide poll 58% of the respondents were shown to be in favour of the IKV proposal. Ironically this poll was held on behalf of the Secretary of Defence and the results became known without his approval. A few months later a local IKV group in Nijkerk, a predominantly conservatively voting village, took the initiative for a house-to-house request to sign a letter to parliament supporting the IKV proposal; 60% of those contacted agreed. The national board of IKV decided to use this method of polling on a local basis as the main vehicle in wider mobilization of public support for the goal of the campaign. In September, October and November of 1979 more than 100 local polls were held all over the country, in cities as well as in villages. All IKV groups who did the polling received the same materials and instructions on taking a sample, counting, etc.[13]

The poll was introduced by a letter on a Wednesday. On the following Friday a 4-page pamphlet with the arguments for a positive reaction to the IKV proposal was handed out to whoever opened the door, and voting cards were left behind with the request to think over the proposal during the week-end, to fill in the card and give it back on Monday. The only question the respondents had to answer was whether they wanted the party of their choice to endorse the IKV proposal that 'in the next cabinet period nuclear weapons must be removed from the Netherlands' in the 1981 election programme. The answer categories were: agree, disagree, do not know/no opinion.

Although not all results of the local polls are yet available, much can be said. Around 200 000 persons have answered the question. In most cases about 70% of the population is in favour of the IKV proposal. The number of people who refused either to accept the pamphlet or to return the card varied from 10 to 30%*. The reasons for refusal show a wide variation: general apathy, wide alienation from the political process, 'do not belong to a church', 'church should abstain from politics', mistrust, disagreement with the proposal and so on. In most places, when all refusals to participate are counted as negative, the majority is still in favour of denuclearization of the Netherlands.

Shortly after these results became known, several attempts were made to discredit them. In the first place it was said that the IKV findings were not reached in an 'objective' way, because those interviewed were informed beforehand of the arguments for the IKV proposal and the proposal itself. Therefore, the argument runs, the IKV poll should not be regarded as 'objective' public opinion research, but as an experiment in social psychology.

The IKV has refuted this argument as follows. As in all social research, publication of data must be accompanied with information about the ways and circumstances in which these have been gathered. Without the context the results cannot be judged. Further, the IKV has reasoned that the 'objective' character of public opinion research does not depend decisively on whether the interviewed are given information before or not. Much more important is whether those interviewed are given a fair opportunity to give a clear response to a clear and non-ambiguous question. In this respect the IKV question can stand the test better than many other 'objective' or 'scientific' public opinion polls. Those interviewed were left in no doubt about the meaning of the question, the background of the organization which organized the polling, or the 'one-sidedness' of the arguments in the pamphlet. Moreover, the IKV polls were held against the background of a very wide debate in Dutch society, from which the controversial character of deterrence strategy with nuclear weapons in the Netherlands was widely known.

In a nationwide survey by the Netherlands Institute for Public Opinion Research (NIPO) on public attitudes concerning West European armaments one of the questions directly concerned the IKV proposal: 'IKV has launched the following appeal: free the world from nuclear weapons, beginning with the Netherlands. The IKV pleads that within the near future, to be precise within the next cabinet period, the Netherlands should be denuclearized. Do you think that such a decision can be taken unilaterally or only after consultation and in accordance with the other countries of NATO?'. The results were: 74% in favour of the last point, 13% thought the decision could be taken unilaterally and 13% had no opinion.

The IKV commented that NIPO had in 1978 held two opinion polls on the IKV proposal, one with 54% and one six months later with 58% in favour. Further, the question was put in such a way that one could conclude that 87% agreed with Dutch denuclearization; the mistake made by the NIPO researchers was, of course, that they did not differentiate between denuclearization of the Netherlands and the manner in which it might be accomplished. The wording of the question stated that a decision could be taken unilaterally by the Netherlands which might easily be understood as a factual point in the sense that it would be possible by the rules of NATO that the Netherlands could decide unilaterally.

The main objection of the IKV to this question (and other questions in the same questionnaire) was the wording of the questions concerning the IKV proposal in terms which stressed the difficult points in the proposal, in this case the point of loyalty to one's allies. This is an attitude rooted deep in our culture and it is very difficult to oppose, even in answering a questionnaire. If there is no indication of the reasons why in very special circumstances the loyalty expected by one's allies cannot be automatic and why it is necessary also in the interest of one's allies. to act unilaterally, then it may be expected that the answers will show assent to what every body takes for granted.

The IKV has concluded that if what its proposal means by unilateral initiative is explained and the arguments set out, a clear majority will agree with such a policy. If the explanation is not given and the questions are put without mentioning any dilemma, in such a way as to elicit conditioned answers, these cannot be regarded as a rejection of the results of the IKV polls, neither is it admissible to denigrate the meaning of public opinion on this specific policy proposal.

What we are seeing, it seems, is a manifestation of attitudes which have been growing slowly over the last 5-10 years and have remained latent for lack of a suitable means of political expression. Both the campaign against the neutron bomb (about 15% of the electorate signed the petition) and the IKV campaign provided tangible forms of action. This development fits in well with traditional long standing elements in Dutch foreign policy. As a small, open country with many foreign commercial and maritime interests and with a culture heavily influenced by Calvinistic moralism and degrees of self-righteousness, foreign policy in the Netherlands (by virtue or necessity) has been characterized for a long time by a strong abhorrence of the realities of power politics (since the Netherlands ceased to be a major power itself) and persistent feelings of neutralism, legalism and internationalism characterized by a belief in international agreements and organizations, and strong feelings of moralism and a general sharing of the idea that the Netherlands should serve as a model and 'moral example' to be followed by others.

There is a good deal of honesty in the idea that the Netherlands should guide the world, but also traces of moral arrogance and self-styled messianism. This idea is widely accepted: in a recent survey of foreign policy 54% of the elite sample thought that the statement 'by giving a good example the Netherlands can promote desirable developments in the world' was correct and among the generally more cynical top officials of the Ministry of Foreign Affairs this was only slightly lower (49%)[15].

The purpose of the campaign need not be, therefore, to raise general concern, or to bring about 'a change of mentality'. People generally are already convinced that nuclear weapons should be removed from the Netherlands. What matters, is how one can organize sufficient institutionalized political support to put this policy into effect.

Prospects of political support

The result of the IKV campaign can be measured in terms of the degree of general support as well as the degree of effectiveness in obtaining the expected results. Support can be defined in two ways: first the number and importance of individuals and institutions subscribing to the proposal and second a more general shift in opinions and policies in the direction of the proposal, but falling short of actually adopting it.

National level

We have concluded that potential mass support for the proposal exists already. Three minor parties on the left fringe have subscribed to the proposal (Communists, Pacifist Socialists and Radicals). Decisive for the future political chances of the proposal is what will happen in the main parties occupying the left and centre of the political spectrum: the Social Democrats (PvdA) and the Christian Democrats (CDA), which probably will be partners again in the next cabinet (the PvdA is now in opposition).

We have already referred to the strong protest movement against both the introduction of the neutron warheads and the modernization of NATO's nuclear weapons. In the latter case the opposition finally scored results in December 1979, when, shortly before the decisive meeting of the NATO ministerial meeting, the opposition parties in the Dutch parliament succeeded in getting a majority for a motion that the Netherlands should not agree with the intended production and deployment of the new missiles. This success was obtained through the support of 10 dissident members of the Christian Democrats, who voted with the opposition. This was the culmination of months of feverish political activity, pressures and counterpressures, the latter coming especially from abroad, from NATO, the USA and the Federal Republic. In the debate an *ad hoc* alliance had been formed between those who, while supporting the necessity of the deterrence system, were afraid of a decoupling of European security from the American strategic guarantees, producing a new nuclear arms race in the European 'theatre' and who wished to explore the possibilities of arms control measures first, and those who, like the IKV, argued from a principled rejection of nuclear deterrence as such. All the traditional methods of pressure were used: mass meetings, local discussions with members of parliament, top level conferences. The National Council of Churches and the member churches again raised their voice. The IKV lobbied the 10 opponents of modernization in parliament.

Under the threat of an impending cabinet crisis the government tried to appease both NATO and the Liberal Party (also a member of the coalition), which insisted on agreement to both production and deployment of the missiles, and the Christian Democrats, who wanted to postpone a decision on deployment. This could only be brought about through ambiguity. The final NATO communiqué mentioned the agreement of all members to the necessity of modernization. The Dutch proviso that it wished to defer a decision on deployment for 2 years, was not mentioned but only referred to in a footnote to the secret integrated decision document. In the final debate in parliament the Prime Minister, Van Agt, evaded a precise answer to the question whether the Netherlands were co-responsible for the NATO decision on production. Efforts by the opposition to dissipate the fog were unsuccessful. A motion rejecting the government's behaviour was rejected, because the 10 dissidents mentioned previously let considerations of domestic and party politics prevail and voted with the government. Thus the government was saved. The lack of clarity as to the degree to which it is bound to the NATO decision persists at present. Thus the stage was set for the next phase: the elections of 1981 and the ensuing formation of a new cabinet.

Within the Socialist Party (PvdA) a critical attitude toward NATO and nuclear armaments has been growing steadily. Its party congress in

1979 voted in favour of including the IKV proposal for unilateral disarmament of the Netherlands in the new election programme. The parliamentary group of the PvdA has, however, always rejected this trend, despite the pressure of the nuclear pacifists among its members. Early in 1980 the leader of the party and of the opposition, Den Uyl, made it known that he would not be willing to lead the party in the coming elections if the IKV slogan were incorporated in the party election platform for 1981. Under this pressure the party programme (despite the 1979 resolution of its congress) only includes a rejection of the modernization decision of December 1979, a unilateral reduction of the nuclear tasks of the Dutch armed forces to 'one or two' (probably the Lance missile) and urges steps at the international-multilateral level, which could lead to a reduction in the number and role of nuclear weapons. This would make a renewed coalition with the Christian Democrats difficult, but not impossible. Socialists and Socialist ministers in particular are still labouring under the necessity of showing that they too are loyal patriots, to be trusted with such departments as Foreign Affairs and Defence. There is therefore a divergence between the leadership and the rank and file. In the Christian Democratic Party ideas are on the move as well. The role of the 'dissidents' has already been mentioned. Strong divisions of opinion exist as to how far the party should accommodate pressure from church and other groups and opt for unilateral steps to reduce the role of nuclear weapons. Recent debates have shown that it is no longer sufficient to pay lip-service to 'ethical' considerations, and pass to the reality, but that something should be done. On the other hand they have been restrained by loyalty to the government and the Defence Minister in particular, which has rejected all proposals to reduce unilaterally the nuclear role of the Dutch armed forces[16]. Although some of the 10 'dissidents' were 'punished' by their party constituencies by being moved down the list of candidates for election in 1981, it is possible that both in party programmes and within parliament there will be a strong shift toward the nuclear pacifist position. It remains to be seen how much this will affect the policies of future governments, but we may expect that those rejecting unilateral nuclear disarmament, as proposed by the IKV, will at least be forced into a search for less 'drastic' intermediate steps, which could alleviate the pressure.

Although the influence of the churches should not be overestimated, neither can it be fully discounted. It should not be too difficult for the IKV to make headway at the level of the church leadership (synods, bishops etc.). The churches did not turn their backs on the IKV when it developed from a council for information and reflection into a pressure group. On the contrary, churches and church leaders have praised it for bringing new life into the discussions within the churches on the nuclear armaments question and on disarmament. None of the large churches however has come out so far with a statement in favour of the IKV proposal as such, although they are under considerable pressure from many quarters to take a stand of their own on this matter. Thus, it seems likely that the synod of the Dutch Reformed Church (to which 25% of the population belongs) will adopt a statement in 1980 rejecting the possession of nuclear weapons (the use of nuclear weapons was rejected in 1962) and giving conditional support to the IKV campaign. Other churches will probably go less far.

There is one difficulty in this respect. As we have shown elsewhere, there is a considerable discrepancy between the attitudes of the church leadership and elite and the rank-and-file with respect to matters of deffence and security, the latter being more conservative [17]. This will lead to friction and will reduce the impact which the churches have on political behaviour. Also in the second half of 1979 there were strong indications that opposition to the IKV was increasing within the churches. Pressure was being organized in the form of committees and reports to counter growing support for the IKV proposal at local and national level and the debate is becoming more intense and acrimonious.

International response

Space permits only limited attention to the chances of success for the proposals at the international level. But of course this is a crucial question. To the argument that denuclearization of the Netherlands would lead to its isolation within NATO and rob it of any influence in nuclear matters, the IKV answers that this isolation could indeed take place. But the influence of the Netherlands is at present small, anyhow, and even with existing nuclear weapons it would not be able to prevent the deployment of new ones, let alone change course towards disarmament. These steps can only be expected if strong popular pressures in many countries develop to counter the prevalent idea that negotiations can only be successfully conducted from positions of strength and that negotiations themselves are to be considered as a form of power struggle. Were the government of the Netherlands persuaded or forced by domestic pressures to abandon its participation in the nuclear arrangements of NATO, this would be the result of a process taking place over a number of years during which other countries would be able to accommodate themselves to this decision. It cannot therefore be said that this would be a highly destabilizing overnight decision.

On the other hand it might be expected that the example of one country divesting itself of nuclear weapons (however unimportant and irrelevant in military terms this might be for the total situation) would greatly stimulate similar movements, organizations and campaigns in other countries. It would then be a proper object of Dutch foreign policy to support and strengthen these movements, each directed toward unilateral commitments on the part of its own government.

The IKV therefore does not count on much government-to-government influence, but instead on parallel domestic developments, in both West and East. In the West it is often said that no positive reply in the form of similar acts of self-obligation will be forthcoming from the East and, in particular, that a strong popular movement requiring such unilateral steps in these countries is simply unthinkable. Indeed the peace movements in the socialist countries have often been one-sided in their criticisms of the policies of other countries and blocs, while neglecting the contributions of their own governments to the maintenance of the war system and all that it implies. This will have to change. If, after an initial number of steps, comparable signals (which could be distinguished from the general noise of internation intercourse) are not forthcoming, the strategy will come to a natural end, because domestic support in the West to continue in this way will dwindle or it will have to be called off for reasons of security.

However, this may not happen, for the following reasons. The socialist countries have always persistently stressed the desirability of disarmament both domestically and internationally (even if this was often merely propaganda and their actual behaviour quite different). If they decide on a policy of initially non-negotiated mutual examples, they will therefore have to face much less direct domestic opposition than would be the case in the West (cf. for instance the price which was attached to an acceptance of the SALT II agreement by the US Senate). Furthermore, evidence of unilateral steps taken within the Warsaw Pact group does not rule out entirely the idea that individual countries might be willing to follow western examples. Finally the defence burden in the East even more than in the West prevents the fulfilment of many unsatisfied needs, which may increase domestic pressures toward the acceptance of the principle of unilateral commitments.

In this connection it was deplorable that the steps announced by President Brezhnev in October 1979, to withdraw 1000 tanks and 20 000 soldiers (though made with clear intent of forestalling the NATO modernization decision) in order to facilitate negotiation and agreements with respect to the so-called 'grey area' weapons, met with little positive response. This is especially deplorable, since a true chance to arrive at a moratorium concerning the deployment of a new generation of nuclear missiles seems to have been missed. This, together with the refusal to ratify SALT II in the US Senate (indeed the modernization decision itself can be seen as an effort to circumvent the treaty, even before it was ratified) contributed to a climate in which the Soviet Union felt fewer qualms about its intervention in Afghanistan.

The events of 1979 have also shown the necessity of cooperation between the peace movements in the various European countries. The cross-national effects of the opposition, especially in the Netherlands, were already by no means negligible, as can be seen by the efforts to restrain the 'contamination' and force a unanimous decision in NATO. But they also show that a strong peace movement in one country makes little sense if it operates in isolation from movements in others. This international coordination seems all the more urgent now that the Belgian government has joined the Dutch in postponing a decision on deployment of new missiles. Together with the existing reluctance in the Scandinavian countries and the West German efforts to search for new ways to reopen negotiations between East and West, this seems to offer a chance still to prevent new and dangerous rounds in the arms race. While there is much reason for scepticism and pessimism, if the analysis of the dangers inherent in the present way of organizing security is correct, we cannot afford not to be optimistic.

Peace education: institutionalization and content

We now return to some of the more general aspects of education for peace and disarmament in the Netherlands. In particular we should like to compare the activities described previously, which we consider to be a particularly important part of disarmament education, with other forms, both with regard to their institutionalization and their content. In doing so the temptation of comparing the efficacy of peace education in schools with that of the work done within and by the churches must be avoided. Rather, it makes sense to exploit the intrinsic opportunities offered by either field of activity, and particularly to consider in what ways the results of the work done in either should supplement one another.

Institutionalization of disarmament education

With respect to its institutionalization it is noteworthy that in the Netherlands the opportunities for peace education and in particular for its latest offshoot, disarmament education, are considerably more plentiful in the area of the churches than in that of education in schools. As a consequence of being tied to the Scriptures, the churches have always assigned themselves a task in the teaching and promotion of peace and justice. Naturally, there have been and are considerable differences in the way the individual churches view this task and how concretely they should engage themselves in it, due to differences in political orientation and in the way in which they see their political responsibilities. But from a strictly 'formal' point of view they are in agreement on the existence of this task. As a consequence they have created many organizations for its execution. Thus in the Roman Catholic world the papal commission *Iustitia et pax* with its many national commissions was created, as well as the international peace movement *Pax Christi*. In the world of the Protestant churches there are the various programmes of the World Council of Churches and their national counterparts.

In the Netherlands the IKV was created for this purpose, though its relations to the churches which established it have not always been harmonious. Its work and activities have been criticised by both ordinary churchgoers and church leaders, on political, theological and other grounds, yet up to now none of the churches has turned its back on the IKV. It seems evident that there is a feeling among church authorities that, despite occasional or more frequent misgivings, it is part of their peace task to provide room for an institution which challenges the churches and their members to attach concrete consequences to their evangelical convictions, which reach much further than is generally accepted. It appears that the churches, at least in the Netherlands, are conscious of the fact that they tend to compromise in their views and standpoints towards violence and armaments. They want to provide room for and give a special mandate to those of their members who desire to remind them of the more radical ideas which the Scriptures also contain, and make their activities financially possible. Sociologically the result is a rather rare configuration: a large social institution which is willing to cover by its authority and standing in society bodies which are free to put the church itself under criticism and to challenge its views, and which also take a critical view of the standpoints and behaviour of other social institutions. The only distance the churches maintain is that the IKV may not speak on their behalf. It can act and vent its opinions freely, but on its own responsibility. As far as we know, this structure is unique.

With respect to education on peace and disarmament in schools, the situation is rather different. There is no similar institution which, supported by the highest educational authorities of the country, is able and allowed to bring about changes in education with respect to, for instance, the generally apolitical nature of education and the absence of any 'global' political schooling. This means that all efforts in this direction depend on individual initiatives, meet with fierce opposition and need tough fighting.

As a consequence of this situation over the last 2 years the IKV has developed into the central and outstanding focal point around which resistance to armaments and efforts for disarmament education are being organized. This also holds for those forms of resistance which are not based on any Christian convictions. The main reason is that similar focal points have not arisen in any other social sector. This is also true to a large extent of the political sector, despite the fact that, for instance, a Pacifist-Socialist Party has existed for a long time. This implies that the institutional basis for resistance against armament, which is primarily offered by the IKV, is too small and vulnerable. It could happen, for example, that further tensions develop between the more 'progressive' church elites which protect the IKV, and the much more conservative rank and file of the churchgoers, which would force the hand of the leadership. In 1972, for instance, a number of clergy took the initiative of printing and distributing freely their own 'peace paper', intended to counter the activities of the IKV. Countergroups were also being organized. This means that the IKV will have to look carefully at its relations with the churches and that strong efforts must be made to develop footholds in other sectors of society as well. Moreover these footholds must be acknowledged within those sectors, if they are not to wither away again quickly.

Content of disarmament education

The other aspect which merits closer attention is that of the content of peace and disarmament education in the school curriculum, compared to its place in peace action. Despite what has been said on the appropriateness of combining and integrating peace education with peace action, it must be made clear that in our opinion disarmament education should not take place exclusively within the context of peace action against the arms race. On the contrary, teaching and learning in the classroom — about the balance of terror, the causes of the arms race and the constant failure to stop and reverse it — can make a valuable contribution towards an improvement of the quality of public opinion on this point. And this could probably become an asset at times when people are tempted by political leaders and specific circumstances to agree to new rounds in the ongoing arms race. A distinction must also be maintained between peace education, which should take place in schools as well as other sectors of society, and peace action, which should take place outside schools.

The school systems, as they exist in countries like the Netherlands, should not be asked directly to further the involvement of the pupils in peace action, because this is, in our definition, quite a specific thing. It implies identification with specific policy proposals, compliance with a defined strategy to get them implemented, a willingness to be organized and an outspoken will to influence actively the course of political developments. Schools do not have the right to claim involvement from pupils in their formative years. Schools will also have to be very careful not to allow the pupils to become internally divided on political issues. However, there are possibilities for a kind of genuine political education on war and disarmament questions that is suitable in the context of an ordinary school, through the introduction and integration of this kind of education is not at all an easy process.

One of the reasons referred to earlier is the lack of a strong accepted institution within the educational system constantly promoting political education on the problem of war. But there are other well-known obstacles. Here we would like to focus on just one.

Particularly in the field of disarmament education it is absolutely essential to hold to the principle of giving a balanced presentation of the issues. This does not imply a neutral presentation, but one that includes the real dilemmas in the disarmament problem. Disarmament education should focus on the evaluation of different political lines and help pupils to formulate their own political standpoints. The importance of such a political education in the school must be stressed. It is one of the few opportunities to confront the new generation with facts, theories and opinions they will seldom be exposed to later in life. So there are differences between peace education within the schools and within the peace movement.

When it comes to the content of peace education, the main questions for research and teaching are identical. In both contexts, but especially in the context of the school, it must not become bogged down in an intellectual exploration of the military, political and technological aspects. This may happen quite easily, because of the widespread fascination with such things as technology and competitive sports in our culture. We do not doubt that it would be senseless to let pupils repeat once more the political and strategic discussions in society. The only thing that makes sense is to try to make them realize what are to be seen as the hidden questions, through handling the main characteristics of the arms situation. Often these are questions of a more *weltanschauliche* nature. They must lead to a real evaluation of the arms situation, of the present course of action and of other suggested courses. Four questions may be briefly mentioned.

In the first place it has been pointed out by Barnaby and others that in academic discussions on nuclear strategies the suffering of the victims has slipped out of sight. The victims of an atomic war are so repressed in our thoughts that they cannot influence discussion in any way. Their presence would disturb the political situation. According to the Jewish philosopher, Levinas, you should show your force and not the trembling of your hands, you may not open your minds to the suffering of the victims. Peace education should let the victims speak, because only when we look at the victims and see their eyes, can our conscience wake up.

A second theme, closely related to the first, is not the suffering of others, but the suffering , the sacrifice, the willingness to endure which we ourselves are willing to accept or, on the contrary, are rejecting completely. A basic principle governing all our deeds and omissions in the field of disarmament is the idea that we can overcome the present deterrence system with weapons of mass destruction, without any consequences for our own society and for ourselves. The idea that we could and should pay a price for the abolition of this war system is absent from our political culture. All thinking in these directions is looked upon as being essentially contrary to the core of power politics, which categorically reject any policy whereby no one would take a chance that his own side will have to endure something from the other side. The motives and emotions lying beneath the surface of power politics and deeply rooted in our culture, are a second main theme.

The third theme is that of 'the enemy'. In the narrow political/military discussion on nuclear arms the enemy is an abstract, arming himself to the point of absurdity. Disarmament education is education about the enemy, not with the intention to smooth over his faults or the bad characteristics of his system in order to reassure one's own people, but only to verify and confirm that no opportunity to improve the situation is neglected.

The fourth theme is that of the powerlessness of ordinary people, the deterrence system and its tense relationship with a democratic system. The politics of deterrence systematically influence and sustain the feeling of helplessness, which undermines the functioning of democracy in this vital area. It is specifically within this theme that pupils can be informed about those groups of people who try to overcome their feelings of helplessness. In the end this leads to an inquiry into the spiritual and cultural sources of our societies, from which we may hope to derive the spirit and the endurance needed for our struggle against the deterrence system.

Notes and references

1. See for instance: Peace research in transition: a symposium. *J. Conflict Resolution*, 1972, 16, 4. Dedring J. *Recent advances in peace and conflict research: a critical survey*. Beverly Hills/London, Sage Library of Social Research, 1976, 27. Väyrynen R. Peace research: problems of application, research organization and finalization. *Internat. Peace Research Newsletter*, 1976, 14, 6. Everts P. Polemologisch onderzoek en de vredesbeweging. *Transaktie*, 1979, 8, 2.
2. Rapoport A. Can peace research be applied? *J. Conflict Resolution*, 1970, 14, 277.

3. Everts P. Protest tegen de bom is verdampt. *Vredesopbouw*, 1976, **13**, (9) 7.
4. Everts P. Developments and trends in peace and conflict research 1965-1971: a survey of institutions. *J. Conflict Resolution*, 1972, 16, 477.
5. Maessen P. Wie stopt de neutronenbom? Besluitvorming en pressie rond de invoering van de neutronenbom. Thesis, Leiden, 1979.
6. This poll was undertaken at the initiative of the Ministry of Defence. Remarkably enough, its results were never published despite requests.
7. Nederlands Instituut voor de Publieke Opinie en het Marktonderzoek. *Bericht* no. 1909, 3 May, 1978. It should be taken into account however that this was a poll taken among the whole adult population, the results of which can, of course, only be considered to a limited extent as representative of the attitudes of those who signed the petition.
8. Maessen P. *Op. cit.*, 122.
9. Press reports, confirmed by the Dutch Foreign Office, mentioned that the former Soviet Ambassador to the Netherlands, A. Romanov, had received a decoration upon his return to the Soviet Union 'for his contributions to the success of the campaign against the neutron bomb in the Netherlands'.
10. Further information on the IKV, its structure and its activities can be obtained from the Secretariat, Anna Paulownaplein 3, The Hague.
11 C.E. Osgood's ideas for a scheme of graduated reciprocated initiatives in tension-reducing (GRIT) are collected with other articles and essays in *Peace Research Reviews*, 1979, **8,** 1 and 2. See also Granberg D. GRIT in the final quarter, reversing the arms race through unilateral initiatives. *Bull, Peace Proposals*, 1978, **(3),** 210 and Czempiel, E.O. Peace as a strategy for systemic change. *Bull. Peace Proposals*, 1979, 10 (1) 79.
12. Source: VARA-enquête, de Rode Draad, 23 December, 1978. See *Bijdrage 5 van het IKV aan het Logboek van het Verbond tegen de Kernwapens.* Den Haag, IKV, March 1979, 168.
13. See *Hervormd Nederland,* 30 June, 1979 and *Kernkrant IKV,* September 1979
14. Nederlands Instituut voor de Publieke Opinie en het Marktonderzoek. *Report A-417 42.* 7 November, 1979.
15. Baehr P.R. The Dutch foreign policy elite: perceptions and attitudes. *Internat. Studies Quart,* 480, 24, 223-261
16. See *Haagse Post,* 30 June, 1979.
17. Everts P. The churches, religion and attitudes on foreign policy in the Netherlands. Paper to Workshop on Religion and Politics, European Consortium for Political Research, Brussels, 17-21 April, 1979.

11. Disarmament education through action: the International Disarmament Relay, Helsinki-Belgrade, 1977

Gerd Greune, *Chairperson, German Peace Society*

Guido Grünewald, *International Peace Bureau*

'The demand that Auschwitz and Hiroshima shall not happen again is the basic, primary demand in all education'[1]. The legitimate intention of such education to prevent another holocaust needs no further justification. It provided the background of the 1980 UNESCO World Congress on Disarmament Education and is the basis for all public education on social and political affairs.

When it is accepted that political education in its widest sense does not simply mean an affirmation of traditions but, on the contrary, a 'critical appraisal of the coherence of actions and motives'[2], then it is essential that an historical-political understanding has to lead to a critical review of history with a willingness to accept constant revisions of the constructions of the past[3].

If we look into popular school books on history and politics we find in most cases that the general tendency is to see mankind's history as a long series of warlike conflicts, depicted mostly as a history of the victors. The conquered, the victims, or those who opposed war, are hardly mentioned[4]. The experience of people educated in this traditional way makes it difficult to arouse wide interest in problems which appear to have no immediate relevance, and raises no more than a passive attention towards the more practical relationship between military politics and security. Even when an emotional response to these problems can be evoked, there is often an attitude of helplessness because there seems to be no way for ordinary people to participate or to make critical demands on the existing powers and structures.

In view of the fact that arms have greatly proliferated since 1975, the second Review Conference on the Non-Proliferation Treaty (NPT) should be greeted by large public protests. To do this would demand the creation of many public demands to change the deteriorating 'security' policy while adhering to the policy of detente, by using such well-known slogans as 'In both East and West, disarmament is best'.

Disarmament is still generally thought of in negative terms of dishonour, defeat and weakness, while armaments attract the opposite emotions of honour, victory and strength. It is therefore necessary to encourage more positive concepts of an unarmed society to enable people to accept that military power and continuing arms production provide the very insecurity for themselves, their families and their countries that they seek to avoid. If present political assumptions are to reject the present idea of an 'institutionalized peacelessness' then it is obvious that all have to learn to meet the challenges which arise from continuing cooperation between political and military institutions. Historical, educational-psychological and political sciences are capable of analysing historical and political structures, and of providing critical examination of single examples, and thus overcoming traditional thinking[6].

To understand some of the special difficulties to which a prejudiced public opinion is exposed, one must take into account that in West Germany, for example, where the conduct and effects of World War II were among the fiercest, we are confronted with:

1. an irrational anti-communism which will exist as long as the memories of the 1930s and the World War II settlement remain;

2. the strong remilitarization of West Germany in the 1950s;

3. the fact that all opposition to armaments is deemed to be specifically communist propaganda designed to weaken West Germany's defences.

Nevertheless, since 1956 there have been more than 300 000 conscripts in West Germany who have refused military service on conscientious grounds. In spite of this strongly-expressed opposition to militarization, the activities of peace societies are hardly referred to in the mass media and are often boycotted by public figures. This leads to a frustration and an air of resignation among peace workers so that an effective opposition to arms production seems to be absent and, with the pressures arising from its place under the USA's 'umbrella', West Germany has become the strongest NATO ally in Europe[7].

The Disarmament Relay took place between 15 April and 15 June in 1977, and actively involved about 500 000 people in 1000 cities, towns and villages on its way from Helsinki to Belgrade. Its decentralized organization encouraged active participation and gave local groups the opportunity to develop their own form of public action and education as the relay passed through their areas. This gave all the consecutive stages of the relay concrete tasks to perform, all related to local circumstances or institutions in the regions through which the relay passed — military training camps, arms factories, peace research institutes, parliamentary bodies or bodies conducting actual arms negotiations. The three examples particularly referred to here concentrate on activities in a large town and a village in West Germany, in Scandinavia and in Yugoslavia, including special events at the start of the relay in Helsinki, talks with members of MBFR in Vienna and the arrival in Belgrade.

To overcome general apathy appears to be the most important task for all peace education, which has to take into account the actual requirements and day-to-day experiences of those who are to be addressed. Education takes place not only in schools and universities but in a multitude of interwoven personal contacts in families, market places, streets, factories and shops, and the mass media: to be effective it has to take account of the typical situation in which this type of natural education takes place. This does not mean that the goal has to be the complete reduction of education to micro-areas, but the connection has to be made between the military hardware and the power structures, how the arms requirements are presented and the actual arms produced. Thus we present below a more or less successful example of an international action in 1977 which demonstrated the possibilities of a kind of alternative education process, which it seems to us should be made more widely available. The results, of course, are relative; no actual disarmament was achieved by any of these efforts, but there were positive results which greatly encouraged those who took responsibility and the others who participated.

Aims of the International Disarmament Relay

The International Disarmament Relay, Helsinki-Belgrade 1977, is an example of an action-orientated, self-stimulating, collective action with close links to the political forces related to arms production in 35 European states, together with Canada and the USA, which held a conference on security and cooperation in Europe in Helsinki in 1975, where declarations of urgency regarding disarmament were made. A determination to meet again in Belgrade in 1977 to review progress was expressed then, and the aims of the relay are related to the declaration presented to the First Review Conference on Security and Cooperation in Europe on 15 June, 1977, in Belgrade. The demands contained therein were put before the public at every stage of the relay and signed by thousands who contacted the relay bus en route.

The initiative came from the German Peace Society, one of the largest western European peace organizations, with some 20 000 members actively engaged in 215 towns in West Germany. Under the general sponsorship of the International Peace Bureau (IPB) in Geneva and the War Resisters International (WRI) in Brussels, preparations were undertaken simultaneously in Finland, Sweden, Norway, Denmark, Austria and Yugoslavia, as well as in West Germany where most of the action took place. The following tasks were set:

1. to make people aware of the discrepancies between the disarmament hopes and sentiments expressed in the final act of the European Conference on Security and Cooperation (ECSC) in Helsinki in 1975, and the continuing military development resulting in an accelerating arms race with absurd overkill in both East and West;
2. to mobilize the people to understand that their active participation was essential to press governments to make stronger responses to the industrial-military complex;
3. to talk directly to participating governments in the countries the relay passed through, especially those which have disarmament questions on their agendas, for example Austria.

To accomplish these tasks a special bus was used which provided material in written, audio and pictorial form. The relay bus was the centre for all further meetings which took place in streets and open places, halls, schools, universities, factories and other social centres. Hundreds of meetings were organized in villages, towns and country areas to welcome the relay bus. Messages of support were carried in many forms. Many participants travelled by bicycle, on foot and by car to the advertised central relay points. Street theatre and sketches and a variety of cultural programmes were also incorporated. Special musical and other contributions were made by local and regional groups and these, being of an informal nature, contributed immensely to increased personal contacts of a friendly and informative kind. Signature lists were delivered to the relay bus by hand carts.

The connection between the different people and their varying activities relative to the central aim of the relay was the most important aspect of the whole programme. In the course of the relay, 15 issues of a relay news service were given to all participants and were much used by the media.

Preparation

The decision for this action was taken by the Federal Congress of the German Peace Society (DFG-VK) in 1976 in Bremen, and International Secretary Gerd Greune was asked to take immediate steps to contact peace and disarmament movements in all European countries to evaluate their interest and ability to join this action. After some negotiation seven coordinators in the participant countries organized and initiated the activities on regional and local levels. Preparation meetings took place in Essen, Gothenburg, Vienna, Geneva and Brussels. As described already, most of the preparatory work was in the hands of single activists in local areas and was reported back to the central coordination point in West Germany (FRG).

The relay bus was brought to Helsinki on 12 April and the opening meetings took place in the Finnish capital on 15 and 16 April with participants from both governmental and non-governmental sectors. Messages were received from the Finnish Ministry of Foreign Affairs and members of parliament. The relay bus went via Turku to Sweden, arriving in FRG on 7 May. Contributions of information material were received from SIPRI (Stockholm) and IPRA (Oslo). Slides, films and exhibitions were carried with the relay bus. Postcards for signature were distributed as well as signature lists. Special leaflets and booklets were produced with extracts from the final act of the ECSC and the UN Charter. In many regions UN Associations contributed to the relay. The relay bus used loudspeakers which spread the relay message on the way through towns or villages and invited people to stop for discussion.

On the outside of the relay bus there was a map of Central Europe with the major stations of the relay on it; the symbol of the UN and of the WRI and IPB in addition to those of the major towns to be visited, A special piece of music was chosen for the relay which was played as towns and villages were entered.

The press was prepared for this event mainly by local groups who gave information about the whole action and especially about their contribution to it. Generally there was good coverage in the press and on the radio about the local meetings.

In Helsinki an international press conference was held with Nobel Peace Prize winner, Sean MacBride, who sponsored the relay. International press agencies took only news from Scandinavia, and later, Yugoslavia, where the Scandinavian Press Agency and Tanjug distributed news. Other international reports were not given. In Yugoslavia each relay day was reported in the daily news on TV and the radio news; interviews were also given, and the reports covered the front pages during the whole week.

Poor coverage was given especially in FRG where some newspapers deliberately boycotted news of the relay. In some cases this led to protest briefings in front of the press offices.

Practical steps during the relay

The Disarmament Relay started on 16 April 1977, with an international press conference in Helsinki at the office of the Finnish Peace Council. Members of the international preparatory group from Scandinavia, FRG, France and the UK reported on the state of the organization in their areas. Messages were received from WRI and non-governmental organizations which cooperate in the special NGO Committee on Disarmament in Geneva. A message was also received from the Minister for Foreign Affairs of Finland. Sean MacBride, president of the IPB, addressing the opening meeting at Koitto Hall where some 500 people overcrowded the first stage of the relay, said:

> This relay carries a simple truth through Middle Europe, the truth that general and complete disarmament is possible, contrary to the will of the leading political and military circles. The most important task of the relay will be to inform the people about the solution of the problem, and to reveal the lies and misrepresentation of the opponents to disarmament. Whoever says that general and complete disarmament is too complex and not achievable, does not, in fact, want it.

An important contribution to the relay was the presence of Japanese members of the Council Against A and H Bombs, who stressed the special importance of outlawing the use of nuclear weapons. The Finnish member of parliament, Mrs Mirjam Viren-Touminen, gave the relay some thousand signatures which had been collected in previous weeks on the way from northern Finland to Helsinki.

Although the Finnish press reported well on the start of the relay, it was important to find a press agency through which a first telex and photo could be sent out to all press institutions in Europe; and Swedish broadcast news was produced to prepare the public about the coming relay a few days later.

The relay bus left the Finnish capital on 18 April, accompanied by a car caravan.

Stockholm

About 1000 inhabitants of Stockholm who were waiting at the Vennergren Centre heard from afar the loudspeaker of the relay bus and welcomed the international crew with great applause. Members of the Swedish Peace and Arbitration Society had formed a large Anti-Nuclear Weapon Symbol which was later carried like a banner. All over the town posters gave information about the 'relay day' in the Swedish capital. 'Ingen framtid utan avrustning' was written on a large transparency, which soon formed the head of a large demonstration through the centre of the city, where another 1000, mostly young people, joined the crowd. At the final demonstration, Anders Fogelström and Britt Tehorin, both members of the Swedish Parliament, spoke to the public, described the task of the relay and referred to the Japanese participants presenting the demands of the victims of A-bombed Hiroshima and Nagasaki: 'No more Hiroshima! No more Nagasaki!'

Signatures were collected on yellow post cards to be carried to the

Belgrade follow-up conference in June. A hand-made carpet from mid-Sweden with hundreds of knots, each indicating the names of supporters of the relay, which had been collected from door to door in the previous weeks, was presented to the relay crew.

A popular music group played — though the weather was not too friendly — and crowds of people stood for hours to discuss the danger of the arms race and the need for immediate steps for disarmament, raising such questions as: What could Sweden in particular do? Was it not more a task for the two major powers or the military blocs? But why then was Sweden at all involved in the arms race with its highly developed technology? Was there not a good reason for countries like Sweden, which play diplomatically such an important role in disarmament talks in the UN, to take unilateral steps on disarmament? The discussion continued in the evening when about 100 people moved to the SFSF meeting room, among them many new faces, young and old. The press in Stockholm reported fairly well, as did also the TV and radio station, which took interviews from relay participants.

Cologne and neighbouring areas
Nearly 4 weeks after the start, the relay arrived in Cologne, the Rhine metropolis in FRG. About 30 groups had been involved in the preparation for weeks before, and their activities covered an area of about 100 km around Cologne.

At a meeting of the Federal Union Federation on 1 May, 1977, where Federal Chancellor Schmidt and union leader Vetter were speaking, about 100 peace activists participated, with banners carrying the motto 'No future without disarmament', among them Buddhist monks from the Buddha Sangha, drumming their gongs, who directly after the demonstration started on foot via Bonn to Siegen, about 100 km to the south-east. Many friends accompanied them along the River Rhine. Their halts in Bonn and several smaller towns were celebrated by the local peace groups with smaller public meetings, often in towns where the issue of disarmament had never before been publicly raised. The reaction of the people was extremely positive, especially that of older people, impressed with the courage of the Japanese friends, who carried a small photo exhibition of Hiroshima and Nagasaki with them to show on the streets where they stopped.

In Cologne meanwhile a special leafleting action took place: the German proverb 'Don't let anybody tie a bear to your back' (which means, do not believe everything you are told) was used, symbolized by someone costumed in a bear skin. On several Sundays leaflets were distributed in front of the zoological garden in Cologne informing the public of the truth about the arms race and the false propaganda for so-called armed security.

The mid-Rhine section of the DFG-VK had prepared a number of coordinated activities for the coming relay day. In Siegburg, 50 km south of Cologne, there was action around a military camp of Belgian troops with participants from Belgium. Distribution of leaflets in front of the Belgian barracks led to intervention by the Military Police and raised conflict between Belgian and German authorities. Slide shows on the history of the arms race and mini-exhibitions on the efforts for disarmament were shown elsewhere in several schools around the town. A small demonstration in Sieburg with a large musical and political manifestation in the market place with speakers from German and Belgian groups marked the main event; hundreds of people, mostly young, gathered discussing the future of a disarmament policy. They joined the organizing groups in an evening discussion with some political songs presented by a group of Young Socialists and an address from a Protestant churchman. On the relay day about 100 cyclists with decorated bicycles started from Bonn and Dusseldorf, collecting friends on the road, passing through many villages ringing their bells. Though rain was falling on this morning, they sang on their way such songs as 'We shall overcome'. After some hours of touring they arrived in the square in front of Cologne Cathedral where the relay bus was expected to arrive from Dortmund at 3 p.m.

The bus, which entered the square with the loudspeakers playing 'We shall overcome', was enthusiastically welcomed. Transparencies in various languages, peace doves flying into the sky, symbolic contributions as well as thousands of signature lists were given to the relay crew, which had now covered about 1000 km. Helmut Vogel, the relay head and chairman of the DFG-VK, addressed the demonstrators, who left after an hour to a large bicycle rally at the educational centre in Cologne where the evening meeting was to take place. Previously, the Dormagen group had presented a street theatre performance on 'Civil defence in a nuclear attack', a satirical approach to the propaganda for civil defence measures in case of a nuclear emergency.

More than 1000 people joined the international peace manifestation at the school centre in Zollstock, among them eight foreign groups, from Greece, Turkey, Vietnam, Chile, Spain, Iran, Italy and Portugal. A famous music group from Cologne, the Bläckföös, opened the proceedings. Addresses were given from all participant groups and the relay crew, and messages presented from Belgium, Luxembourg and the Netherlands. Political poems from Brecht and Tucholsky, and political songs from the antinuclear movement led an overcrowded hall of young people into apparently endless discussion. But when the Ven. Teresava from Japan presented his slide show on the damage and aftereffects of Hiroshima and Nagasaki none of the 1000 participants dared to make a sound.

Maribor

The relay arrived at the Yugoslavian border on 6 June and was welcomed by members of the city council, by journalists and TV. The mass media had never before reported the relay in such a comprehensive way as in Yugoslavia. Though street activities were not prepared, the bus was surrounded immediately when it stopped in front of the city hall and discussions started, signatures were collected, and leaflets distributed.

The youth organization of the UN Association invited the relay members to a discussion in the city hall and around 300 young pupils and students joined the meeting. The introductory speeches of the Yugoslavian group and the relay crew led to many questions and discussions on all issues linked with the follow-up review conference in Belgrade, the possibilities for arms reduction in Europe, the role of the major powers and the contribution of youth when refusing to serve in the army. The relay crew received all cooperation from the local and national authorities and was supported by the police, received by local mayors and interviewed by national and regional radio stations. The front pages of the newspapers showed photographs of the relay bus and its crew, and real friendship was developed with the participating people.

In Maribor we sat together until well after midnight following a dinner with the local council members, and many participated in the discussions. The need for unusual activities to spread disarmament ideas was well understood, and the relay was seen as a remarkable attempt to encourage people to learn that they have to do their own thinking, make up their own minds, and not wait for a miracle to take place in the diplomatic and political negotiations.

References

1. Adorno T. Erziehung nach Auschwitz. *Erziehung zur Mündigkeit,* Frankfurt 1970, 92
2. Kuhn A. *Einführung in die Didaktik der Geschichte.* München, 1974, 12
3. Hartwich H.H. Democratieverstandnis und Curriculumrevision, *Gegenwartskunde* 1973, **22,** (2) 141-154
4. Greune G. *Kontroverse Uberlegungen zu Abrüstungsstrategien unter Einbeziehung von Bürgerinitiativen.* Siegburg 1977 8
5. Wehler H.U. *Geschichte als historische Sozialwissenschaft.* Frankfurt, 1973; also Schmidt A. *Die kritische Theorie als Geschichtsphilosophie.* Munchen, 1976; Habermas J., *Zur Rekonstruktion des historischen Materialismus.* Frankfurt, 1976

6. Schorken R. Lerntheoretische Fragen an die Didaktik des Geschichtsunterrichts In: Süssmuth H. *Geschichtsunterricht ohne Zukunft?* Stuttgart 1972, p. 65 ff; also Narr W.D., Logik der Politikwissenschaft — eine propadeutische Skizze. In Kress/Senghaas, *Politikwissenschaft*, Frankfurt 1972, p.22ff und Senghaas, D. Zur Analyse internationaler Politik, *op cit.* p.347

III. CASE STUDIES IN FORMAL EDUCATION

12. Disarmament education in Norway: present state and some thoughts for the future

Birgit Brock-Utne, *Institute for Educational Research, University of Oslo*

This report deals with disarmament education at different levels of the publicly financed educational system in Norway. Disarmament education will here be used both in the sense of education *about* disarmament and in the sense of education *for* disarmament.

Though some concrete examples of disarmament education in Norway are given it is important to bear in mind that not much has been done in this field in Norway. The concept itself is relatively new and has not as yet received wide recognition. At a seminar recently held in Norway in preparation for the World Congress on Disarmament Education, several teachers expressed anxiety that a programme of disarmament education would easily be regarded by many parents as 'leftist'. Some thought it wise not to use the expression 'disarmament education' by itself but rather to talk about education about disarmament human rights, war and peace. Others claimed that education *for* disarmament could be taught under less controversial headings such as 'education for tolerance', 'education for peaceful co-existence', 'education for democracy'. Those expressing such concerns were teaching in elementary schools located in an area with inhabitants of high socio-economic status. These teachers pointed out that many Norwegians look on disarmament as a threatening process; a process which threatens the national security.

Building national security on military arms has a long tradition in Norway. Disarmament is not regarded as an alternative and possibly safer way of maintaining security, but as a loss of security. Few people pose the question of whether nuclear bombs can defend anything at all. Membership of NATO is backed by the great majority of the population and is hardly ever disputed. There are, however, some hopeful signs that the public is demanding better information about military dispositions and possible agreements before these have been reached. One of these signs is the 'Women for Peace' movement which has organized thousands of women in all the Nordic countries in a campaign for peace and for a halting of the arms race. Another sign is represented by the 'No to new nuclear arms' movement. This was started as a campaign against the so-called 'modernization' of NATO's nuclear arms. Although this decision was reached in Brussels in December 1979, the movement has not stopped its work. In the autumn of 1979 quite a number of people became aware of the dangers of the nuclear arms race. The 'No to new nuclear arms' movement has been using this new awareness to build up an organization which disseminates information about and debates on the arms race.

Disarmament education at the elementary school level

Elementary school in Norway comprises 9 years of compulsory schooling. Schooling is free and publicly financed, and there are very few private schools. The teachers in the rest of the schools are guided by the Curriculum Guidebook for the Elementary School. In this book the word 'disarmament' is mentioned only once — as one of the topics suggested for study in social sciences, and it is suggested that this subject be studied in the ninth grade. Here lies the rationale for teaching *about* disarmament. Though the word disarmament is only mentioned once, the Curriculum Guidebook stresses the responsibility of the school to work for international understanding and peace between different nations and ethnic groups. The expression 'education *for* disarmament' is not used, but the main ingredients of this concept are to be found in the guidebook.

Teachers who wish to engage in disarmament education in the Norwegian elementary school should find a backing both in official documents about disarmament and in the Curriculum Guidebook. But the following episode highlights earlier remarks about the controversial nature of the subject.

In 1974 the National Council for Innovation in Education developed and published a series of booklets as part of a project aimed at some integration of the teaching of the Norwegian language and social studies in the upper part of elementary school. One of the booklets had the title 'War'. It contained pictures of dead soldiers, women in concentration camps, dead mothers, crying children. Many of the pictures were from World War II and showed German troups in Norway, Jews in concentration camps and also the bombing of Dresden in February 1945, when more than 200 000 people were killed. There were pictures of Hiroshima and Vietnam. Between the pictures were poems and abstracts from books dealing with the same sad events, or songs like *Strangest dream* by Ed McCurdy and *Le deserteur* written by Boris Vian against the Algerian war.

This booklet was well received by teachers and pupils in the schools in which it was tried out, but after a well-known conservative Member of Parliament accused this booklet of bringing leftist propaganda into schools, there were strong negative reactions from a number of parents. A fierce newspaper debate followed. It was held that the booklet represented a conscious attempt to destroy the values most parents were trying to build in their children, producing negative attitudes toward the Norwegian society, culture, religion and military system. The criticism of the booklet went so far that it was brought up in parliament through a question to the Minister of Church and Education. He said that the booklet was being tried out and that the final version, to be accepted by the Ministry for use in schools, would have to be revised. Some of the pictures and poems would be taken out and replaced. The authors of the booklet were asked to revise it according to the criticism; they did not want to do this and the Council for Innovation in Education had to withdraw the booklet.

The episode also highlights one of the two prerequisites for engaging in disarmament education: support of the parents, discussed later.

Not much is known about the extent of disarmament education at the elementary school level in Norway. There has been no survey to assess its extent. Defining disarmament education as education *for* disarmament would also make such a survey extremely difficult to conduct. What is known is that the UN Association in Norway has produced excellent teaching material to be used at the elementary school level. There is reason to mention especially a series of four pamphlets concerning war, peace and disarmament produced with financial support from the Advisory Board for Arms Control and Disarmament. The series gradually moves from education *for* disarmament to education about war, peace and disarmament. It starts by looking at conflicts in the child's immediate surroundings, using news items about children having been beaten in the school playground by their fellow pupils, and giving questions to discuss in class. The questions are well suited for group work as they are posed in a way which connects the piece of news to the child's everyday life. Are there pupils in your class who are treated badly by the others? Why is this so? What could we do to avoid this? There are suggestions for role-playing, for games and simulations.

Even when the pamphlets move more in the direction of world problems the connection to the immediate surroundings of the pupils is not lost. For example a picture representing a modern jetplane of the F16 type is given with the information that the cost of this plane is about 30 million Norwegian kroner. They are asked to find the building costs of some recently built institutions in their neighbourhood, such as a hospital, a day-care centre for children or a home for the aged. These costs are to be compared to the cost of the jet plane. The four pamphlets were first produced in 1972, and are now available in a revised edition.

In 1978 the UN Association in Norway devoted a special issue of their periodical *Alternative* to the theme 'Education for international understanding.' Here there were articles about disarmament and development, about the UN special session on disarmament, about education for peace in schools. In the same issue concrete examples of teaching units on the themes of war, peace and disarmament were given. These teaching units have been created by teachers and tried out. The teachers have been working together, helping each other to find literature, films and songs, and to compose role-playing sequences.

This demonstrates the other prerequisite for engaging in disarmament education at the elementary school level: cooperation between teachers. These two prerequisites are now examined more closely.

Cooperation between teachers

There are several reasons why this cooperation is so important. Disarmament education will have to be taught as an integrated discipline. It will be necessary to draw on knowledge from disciplines such as mathematics, chemistry, history, geography, literature, music, arts and crafts, psychology and political science. It will be difficult for one single teacher to possess enough expertise to deal with such a variety of subjects. It is also stimulating for the pupils to meet the same theme in different subjects and for the teachers to learn from each other.

At a recent seminar in Norway a group of teachers from various elementary schools and with different professional backgrounds met for the first time. The group worked very well together informing each other of teaching units they had tried out, and constructing new ones which they were going to try out when they returned from the seminar. The group has been meeting regularly ever since. Among the work it produced were tasks such as finding out how much was destroyed by the Hiroshima bomb, what part of the surroundings of the pupils would be destroyed from a bomb of the same size, how many bombs of that size are there in the world, etc. The group worked also to find literary texts about war, peace and disarmament. They found that there was much literature to be found from World War II but very little about the more than 100 wars which have been fought since that time.

Another reason why teachers should cooperate, especially teachers at the same school, is that they can support each other, not only with practical work but also morally. It is extremely difficult to introduce a new way of teaching as a lonely teacher. It is easier for a *group* of teachers to gain the confidence of the school administration, their colleagues and the parents. If pupils are to be taught to cooperate, it is important that they see their teachers cooperating.

Support of the parents

There are also several reasons why the support of the parents is important. The example given earlier shows that the parents can actively prevent disarmament education if they consider the teaching material used is controversial. Parents should not learn about the teaching their children are subjected to on controversial issues through a heated newspaper debate. It is important that the school informs the parents about and discusses with them the treatment in school of topics of a controversial nature. It is important in this connection to have official national and international statements to refer to. Several research findings have indicated that the school is not the most important agent when it comes to the creation and maintenance of racial stereotypes and attitudes towards other people. The family background, the home environment together with the mass media, especially TV, are more important factors contributing to attitude formation.

In a research study of Norwegian elementary school children's stereotypes of other nations, conducted by the present author and two other researchers, it was found that the stereotypes held were only to a very small degree acquired at school. To be effective in this area the school has to work together with parents and the mass media. The study related school children's stereotypes according to where in Norway the children lived. It was interesting to note that the stereotype of the Soviet Russians was positive in the north of Norway, in a town near the border with Russia. Here the majority of school children had met Russians, and their parents had Russian friends. In a well-to-do suburb in the south, near Oslo, where hardly any children had met Russians, the children had a negative stereotype.

If the parents become engaged in disarmament education they may represent a valuable resource. Among the parents of a school there is usually considerable expertise which the school may draw on. Parents often like to be able to contribute to the teaching in school instead of just being informed about the school curriculum.

Disarmament education at secondary school level

Norway has a 3-year publicly financed secondary school system. The great majority of Norwegian youngsters in the 16-19 age group attend these schools, though they are not part of the compulsory school system. The school courses consist in part of theoretical subjects preparing the students for advanced study at university or district colleges, and in part of vocational courses preparing the students for practical vocations. Most of the students attend the vocational courses. In these areas it has been difficult to devote time to the study of war, peace and disarmament.

Of the theoretical branches there is only one, social sciences, which includes the topic of disarmament as an obligatory subject for all the students. But all the theoretical branches offer opportunities for teachers and students to study this topic if they want to. There is a great freedom of choice within many subjects, especially in the social sciences and literature. The need for teaching material and new textbooks is urgent here.

At the recent seminar referred to earlier the teachers working in secondary school pointed out the necessity of producing teaching material which showed how conflicts of a kind which had sometimes led to wars and military aggressions had at other times been solved by peaceful means. Would not this be a meaningful research project for some UNESCO experts? Most history books are centered around men, 'heroes', kings and wars. Pupils may get the notion that war is the inevitable way of solving conflicts between nations.

Little is known about the extent of education on disarmament at the secondary school level, although a teacher from a secondary school in the west of Norway has constructed and tried out a teaching unit about war, peace and disarmament in literature covering 20 school lessons.

Recently a textbook on human rights and disarmament has been produced in Norway especially for the secondary school. This has been a joint venture from the Norwegian sector of Amnesty International and the Red Cross. The book contains photographs, and on every page actual examples of rights and realities, quotes and paradoxes, to illustrate the text. Those initiating work with this textbook have been wise enough to seek collaboration with professional educators with factual knowledge of the vocabulary which most pupils of this age range command. Much of the available literature about disarmament by peace researchers or governmental bodies is written in a language which it is impossible for secondary school pupils (and almost everybody else) to understand.

Disarmament education at higher level

Universities

At the seminar members of the university/teacher-training group agreed that it would be important to work for the establishment of an institute of disarmament education at all four universities in Norway.

This same suggestion has been discussed by the Advisory Board for Arms Control and Disarmament and also by the Labour Party in its defence policy group. The idea is to establish a small institute with educators and researchers from different professional backgrounds. The establishment would have to be politically initiated and funds for this would have to come from sources other then the regular university budgets. Why not use some of the money earmarked for defence for this purpose?

The people working at such an institute would have to have a special obligation to popularize and simplify their findings and to work on the educational aspects of their topic. When appointing teachers to these institutes, pedagogical qualifications would likewise have to be regarded as important.

The development of teaching materials for different school levels would be a special obligation these institutes would have to fulfil, and the development of such materials would have to be undertaken in close cooperation with teachers working in the field. It would be wise to have such teachers connected to the institutes for short periods. If the institutes could be established in the near future, they would be likely to have responsibility for coordinating Norwegian participation in the development of teaching material about disarmament which is to be a joint Nordic venture.

The Minister for Church and Education announced in Parliament on 9 May 1979, that his Ministry would ask the Advisory Board for Arms Control and Disarmament to assist in the early development of teaching material about disarmament on a Nordic basis. Teaching material as a joint Nordic venture has been developed earlier, on environmental questions and consumer affairs.

Apart from the proposed creation of institutes of disarmament education at the four Norwegian universities, the university/teacher-training group at the seminar also had plans for integrating disarmament education into the teaching of already existing institutes at the universities. It was suggested that the Advisory Board for Arms Control and Disarmament should give scholarships to advanced students who were willing to do textbook analysis or develop teaching material about disarmament as part of their degree courses. It would be possible to arange one-term and even two-term seminars about disarmament education as part of the teaching offered to students. Such seminars should be arranged through cooperation between several institutes, for instance the Institutes for Education Research, Political Science, Psychology and Sociology. At the University of Oslo there is an intersectorial seminar on development studies which was started as a result of student initiative. It is now organized on a more official basis and gives credits to the students

B. Brock-Utne

attending it. It could well serve as a model of what it is possible to start in the field of disarmament education at the university level — before institutes in this field are set up. To get such seminars going, it would be important for the university authorities to have UN and UNESCO recommendations in this field and to be asked what had been done about them at their university.

Regional colleges

Apart from the four universities there are in Norway several undergraduate regional colleges of recent origin scattered all over the country. To begin with they offered mostly technical and administrative courses but of late they have also started offering courses in education, special education, history, the social sciences, literature and the arts, Several of the colleges thus have staff with wide expertise. Since the regional colleges are still in their infancy and are not such established institutions as most of the universities, it should be possible to initiate courses in disarmament education at some of them. Regional colleges located near to teacher colleges would be particularly suited to offer such courses.

Teacher training colleges

Work on disarmament, human rights, war and peace should be an obligatory part of any teacher training. In Norway all the teacher training colleges are guided by the same Curriculum Guidebook. It is important that questions concerning disarmament education should be put into this guidebook when it is revised. Such questions should be dealt with in education and social studies. It should also be possible to have obligatory teaching units in this field, comprising many of the subjects taught in elementary school. In the field of education it will be especially important to make the prospective teachers familiar with the ideas behind education *for* disarmament. How can conflicts be solved? How can conflicts in the immediate surroundings of the child be used as a starting point for discussion and understanding of conflicts on a national, regional and international scale? Apart from having disarmament education as an obligatory part of the curriculum in the teacher training colleges, it is also desirable that the various colleges arrange optional half-year and all-year courses in teaching about disarmament, human rights, war and peace, as part of a more advanced degree in teaching. Such work has already started at Kristiansand Teacher Training College in the south of Norway. At this college the students may choose a half-year course in democracy comprising three main components: democracy in a historical perspective, democracy in a comparative perspective, and education for democracy. The course has been created as a result of cooperation between teachers in education and social studies. These teachers have also been cooperating with elementary school teachers, so that theory and practice have formed an integrated part in this course. A half-year or all-year course in disarmament education could well make use of experience drawn from work at Kristiansand.

Research and development work

The prospects mentioned by the former Minister of Church and Education, of developing teaching material in disarmament education on a Nordic basis, have already been mentioned. No matter who is to be in charge of the developmental work it will need some extra funding.

The university/teacher-training group at the seminar proposed that one of the areas for future research and developmental work of the Ministry of Education should be education about disarmament, human rights, war and peace. The idea here would be to fund projects which would develop teaching material in this area. Projects surveying the teaching actually going on in this field throughout the country would also have high priority as would analyses of existing teaching material. The teaching material to be developed should focus on the reasons why the UN resolutions about disarmament have not had any effect. As already mentioned it is also important to develop alternative history books showing how conflicts have been solved by peaceful means, focusing on peace heroes and on dramatic campaigns for peace.

Adult education

One serious difficulty experienced by those working with disarmament education at the adult level is the lack of adequate teaching material. Most of the official documents and research reports are written in a technical, dry and exclusive language. There is a great need for simplified versions, films and teaching material which has proved successful with adult learners. What sort of questions have been discussed? Who are the outside lecturers who have been used? What songs and music have been used, what literature? How can role playing, simulation games, drama and art be integrated within disarmament education?

An information centre on material for adults would have the responsibility both of developing teaching material and obtaining already existing teaching materials. It would have to keep a stock of suitable films, video tapes, slides, records and tapes for distribution, together with books, reports and other publications. At the seminar about disarmament education the group working on adult education outlined plans for such an information centre and even suggested how it could be financed. They claimed that the creation of such a centre would be a

B. Brock-Utne

great help to all the voluntary organizations working in this field. Two examples of disarmament education in Norway are given below.

Fridtjof Nansen Academy

The Nansen Academy offers half-year and shorter courses for adults wishing to study a topic in depth for some time without the pressure of examinations. The academy, being named after Fridtjof Nansen, calls itself a humanistic academy. The teaching offered has mainly centered round philosophy, ethics, literature and the arts. In the winter course of 1978/79 one of the teachers at this academy offered a course in peace education running through the whole term (half a year) with 2 hours each week. The course was called 'Rearmament for peace?' In a report on this weekly seminar the teacher stressed the importance of establishing a non-authoritarian learning climate. Peace education cannot be taught in a hierarchical set-up. He mentioned the themes which were dealt with at the seminar, the type of discussions the group had had and the literature and the guest lecturers thay had used. At the end of the seminar the group arranged a large exhibition showing the arms race during the last 10-15 years. In the exhibition they made use of graphs, pictures and captions. Through this exhibition they managed to share their knowledge with fellow students who had not attended the seminar. The group also edited a collection of short articles which were framed by poetry.

In evaluating the seminar the teacher responsible said that the definition of peace as the absence of war, which they had used, was too narrow to work with. On another occasion he would use a wider definition, including also the absence of structural violence. Peace was not only a question of eliminating the use of arms: it was also necessary to alter the political and economic structures which are killing millions of people through starvation and poverty. By focusing also on structural violence, the students would see the connection between this type of violence and the use of direct military and physical violence. In the current course at the Nansen Academy this wider definition has been used. The course has also covered more sessions per week.

Preparatory school for Civilian Defence

The young men who find it incompatible with their moral conscience to do military service may in Norway do various types of civil defence work. During the last few years there have been about 2000 young men each year refusing to do military service, about 10% of those in Norway doing military service.

During the first years after World War II those refusing to do military service usually had to do work within agriculture or forestry, but from about 1960 these young. men were mostly set to do work within the health and social services. Their main concern, however, was that the time they spent on civil defence should be used for peace-building activities. They found it to be a move in the right direction when in 1963 it was decided that earnings made by civil defenders through their period of service would be earmarked for UNICEF. Another positive move was represented by the fact that the UN Association in Norway was accepted as a place where civil defence workers could do their service. In 1968 there was a debate in Parliament about civil defence, in which it was pointed out that while those doing regular military service had a common initial training there was no such training for those doing civil defence work. Parliament asked the Ministry of Justice to work out plans for such an initial training or preparatory course. Plans were worked out and an agreement to try these out in practice was reached in 1972. The preparatory course was run for three consecutive years, each course lasting for three months, with a total of 450 lessons; of these 300 formed a common core while the rest had to be chosen from a variety on offer. Peace education was given 70 of the 300 obligatory lessons and was also one of the options to choose from.

Peace education at the Preparatory School for Civilian Defence consisted of three main parts: non-violent defence, theories of social and political development, and study of peace and conflicts. This field of peace education has been regarded as the main subject at the preparatory school. In the official documents outlining the curriculum, it has been described as follows:

The reason why civil defenders refuse to do military service is that they, for various ethical reasons, do not accept the solution of conflicts through violence. Peace education will accordingly have to be the most basic and central subject studied in the preparatory school. The aims of the subject should be:

to strengthen the civil defender's non-violent attitude;
to give knowledge and training in the solution of conflicts through non-violent behaviour and measures;
to study in depth the theories on how conflicts between people, groups of people and nations are created.

Since this Norwegian example of having peace education as a main subject in the initial training of men doing their national defence service seems to be unique, some of the main topics for focus within the three main parts of this subject are worth mentioning.

1. Non-violent defence:
discussion of various ethical attitudes to non-violence, among

them the Christian ethical attitude, the humanist ethical attitude and Gandhian political ethics;
introduction to different forms of non-violent strategies;
historical accounts of earlier use of non-violent strategies;
principles behind the use of non-violent defence;
simulations and role-playing;

2. Theories of social and political development:
various models for development;
the relationship between industrialized countries and developing countries;
the relationship between between nations with differing political systems;
conflicts between industrialized countries;
conflicts in relation to the developing countries;
the theory and practice of aid to developing countries;
factors influencing the developing of Norwegian society

3. The study of peace and conflicts:
general theory of conflict and peace;
what actions are usually brought about under the threat of conflict?
alternative actions and methods which can be developed to be used in situations of conflict.

The preparatory school for civil defenders was an experiment lasting for 3 years. It was housed in temporary buildings and parliament had to find money to secure a permanent location for this school. This was done in 1979. The school is now under construction but the content of the courses has not been finally agreed on. It is likely that the main ingredients of the subject of peace education will still constitute an essential part of the school curriculum. It is a hope that these ingredients will also constitute a part of the learning at the preparatory school for those doing military service. So far there has been nothing about peace education, about the use of non-violence or about disarmament in their education.

As I am a Norwegian let me end by quoting a Norwegian fighter for peace, Fridtjof Nansen:

There will be no war unless we human beings want it. War is not a result of a natural catastrophe, it is a work of the human race, it is our own shame. Through sensible political actions it should be comparatively easy to put an end to the phenomenon of war.

13. A future studies approach to disarmament education

Philomena Fischer, *Fordham University, New York*

The purpose here is to describe what 'future studies' in education are, and to explain how they can be applied to global issues of the arms race and disarmament for high school levels and above. A brief theoretical rationale behind the future studies of the arms race* will be given, before a step-by-step teaching procedure is presented.

The idea of future studies was advocated by leaders of the progressive education movement in the 1930s and 1940s in the USA. The aim is a cognitive understanding of contemporary issues through 'futuring', a 'look at tomorrow today'[1], and the main theme is that choices being made today influence what will happen tomorrow. Futuring puts special emphasis on thinking in an anticipatory way about future consequences, which serves two purposes. First, it helps students to look for and recognize future trends (e.g. increasing military expenditures, especially in the Third World). Second, it will make them realize what is happening in the present (the arms race nobody can win), help them to conjecture possible futures that can grow from the present (probability of nuclear war, damaging effect of military weapon testing on the ecosystem and public health, etc.), and understand more fully what has to be done now to prevent the undesirable and create a more desirable future (campaign to help the public realize the senselessness of nuclear war and thus help form pressure groups for mutual disarmament).

Cognitive understanding, at which future studies aim, is theoretically assumed to stimulate the development of a sense of justice which will often serve to motivate a person into action[2]. Especially when the cognitive understanding is combined with self-evaluation of a person's specific values and related attitudes, it can result in a change in those specific values and attitudes, and thus produce behavioural changes[3]. In other words, some specific values such as a world at peace, respect for human life and equality seem to be determinants of attitudes toward war and peace. A pilot study with members of the International Peace Research Association and with college students in Geneva has shown clearly that the higher those values are ranked within a list of

---

* This is based on a pilot experimental study for the author's doctoral dissertation.

18 selected values, the more peace-oriented the attitude exhibited; more participation in social action was shown with much stronger conviction[4].

If the goal of disarmament education is to help students or workshop participants to become more action-oriented (active participants in social actions) or more structure-oriented (active participants in restructuring national and international systems in alternative ways) towards a disarmed world, future studies of the arms race and disarmament can serve as a practical stepping stone toward the achievement of that goal in the area of education. A step-by-step future studies approach is described here.

Creation of a 'threat-free' atmosphere

In the future studies programme, students are supposed to participate in the learning process as active learners, going through information-processing on their own initiatives; thus teachers or workshop sponsors remain as facilitators and/or information suppliers.

In order to ensure that each student can freely participate in a group, 'magic circle' rules[5] should be observed. Those rules are: students sit in a circle, each student takes a turn with a fair amount of time to express his or her own opinion, and everyone's opinion is accepted with no criticism and no put-downs. Discussion topics such as 'what I enjoy most', 'what I treasure most,' etc., are introduced for magic circle sessions.

For each session, once each student has had a turn in the circle, students express what similarities and differences the circle members have and exchange what they have learned from that session. Then, a game 'where is my orange' is introduced. This game can be enjoyed from sixth grade upwards — even by adults. A bag of oranges (the same number as there are circle members) is placed in the middle of the circle. Each student takes one orange out of the bag, and examines it carefully. Then all the oranges are collected, put back into the bag, and poured out on the floor. Each student has to find his or her own orange. A funny name and personality can be imaginatively added to one's orange and introduced to the whole group. It is a fun game in which there is no winner and no loser, and which allows students to get to know each other better in a relaxed atmosphere.

Future studies of the arms race and disarmament

Glenn has described a procedure of 'futuring' in detail for classroom activities. An outline of the future studies of the arms race and disarmament, based to a large extent on Glenn's procedure is given below.

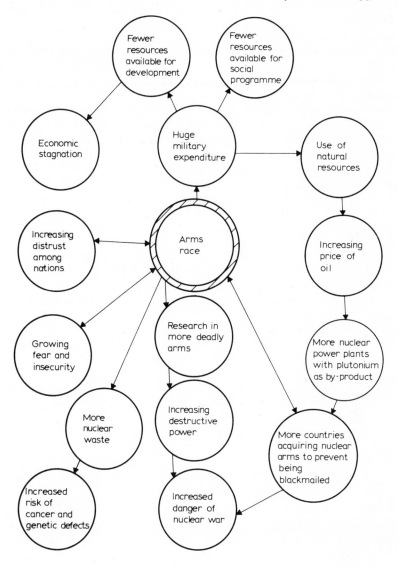

Figure 1. A future wheel with the arms race as central trend. An arrow from circle A to circle B means trend A affects B in some way; a double-headed arrow between A and B means that A and B mutually affect each other

Initial steps

It starts with simple ideas. Ask each student to describe something she or he is able to do today, but could not do in the past. Ask why things have changed since. For example, one may be able to speak a second language today, but could not do so 10 years ago. Between, one had to learn it.

Ask students to describe something they want to do in the future but cannot do today. Ask them to describe what changes will have to take place before they can do it, and in what way they can contribute to bring about those changes.

Have groups list trends that are increasing and decreasing. A trend is defined as an influence on human behaviour that noticeably increases or decreases over time. It must exist in some form in the past and present, and be reasonably expected to continue into the foreseeable future, for example, the increased use of computers and the decreasing number of wild animal species. Put the increasing trends together, and the decreasing trends together. What is the difference between the two lists? It is important in this first step to make sure that every participant understands what is meant by a trend.

Moving to more structured discussion, take a topic as familiar as transportation. Futuring this topic calls for consideration of such aspects as the situation as it is today, the question of using individual versus mass transit vehicles, the availability of fuel supplies, the need to move large members of people quickly, the safety of vehicles, the fact that people will demand convenience and comfort in getting from place to place. Students may think of related aspects — the need to allocate ever more land areas for transportation routes, the possibility of staggering working hours in highly industrial areas to alleviate traffic jams, the significance to the economy of fewer personal vehicles being manufactured if more and more people use mass-transit systems. As students discuss some of these possibilities, their view of today and its problems will lead them to consider actions and decisions that must be taken now to solve future problems.

Further developments

Next, a more highly developed future-oriented teaching process can be adopted. It may be divided into four steps.

Trend identification. Students are asked to list any issues which are related to war and peace, and to discover trends among them. Among the identified trends, let students figure out a central one. The trend of the arms race will inevitably be brought out.

One way to help students understand the complexity and implications of the trends they list is the use of a 'future wheel'. (Figure 1). This consists of a circle with lines emanating from it, with the central trend

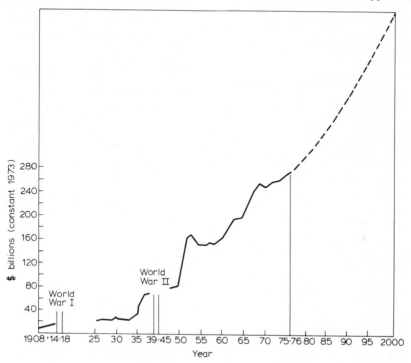

Figure 2. World military expenditure, 1908-76 (from SIPRI 1977, reproduced in Johansen, 1978) extrapolated to the year 2000

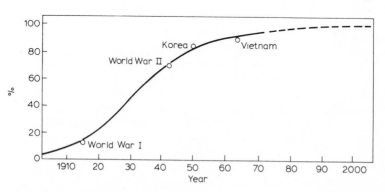

Figure 3. Increasing percentage of civilian casualties from 13% in World War I, rising to 75% in World War II, 84% in the Korean War and possibly 90% in the Vietnam War (after Monez, 1973)

inside the circle. Students have to find its cause and effects and write them at the end of the lines. Real data should be available to students here. Commoner's small booklet[6] and Sivard[7] are very useful.

This technique clearly demonstrates that a single trend cannot be thought of as isolated from other factors in society. For instance, a 'future wheel' concerned with the arms race will help students to think of what is increasing and decreasing in this particular area. Military expenditure, research in deadly weapons, public health hazards from testing of nuclear weapons, the size of the nuclear club and distrust among nations are among increasing trends. Those trends which are decreasing with acceleration of the arms race are social expenditures, the rate of economic growth, natural resources, etc. There are many other factors and trends involved in the arms race; therefore, the future wheel shown in Figure 1 is by no means exhaustive. While making a future wheel, let the students look not only at the aspect of possible direct violence, such as nuclear war, but also at structural violence resulting from military expenditure, especially in the developing countries. Comparison of each country's military and social expenditure (education and health) throughout the world can be made by students themselves with real figures given by Sivard[7].

After trend identification, let us examine where such trends might take us.

Future projections. Individually or in groups, students make projections to a future date describing what life may be like, determined solely by those trends identified in the first step.

Teams of four or five students might get together to put their trends on one wheel for projection or put them together on a graph. Many future forecasts are made simply by graphing. A trend is plotted from some point in the past to the present, then with a dotted line the curve is continued to the date to which students wish to project. Military expenditure and the increasing percentage of civilian casualties in wars can be projected to the year 2000 by students (Figures 2 and 3).

Another way in which students can put their trends together is in a cross-impact matrix, in order to discover the interrelationships among them. Causes are listed on the left, and effects at the top (a simple example is given in Figure 4). This technique can be used to show the interdependence of almost anything. It is in an excellent way to teach logic and creative questioning. While students are filling in the boxes, they can think about how their projections might affect the whole ecosystem and if they will satisfy human needs.

Future models. Students are encouraged to search out other related literature or to hold 'brain-storming' sessions. In these any ideas relat-

	Destructive power	Military expenditure	Social expenditure
Destructive power	—	Military power of other nations leads to more domestic military expenditure to counter a real or perceived threat of aggression	—
Military expenditure	More sophisticated weapons increase destructive power	—	Fewer resources for social programmes
Social expenditure	—	If more was spent for social programmes (health, education, housing, etc.) then less would be left over for military purposes	—

Figure 4. A cross-impact matrix with three trends, relating to the arms race

ing to the topic are contributed by group members in a random order and are noted on a blackboard; later, the ideas can be developed further and put into a more logical order, and students can choose which theme they want to develop further so that all can participate. With these experiences as background, individuals or groups of students write, paint, create a play or make their projected future models, in order to explain in some way what the future might be like, based on the trends identified — assuming that no intervention occurs to change the trends significantly. The students should decide on a date in the future to which they all wish to project. A scenario expressing a

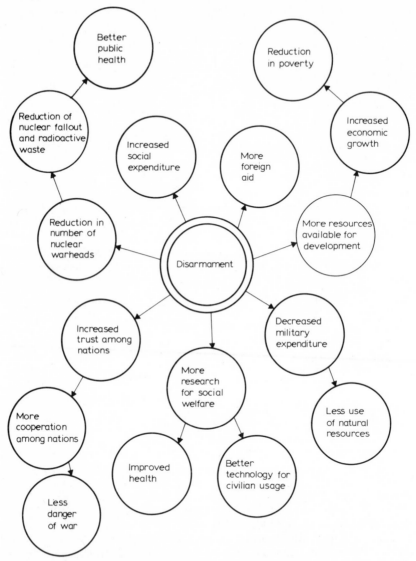

Figure 5. A future wheel with disarmament as central trend

day in that future life should help to clarify students' ideas as to their jobs, family life, environment and other important issues of that time in the future. It should also help them to begin to think whether or not that future is desirable.

If that future state is not desirable, this can easily lead to a discussion of what they believe to be the best future. Students then invent and describe what would be desirable. The students' description of their desirable world, might be followed by a slide show, which explains the reality of the arms race and economic conversion. Students can discuss the plausibility of economic conversion under various conditions. Then, they go back to the desirable world they described previously.

For example, let us assume that the students' vision of a desirable future was of a disarmed world, free of social injustice and inequality. Then, students once again make a 'future wheel' with disarmament at the centre, in order to visualize clearly what is increasing and decreasing as a result of disarmament. What happens to possible direct violence and structural violence with disarmament can be observed by students themselves. An example of a future wheel with disarmament as the central trend is shown in Figure 5. The reduction of military expenditures and increase in foreign aid[8] can be projected on a graph. Another projection can be made with tax rebate and arms reduction in the USA[9]. Students may discuss what sort of political institutions will have to exist in such a disarmed world. Preferred world models can be introduced for reference. The International Police System[9], World Council[10], a UN with two chambers[11] are some examples for a preferred world. They can discuss further how the economy will work, how conflicts can be resolved without resorting to arms, or what structures can prevent or minimize the eruption of conflicts (e.g. a political system with a decentralized distribution of power, such as the federal government structure in Switzerland). Based on their preferred world, students can make future models.

Policy creation. Finally, students work back in time from the desirable future model to the present in order to learn several approaches to what needs to be done to bring about a more acceptable future.

What must be done for a better future? The students' desired future will not come about unless certain decisions and actions are taken first. Can they figure out what are the necessary steps to the future they desire? Do they have a reasonable chance of completing these steps? Suppose students wish to begin putting some of these steps into motion. Assume that they come up with disarmament as a desirable step towards a dependable peace system. The students should look for literature to find what has been done for disarmament so far, and discuss what should be done now. A brain-storming session is in order, to develop as complete a list as possible of all the policies and social actions which must happen to achieve this desirable future, a dependable peace system, e.g., creating an international peace police force non-military defence, negotiation with other countries, lobbying for disarmament, writing to senators and newspaper editors, organizing disarmament groups or participating in peace organizations, persuading people to join peace movements, showing slides about the arms race, etc.

Once the lists are made, have students put them in order, starting with those which are the easiest and provide a positive feedback soon, moving to those which may take much longer or require a certain position of power. For instance, from the examples just listed, showing slides about the arms race to a group is fairly easy and feasible, with a possible quick feedback. On the other hand, not everybody is in a position to negotiate about disarmament with other nations. What is more feasible for most people is to help bring about public pressure to reduce arms and to boycott arms laboratories and arms factories, etc.

References

1. Glen C. A look at tomorrow today. In Torrance E. and White W. (Eds.) *Issues and advances in educational psychology.* Itasca, F.E. Peacock, 1975
2. Kohlberg L. Moral development and identification. *NSSE Yearbook, 1963,* **62** (1) 277-332
3. Rokeach M. *The nature of human values.* New York, Free Press, 1973
4. Fischer P. Self-dissatisfaction as a determinant of changes in students' peace value and attitude towards war. PhD dissertation proposal, Fordham University, New York, 1980
5. Palomares U. and Logan B. *A curriculum on conflict management.* La Mesa, Human Development Training Institute, 1975
6. Commoner B. *Science and survival.* New York, The Viking Press, 1966
7. Sivard R. *World military and social expenditures, 1976 and 1977.* Leesburg, WMSE Publications, 1978
8. Leontief W. Disarmament, foreign aid and economic growth. *J. Peace Research, 1964,* **1,** 155-167
9. Johansen R.C. The disarmament process: where to begin. *Eric Document, 142486,* 1977
10. Falk R. Toward a new world order: modest methods and drastic visions. In Mendlovitz S. (Ed.), *On the creation of a just world order: preferred worlds for the 1990s.* New York, Free Press, 1975
11. Galtung J. Nonterritorial actors and the problem of peace. In Mendlovitz, *op.cit.*

14. Reform of officers' training in the Federal Republic of Germany: an approach to the democratization of the military or a lost opportunity*

Mathias Jopp, *Peace Research Institute, Frankfurt* [†]

Some readers may be surprised to find an essay on the education of officers in the Federal Republic of Germany in a book about disarmament and peace education. However, there are more connections between these two topics than one might at first suppose.

In the mid-1960s the well-known sociologist von Friedeburg declared as illusory disarmament strategies which exclude the military as one of the central supports and participants of the arms race Considering the enormous power of the military organization, its technical and professional structure and the tremendous possibilities it has to pursue its own interests, he came to the conclusion that disarmament strategies would be more easily achieved acting with the military rather than against it. He suggested therefore making 'the problems of deterrence and war limitation, arms control and disarmament into problems for the military organization and military professional conscience itself'.

It would be relatively simple if the problem of permanent rearmament could be solved merely by teaching officers the techniques of arms control. Even if this were regarded as an important step towards breaking the lines of the traditional threatening posture, education towards disarmament nevertheless includes far more than mere command of the appropriate instruments; because real disarmament means a change in the constellations of power and interests on which war and armament are based. Peace education therefore cannot be separated from a general concept of political education with the goal of abolishing illegitimate structures of power and establishing a base for democratic rule in the conscience of the people[2].

Because of this close relationship between peace education and education towards democracy, the democratic and political education of

---

*This is based upon Jopp M. *Militär und Gesellschaft in der Bundesrepublik Deutschland. Das Beispiel der Bildungsreform in der Bundeswehr,* Frankfurt/M, i v im Campus-Verlag, 1980.

† Translated by Annette Baronin Charpentier, Frankfurt

M. Jopp

the military officer becomes a matter of interest. The relationship between the military and democracy is influenced by the ways and means of this education, as is also the chance of enforcement of disarmament and peace strategies.

Since its foundation in 1955, the Bundeswehr has tried to follow the concept of *Innere Führung,* or political education according to the idea of a 'citizen in uniform'. Unfortunately, this goal was undermined during the 1960s, so that it did not have sufficient means to withstand the traditional, authoritative patriarchal ways of thinking and acting, which had been cultivated in the Reichswehr and Wehrmacht[3]. The reform of the military educational system, begun in 1970-71 consisted among other things in a renewed attempt to introduce democratic goals especially for the education of the officers[4]. Although resistance by conservatives within and without the military to such a democratizing approach in educational reform was tremendous, circumstances favoured such a move. The army was then in a crisis about its status which could be overcome only by modernization of the military educational system. Social development in general was in the midst of a reforming period[5], so that it was easier for democratic intentions to be included in overcoming the military crisis.

Unfortunately, the educational reform of the Bundeswehr, one of the most extensive democratizing projects in German military history, has been threatened by decline during the last few years. The aim here is to report the intentions of the reform, its gradual reduction in practice, and finally to point out the necessity of a renewal of reform.

Goals of reform

University study allied to pedagogics and social sciences
The reformers[6] regarded the development of compulsory study for officers as the crucial point in democratization of the military institutions This had been demanded several times before, but was never realized because of the 'education phobia' of parts of the military elite. To the reformers, the sciences seemed suitable for educating officers towards critical thinking and democratic behaviour[7]. The reformers expected that this would arise through various methods of scientific criticism, academic freedom and the possibilities of democratic socialization at universities, for example through student participation. To guarantee the utmost intellectual freedom for officers, the reformers designed the concept of 'university study aligned to pedagogics and social sciences'[8] (called here the Anleitkonzept),which was integrated into the 5-year training programme for officers at the beginning of their military careers.

216

This Anleitkonzept was intended to combine and relate specific science and general social policy. The officer was to learn basic historical and political facts as part of the subjects of the specified programmes instead of receiving titbits of critical education apart from the required courses. Officially the reform of military education aimed at integration of specified courses with pedagogics and social sciences. In addition to the pedagogic elements, there was the concept that the military student would, through his situation as a student, develop the educational perception necessary for his future position as a trainer and senior officer. The social science elements were to prepare him to react critically when working with the military and later in a civil profession, especially as 70-80% of student officers leave the army for civil careers after 12-15 years. So the conception aimed at educating an intellectually flexible officer corps, as well as preventing a major portion of academically educated temporary officers returning to civilian life with one-sided military way of thinking.

'Participation' as a major educational goal
The aims of the educational reform being to produce an officer corps, democratized and familiar with the methods of free academic discussion by developing critical abilities, the first goal when setting up the curricula was 'participation'[9]. This goal had become a bone of contention between the different ideologies during the reform of the normal civilian universities some years before, and it was the same for those responsible for the military curricula[10]. There developed two groups: the *systemimmanente* (inherent system) and *systemkritische* (critical of system), which interpreted the concept of 'participation' in very different ways[11]. The systemimmanent military reformers aimed at introducing a more humane concept of leadership by the extension of possibilities of codetermination, and the spread of a cooperative concept of leadership, but simultaneously maintaining the hierarchical structure. The systemkritisch reformers emphasized that democratization should eventually result in change of all military structures — and with that the military system itself.

The systemimmanent reformers regarded education of critical abilities as an education producing critical loyalty in the same ways as Baudissin's concept of a 'citizen in uniform'[12]. They demanded that the military officer should be involved, creative and intellectually flexible to enable him to deal with the technical, organizational and social problems of a modern army in an industrial society. Their understanding of codetermination was that it was important to enlarge the possibilities of participation within the limits of existing conditions, which would simultaneously produce higher efficiency and stability of the social system of the Bundeswehr.

The systemkritisch reformers emphasized the distinction between their concept of participation and the strategies of participation, which 'serve to stabilize social power'[13]. In their opinion, participation was to be understood as comprehensive involvement in relevant decision-making processes within and without the military and not as 'instrumentalized reduction in the sense of stabilizing the system and providing higher efficiency'. These reformers hoped to achieve flexibility in the 'principle of obedience' through adequate education of the officer in spite of the hierarchical structure of the military system. The deciding issue was that the control principle, the principle of order and obedience, sanctioned by law, was only fully justified in case of war. Only in wartime, when strategic and tactical actions have to be carried out under the premises of smooth efficiency, would the demand for participation become unrealistic. The aim of participation in peacetime military life should be a widening of the involvement of the soldier in the 'processes of information and decision' until the phase preceding military conflicts.

These reformers considered that officers used to university codetermination and scientific criticism would be the supporters of such a strategy aimed at argumentative instead of authoritative processes. As these educational reformers had neither the means nor the competence to change the hierarchical structure of the military immediately, they tried to influence the military organizational patterns by changing the education of the soldier — changing the men rather than the structures.

Elimination of systemkritisch approach

Reformers belonging to the systemkritisch orientation concentrated mainly on the group authorized to set up educational goals for the pedagogical and social elements of the specified courses. This group in a way took a key position in the planning process for officers' studies in general, as it did not deal with the planning of the learning objectives for single specific programmes but with the setting up of the central, general educational goals for the study programme as a whole. The Anleitstudium committee, influenced by the 'Frankfurt School' and the demands for democratization of the antiauthoritarian students' movement, designed a comprehensive learning programme, in which a critique of the structures of power and functions within the capitalist society played not a small part. Officers should be taught for example about 'economic power as an opportunity for political influence', 'the phenomena of distortion of the social *Marktwirtschaft*,' 'theory and practice of codetermination' and 'militarism and problems of resistance' up to 'disarmament strategies' and the 'conversion of armament industries into peace industries'[14]. These guidelines for specified courses, however, found little or no response in the officially sanctioned curricula for the academic education of officers.

Even the regular publication of results was prevented, and with that the influence of the systemkritisch reformers on the concept of the reform itself. The suppression of their intentions arose because they disagreed with the official direction of the reform and the attitude of the Defence Ministry. It was also excluded because of resistance from the officer corps, which was substantial originally, and even threatened to grow when it became known that the new officers' training aimed at a change of the military system.

It was to be expected, however, that the inclusion in officer training of strategies designed to change the system itself would especially turn out to be utopian because of the conservative, hierarchical structure of the military system and the power of the military establishment. The reformers would have been aware of this. Nevertheless, the fact that they attempted to plan a critical study for officers can presumably be traced to the historical situation of a general era of reforms and emancipation in the Federal Republic and to the special opportunities of these reformers and members of an official planning committee.

Although, after the rejection of the Anleitstudium committee's recommendations no official curriculum existed for the pedagogical and social science elements in the specified courses, the Anleitkonzept was maintained as one goal of reform. Integration of general culture into specified programmes was still intended to prepare the critical and reflective officer for his military and later civil career[15]. The major learning objective of the new academic training was still education towards participation. Only the systemimmanent reformers' concept of participation was now important. The educational guidelines towards critical loyalty and a cooperative style of leadership for officers showed very clearly in the specified curricula and materials developed by this group[16].

However, although these goals represented the official attitude, their realization in practice was by no means guaranteed. The plans of the reformers were only recommendations, not compulsory. The curricula set up by them represented an offer for the planned Bundeswehrhochschulen. In these, as in normal universities, the principle of academic freedom was applied. The realization of the Anleitkonzept and the educational goal of participation were from the very beginning dependent on how far the teaching staff of the Bundeswehrhochschulen backed the concept of the reform and on how the Defence Ministry would insist on its complete realization in practice.

Distortion of educational concept in practice

Minor role of Anleitkonzept

The Bundeswehrhochschulen were founded in 1973, one in Hamburg, the other in Munich. Today about 4600 officers study there in 8 departments[17]. They are taught by 262 professors, with 130 senior officers to watch over military discipline. Originally some reformers planned to have the officers take their courses at civil universities, so as to integrate the officer corps as much as possible into civilian society and stimulate them to 'civilian' thinking[18]. They could not carry out their plan without the military establishment who then, as today, feared an ideological conversion of the officer corps[19]. Because of the isolation of the Bundeswehrhochschulen in regard to their academic environment and their special structure, with academic and military departments, the realization of the Anleitkonzept would particularly have been of major importance.

Yet the concept of specified courses aligned with pedagogics and social science elements (the integrated approach) could at no time be realized during the early years at Bundeswehrhochschulen. In practice there developed a pedagogically and social science orientated study, Anleitstudium, on its own, separate from the specified programmes. The relevance of tests and examinations and the lack of staff showed how unimportant the Anleitkonzept had become between 1973 and 1977. In some courses, the pedagogic and social science content sank to less than 2%[20]. And so, things developed in exactly the way that all reformers had sought to prevent from the beginning: the socially relevant topics of the officer training were dealt with as unimportant secondary lessons. The reason for this development is mainly that the Defence Ministry and the professors at the Bundeswehrhochschulen had other aims than the education of a social critical officer.

In opposition to the intentions of the reformers, it became clear quite soon that only a minority of the teaching staff actively supported the ideals of the reform[21]. Some of the professors had applied to the Bundeswehrhochschulen not out of interest in the reforms, but because they could not find adequate positions at other civilian universities and/or felt attracted by the connection between science and military discipline. They dedicated themselves exclusively to their professional reputation and showed hardly any interest in the realization of the Anleitkonzept, the more so as in this concept ideological subversion was often presumed to be a danger. But even that part of the teaching staff which identified with the goals of the reform felt under pressure to put professional interest above educational ideals. As the studies at Bundeswehrhochschulen are limited to 3¼ years with 10 terms, and differ from a normal university study with 8-10 semesters normally taking 4-5 years, their academic value was from the very beginning controversial.

The professors therefore concentrated on justifying the academic credibility of Bundeswehrstudium in compressing the normal 5 years of academic studies into 3 and veered towards achieving the academic demands of ordinary universities rather than to the curricula of the reformers. Through the dominance of specified courses, Anleitkonzept was pushed aside. Under these conditions only a considerable lengthening of the study could have given sufficient time for both specified courses and political education. For reasons of efficiency as well as politics, the Defence Ministry up to now has not been willing to give up the concept of a short study course[22]. Apparently, they do not want the officer corps to study for a long time so as to prevent possible educationally based alienation from military concepts. This retention of the short study course combined with the internal compulsion of the teaching staff to aim at the equivalent specified studies in civilian universities, caused the failure of pedagogical and social science orientated programmes.

Revaluation of Anleitstudium as a result of antisemitic occurences
Presumably Anleitstudium would still have played a minor role in the Bundeswehrhochschulen if the academic education of the officers had not become a target for public criticism during 1977 and the beginning of 1978 because of antisemitic scandals.

In February 1977, there was a mock burning of Jews during a student's party at the Bundeswehrhochschule in Munich. Some time later, swastikas were found on a seminar paper and a car. During a journey to Vienna, some student officers are supposed to have called out in the Judengasse: 'Shoot the Jews!'[23]. Because of these and other neo-nazi events in the army, some newspapers demanded a change in the conditions of admission, stronger supervision, and a return to the reform model. The Defence Ministry was obviously under pressure from such vehement criticisms especially by the foreign press, and began improvement of historical-political education at the Bundeswehrhochschulen.

A conference took place in December 1977 with senior officers, civil servants from the Defence Ministry and professors of the Bundeswehrhochschulen[24]. There was no going back to the ideals of the reform, but the position of political education within the framework of the existing conditions in the Bundeswehrhochschulen was reevaluated. It was decided to reorganize the content and position of Anleitstudium, to increase the teaching staff and to up-grade this subject in examinations. This conference was important not only because political education was revalued. Simultaneously limits were placed on the content of Anleitstudium which were not part of the original goals of the reform. In future, they were to serve only a preparatory function for the military profession and make possible reflection about the officer's position in society. This orientation of Anleitstudium towards the military was completely opposed to the intention of the reformers.

Because most graduates of the Bundeswehrhochschulen enter a civilian profession at the latest after 15 years, a special critical orientation towards civilian life had been intended by the reformers as well.

The limiting of Anleitstudium to the military professions served the interests of opponents of reform in the Defence Ministry and in leading positions of the military establishment. From the beginning, they had interpreted the key-word 'reference to professions' in a military sense. They were not interested in preparation for civilian life: Anleitstudium was rather regarded as a chance to put a military grip around the purely academic phase of the officers' education[25].

This playing down of preparation for civilian professions produced a further reduction of the original reform concept, after the elimination of the systemkritisch intentions and the reduction of the Anleitkonzept to a mere additional component of studies. Also after this conference, people no longer talked about participation as the main learning objective. This trend to reduce the educational concept is certainly a result not only of the resistance to reform because of military interests, but also has to be seen in the context of a decline in the reforming impetus in society since the mid 1970s. In particular the tendency against reform in general educational policy discouraged any development of the military reform concept, based upon emancipation.

The decisions of the December 1977 conference, which aimed at a reduction of the contents and the revaluation of the role of Anleitstudium, were only in the nature of recommendations or directions, because of the academic freedom at the Bundeswehrhochschulen. Its realization furthermore depended on the assent of important committees within them. It was because of these conditions that the development did not take such a negative course as was first expected. Some reform orientated professors at the Bundeswehrhochschule in Munich, for example, succeeded in influencing the reorientation of Anleitstudium towards the old goals.

Foundation of the Department of Social Studies: an attempt to return to the ideals of reform

At the Bundeswehrhochschule in Munich, in contrast to that in Hamburg, as a result of the December 1977 conference a special department for social science elements of Anleitstudium was formed*. In Munich, followers of reform had a strong position within the university. After several disputes with the conservative military men of the Defence Ministry, they succeeded in convincing the professors of technical subjects (who generally took a sceptical position towards the

---

* The pedagogic elements were taught in the pedagogic studies department of the Bundeswehrhochschule.

Anleitstudium) that a department of social sciences should be formed[26]. Professors and assistant professors of social sciences, who before June 1978 had offered their courses in different departments, were brought together. Furthermore, 30 new positions were granted to the new department from January 1979 onwards, so the Anleitstudium Department was not only institutionalized, but also better staffed.

The professors of the new department had high aims. They saw a possiblity of preventing the reduction of the original reform concept to the merely technical and military crafts level[27]. Accordingly there followed a reform of the content of the social sciences courses, which were to be completed between the fourth and ninth terms. A catalogue of learning objectives was set up under the heading 'discrepancy between freedom and power'[28]. In the academic year 1978 seminars were planned under the general topic of German separation; during the academic year 1979 the seminars were oriented to the topic of militarism. Politics, law, history, sociology and a newly developed subject, the social economic consequences of technical change, were taught. It was intended that individual teachers should illustrate the legal, economic, religious or philosophical dimensions of the general topic, taking an adequate broad consensus for granted. By this *topic-oriented* method the Department of Social Sciences aimed at producing a distinct but differentiated political orientation among the students.

The new concept agrees in principle with the limitation of Anleitstudium to the military profession as had been agreed during the December 1977 conference. Nevertheless in spite of this one-sided orientation efforts were made to provide a critical civics course *(Staatsbürgerkunde)*.

Practical relevance of Anleitstudium

Because of the foundation of the Department of Social Sciences and the reform of the social science content, positive and negative tendencies in the development of Anleitstudium are balanced. The institutionalization and organizational stabilization of Anleitstudium by the foundation of a department with its own claims to staff and finances, must be evaluated positively. The structure of the content and the concentration on certain topics and the clarity of the seminars offered have resulted in an improvement in comparison with the former situation. Conservatives within and outside the army would rather have had, as mentioned above, some sort of military professional education as an Anleitstudium, instead of what has been called a 'playground for social science'[29].

The practical relevance of the Anleitstudium in the future remains a problem. Because of the small amount of time (only two lessons per week) the 'foundation of the political education of the officers . . . will remain a matter of secondary importance'[30]. Because of the insignificant demands and because the learning behaviour of the officers is orientated towards efficiency tests and examinations, Anleitstudium will be left as some sort of 'unpleasant' minor subject. Presumably, the improvement of tests in the social sciences for the *Hauptdiploma* will have no influence[31]. Also the lack of interest among the students shows that the possible practical effects of Anleitstudium will remain relatively small[32]. After the reorganization of Anleitstudium the students expressed doubts concerning the available time and the content of the extra work. Results of a continuous survey in Munich make clear that only a few students are aware of the content and aims of the Anleitstudium at the beginning of their courses, and they doubt its necessity. During their studies, most of the students feel that Anleitstudium is too strenuous. They would rather drop these 180 lessons during the 3 year course. This time saved would be of more importance to them than a possible increase of knowledge in the overlapping of normal courses. Only a small part of the students were willing to split up their professional education by taking up options of social sciences or even obtain a further qualification for a future non-military career.

This political disinterest among the students, who are mainly interested in sports and technics, cannot be charged to them alone. As will be shown, it is systematically promoted by the conditions of study at the Bundeswehrhochschulen. The students could perhaps be more strongly motivated by considerably higher relevance of the Anleitstudium. This alone could provoke the attention of the students. Then either the specified courses would have to be cleared of their superfluous material, or the study period in general would have to be prolonged. As both these possibilities are unlikely because of the attitude shown by the Defence Ministry and the staffing structure, the possible effects of civics will be small for the present.

Neglect of 'participation' as an educational goal

Conditions of study at the Bundeswehrhochschulen
The same conditions which caused the failure of Anleitstudium also brought about the nearly complete exclusion of the reformers' curricula set up under the heading 'education towards participation' and designed for short study periods. These could not and cannot be applied as long as instructors have to confine the normal university courses to a context limited by military political requirements[33]. Similarly, as the Anleitkonzept was completely neglected, because of the dominance of the specified courses, this has resulted in an overloading and de-emphasizing of critical topics.

It is nevertheless problematical if political insight and political behaviour can be brought about only on a cognitive level. Political education also needs practical experience. The educational reformers speculated that education in practical politics could be instilled through academic discussion and involvement of the officers by self-administration during their time as students but the possibilities of learning about practical politics are subject to major limitations at the Bundeswehrhochschulen. Under military law, student-officers are prevented from expressing political opinions or forming coalitions, and are furthermore obliged to be loyal to their superiors[34]. Supervision by senior officers, their status as soldiers and the stress brought about by the specified courses do not stimulate political engagement and free academic dialogue. The excess of subjects offered within the specified courses and the permanent control of the knowledge attained do not leave much time for discovering truth by way of discussion, as was the ideal of the educational reformers. The dominance of the specified courses results in the students trying to avoid anything else such as political education, special seminars and working in committees. They have hardly any time for independent reflection, to wholly understand the abundance of subjects. Apparently, the mere learning of facts is dominant, at the cost of problem-oriented knowledge of methods and the appreciations of contexts[35].

Even though the course was prolonged after December 1978 from the original 9-10 terms, because of the high rate of failure in examinations these conditions of study have obviously not changed[36]. Still the short duration of the studies and the organization of the terms seems to have resulted in a 'disadvantageous form of schooling'[37], 'which reminds one of courses typical for the Bundeswehr, with rigid learning by heart, rather than academic university study'[38] The rigid studies apparently force the student officer to study 'economically and efficiently'[39]. This not only results in a superficial gathering of facts, but also 'corresponds in no way to the principles of the *Innere Führung*'[40] — as it was expressed in a declaration, published in 1979 in the student's paper *Druck,* signed by seven students. In the same paper, which dedicates much space to discussion of the situation of the studies and the aims of socialization, another student describes the conditions of study as follows:

> The student is permanently forced to learn receptively; he has to submit permanently to claims from outside. In the extreme this can lead to an internalized principle of order and obedience. He has no possibility of developing other qualifications, which nowadays are demanded of an officer, such as independence of thinking and acting, the ability to solve problems and to evaluate circumstances critically. How can an officer, at least in the services — show responsibility and initiative, if he only has to fulfil orders from

>   superiors and only shows initiative when it becomes important to finish
>   his studies?
> — show tolerance against open situations, if he has never had the oppor-
>   tunity to be tolerant, because of the pressure towards efficiency?
> — be a critical, thoughtful and responsible citizen in uniform if here reality
>   teaches him that because of the lack of time working in committees or
>   other groups of students' self-administration only creates disadvantages
>   for studies?[41]

This description certainly reflects personal experience. It is, however, typical when compared with other statements of students and teachers at Bundeswehrhochschulen. The general tendency shows that the study in these universities cannot be compared easily with study at normal universities[42]. Typical conditions of socialization for students which the reformers had expected to be democratizing and 'civilizing', providing time for independent processes of development, varying opinions, and free space for discussion and reflection, seem to have been eliminated during studies at Bundeswehrhochschulen, to the advantage of a more school-like system.

Keeping the conditions of study in mind, one can project the hypothetical image of socialization at Bundeswehrhochschulen. Many students, especially in the technical disciplines, will be stuffed with a broad knowledge of mere concrete facts and an 'additional' political education, when they leave. They have learned how to solve problems efficiently, following prefabricated patterns; their professional qualifications mainly consist of technically limited rationality. They probably have rid themselves for the most part of the myth of the fighter and the military craftsman of the former officers' generations. Principally, one must doubt how far the studies could provide the 'critical competence for behaviour'[43] which had been the aim of the reformers.

Education towards technocratic thinking
The goals of education, as education towards creative engagement, the ability to criticize etc., could hardly be incorporated in practice in the officers' training. The means to carry out these ideals were only partly established. Anleitstudium was pushed aside; hardly any discussion or engagement takes place. The presence of military supervision, which looks after the observance of discipline, acts willingly or unwillingly as a control of the staff[44]. Between the claim of higher academic attainment on the one hand and the military norms on the other, only the path of least resistance is left to the students. There is not time for criticism or a self-determined learning process, or these are suppressed methodically. The student learns how to study efficiently, and to fulfil as well as possible the academic and military demands. But he has hardly any possibility of doubling these. It is only important to

accomplish a series of gains with a minimum of effort in the shortest possible time[45]. If he succeeds, the diploma is his reward and the path is free for his military career. This training situation induces, although does not compel, technocratic thinking and adapted, career-orientated behaviour.

Furthermore education towards adaptation is one of the oldest and 'best' means of military socialization, to adapt the individual to the functional claims of the authorities' powers — and to keep the military organization functioning as part of the state and its policies. New, however, is the condition that there is no rigid order of norms of these socialization processes[46].

The officer at the Bundeswehrhochschule finds himself in some sort of magnetic field, in which scientific/academic and military claims try to dominate; these are however not clearly determined so that the student has to find out the exact regulations by himself. The socializing effect of the Bundeswehrhochschule as opposed to the classical concept of military academies, reacts in times of uncertainty with overloaded pretensions. This is even more subtle than the classic concept, as the limits between existing individual values and the claims of the environment are shadowy. It is never made clear when demands begin and where and when they end. Such a climate may result in existing individual values being pushed aside, diminished, or transferred to the private areas at the weekends. It hardly ever results in an improvement or building up of a system of inner values which makes possible individual self-realization and the simultaneous existence of functional and society-orientated responsibility[47]. It should be made possible, in the context of reform, to dissolve authoritative patriarchal values by the rationality of technical science, and by these means, to make the officer corps non-political. But there is serious doubt if, instead of the old values of the Prussian officer, new values can be set up, which produce sufficient political and moral judgement for the tasks of the military as well as later civilian professions in democracy. Such a result of 'academic' officer training is, however, as will be shown later, under certain conditions a major problem.

Problem of apolitical socialization

Education towards adaptation and towards technocratic thinking results in a type of person socialized to thinking in conventional terms, but not able to regard certain things from a critical distance, and if necessary to change them, or to propose possibilities for change. Because of their education it is doubtful if the student officers of today will be able to master the problems with which the military will be faced within the next 20 years, beginning with dilemmas of future security related to changes in the strategies of the superpowers[48], and leading to social and psychological problems of a compulsory army in a quickly changing social environment. Apart from future problems possibly facing the army, the results of a consciousness of a professional role oriented to correct and optimal adaptation are already known. If senior officers for career reasons and loyalty to the corps hide the interests of the armament industry, leave deputies in the dark concerning the military usefulness of armament programmes or do not tell the complete truth, the military establishment becomes difficult to understand and control[49]. It is no longer a reliable instrument of politics as far as its functions and social responsibility are concerned, and these are a principal part of each and every decision about armament. The latter function is to be understood not only as the military readiness of a weapon system, but also the action of arming as such, which should not lead to a waste of the wealth or resources of a society. The Vietnam war of the USA has shown the amount of material and human waste and the catastrophes to which technocratic thinking may lead.

These occurrences happened in relatively stable political systems and with relatively well functioning social systems. But what would happen if there were no educational goals to bring about a system of internal values, and a democratic system changed during a crisis to an authoritative one? It can be supposed or at least feared, that technocratic opportunism adapts to the aims of a political system more easily than a straight moral and distinct system of inner values. It is not that we mourn the lost professional ethics of the Prussian officer. The ethic of the Prussian officer was not strong enough to resist National Socialism's claims of power. But their *Gleichschaltung* did not occur without friction and resistance[50]. Furthermore, National Socialism's elite understood very well how important it was for them to eliminate the educational and cultural goals of the Prussian officer. Until 1939, training for the general staff was reduced almost entirely to technical and craft disciplines, in order that the military organization should function solely for the Nazi war machine[51].

A conservative professional ethic is much more susceptible to authoritative developments than a democratic professional ethic. The educational reform of the Bundeswehr had as its goal to educate officers to be democratically conscious citizens and to enable them to be capable of independent, critical scientific thought and action. This does not seem to have been achieved within the bounds of current officers' study. It has only succeeded in pushing aside conservative, traditional values. This certainly can be regarded as progress, but it can be doubted if this neutralization will be a sufficient basis for the future.

The question is, is the presumably apolitical way of thinking in terms of efficiency conducive to an authoritative superstructure, caused by socialization in the services? Traditional ways of thinking in the armed forces exist even on the highest level[52]. The new educational concept up to now only concerns the generation of officers born at the end of the 1950s. In order to resist military socialization and traditional values produced by long term service, there is a definite need for a democratic balance in officer education. To establish this firmly would have been the crucial task of the practical reorganization of the educational system — but the reform stuck at the first steps. Not only for the military organization, but for the civilian society as well, this may have undesirable secondary effects.

The university diploma and officer's certificate will enable the temporary soldier, leaving the army after 12-15 years of service, to take up a leading position in industry and administration. This absorption of temporary officers, with specialized technical knowledge, could create problems. Because of the relatively few 'army-academics' it is not to be expected that the whole of society will be militarized by an elite cadre, trained to function efficiently and control by order within a military organisation. But because of the one-sidedness of the studies at Bundeswehrhochschulen, it could produce a concentration of military trained academics in certain parts of industry and public administration — a kind of military enclave, where it would be easy to maintain military characteristics. In this case a transfer of the military way of thinking and behaving would be possible, together with a 'social psychological militarization'[53] of certain parts of society — with unexpected consequences for society as a whole.

Need for continuous reform and dangers of restoration

No one has so far succeeded in making political education play a major role in the studies at Bundeswehrhochschulen. In particular, Anleitstudium, academic methods of teaching, co-determination of students etc., through which the reformers hoped to bring about democratization have been only partly realized.

It is also hardly possible to make the topics of detente and the problems of arms control and disarmament an important part of the Bundeswehrstudium in the limited context of the Anleitstudium. This goal, set up by the educational reformers and renewed by the founders of the Social Sciences Department, and described in the 1960s by von Friedeburg, has for the most part not developed beyond the planning stage. However, this should not be considered a general failure of the educational reform, even if this is the impression. The present training at Bundeswehrhochschulen seems suitable for educating officers to be technocratic managers of the power organization. Furthermore the studies may not be without the civilizing effects resulting from the relaxing of formal rules, such as wearing of uniform not being compulsory, attendance not being obligatory, free time, etc. But these free spaces only make possible the gradual penetration of civilian influence, the value of which may be unimportant or at least difficult to ascertain. The student at a Bundeswehrhochschule will fall under military influences as well as be isolated from the civilian environments and, in a ghetto situation, be tied to the demands of rigid studies. The school-like atmosphere is hardly suitable for the promotion or development of critical judgement — rather the reverse, as it discourages independent scientific thought and action.

Not only because of the possible future problems for the military and society arising from a technocratic education, it is necessary to go back to the goals of the reform. The need to strengthen all those elements promoting democratic consciousness and critical judgement was made clear by actual events, not only the antisemitic incidents referred to but also in the number of competent criticisms of the poor quality of the political education *(Innere Führung)* and leadership within the armed forces which appeared in 1977 and 1978[54]. If these criticisms are taken seriously, the only solution is a return to the goals of the reform, to make the education towards humane leadership and democratic political thinking important parts of officer training.

The urgent need to strengthen all those elements of officer training, which the reformers had expected would produce a democratizing effect, is also emphasized by Gessenharter *et al*[55] writing about right-wing extremism among student officers. After the antisemitic events and some other known neo-nazi phenomena, the question of potential right-wing extremism at the Bundeswehrhochschulen was raised. One students' paper included the opinion that right-wing attitudes among student officers were by no means unusual[56]. Gessenharter *et al* discovered that there was an 'extreme group' at the Hamburg Bundeswehrhochschule consisting of approximately 10% of the students questioned. According to the analysis, students regarded as 'right-wing', are relatively 'highly hierarchical-authoritative, anti-democratic, dogmatic, intolerant and prejudiced'. They tend to 'think in terms of black and white, to reject democratic criticism and compromises and trust to the development of a strong personality within government'. The authors explain the development of such attitudes by the special attraction of study at Bundeswehrhochschulen and the isolation of these schools from their environment, which creates the feeling of belonging to an elite caste. To prevent the influence or the enlargement of these right-wing attitudes, they demanded a change in the system of selection, the opening of the Bundeswehrhochschulen to civilian students with the aim of liberalizing the academic organization, and strengthening those elements of the studies which make it possible to educate students as citizens and officers.

The realization of these worthy aims, however, has met with difficulties. The interests of the Bundeswehr elite are mainly against further liberalization of officers' study. The Ministry of Defence is determined to maintain the concept of short courses, and the professors are not willing to give up the normal university courses. At present, there is only the hope of using the small freedom left as much as possible for democratic education as long as restrictions are placed on open political education and socialization for officers. The foundation of the Department of Social Sciences certainly improved matters, compared to the former situation, and can be regarded with 'suppressed optimism'[57]. But if officers' education is to prevent the production of only 'militarily trained, career orientated and supposed apolitical officers'[58], it cannot and must not be limited to the present achievements.

The chances of making the democratic and political education and training of those officers who will provide the general staff of the year 2000 into an important and central part of the Bundeswehrstudium are not good. The reason for this is not only to be found in the discrepant interests of teaching staff and Ministry. Unlike the situation 8 or 10 years ago, the political climate within the military and society in general is not ready for reforms. The ideology of maintaining the *status quo* has spread. Even the reform concept in its current existence is in danger. Officers who some years ago accepted the reforms (or at least appeared to do so) today consciously or unconsciously work with those conservative officers interested in the restoration of the old goals. In addition to the general situation, the reasons are to be found in events with Bundeswehr. The elan of the building-up phase is gone; over-bureaucratization and centralization have produced immense organizational problems; the number in the age groups who saw service in wartime decreases continuously. Among older officers, there seems to spread a terrible vision of an army overrun by theory, blocked by bureaucracy and inexperienced in war. For these reasons hostility towards science and theory within the military elite is common, designed to produce a renaissance of traditional military values and openly or secretly trying to reduce reform[59].

So far the attempts at anti-reform by some senior officers have not succeeded but they have succeeded in strengthening the military influence on the 'civilian' academic phase of officer education. The changing of the Bundeswehrhochschulen into military academies, where learning and teaching are based upon order and obedience, has not happened yet, as had been feared by some critics. Apparently the opponents of reform have up to now been interested only in relating studies more strongly to military matters, to ensure educational and

M. Jopp

disciplinary control over the junior military set[60]. But even so, the Bundeswehrhochschulen are more than ever a bone of contention between 'study and steel helmet'[61]. Further development towards reform can only lead in the direction of further 'civilizing' of the academic phase of officer training, together with all its consequences, such as lengthening of the study course and liberalization. Whether this will succeed in the future or whether a stronger orientation towards the military will be enforced, depends not only on how far the Bundeswehrhochschulen themselves are able to resist the anit-reformers. It will especially be of major importance to see how far reform-orientated influences in the military organization and society will perceive the dangers of restoration and work actively for renewal of the goals of the reform.

Notes

1. Friedeburg L. von. Zum Verhältnis von Militär und Gesellschaft in der Bundesrepublik. In Picht G. (ed.). *Studien zur politischen und gesellschaftlichen Situation der Bundeswehr.* Witten and Berlin, 1966, p.55
2. See: Wulf C. (ed.) *Friedenserziehung in der Diskussion.* Munchen, 1973. This volume with essays by Galtung, Vilmar, Boulding, Senghaas and others, respresents in concentrated form the manifold relations between peace education, social criticism and political education. See also: Nicklas, H. and Ostermann A. *Zur Friedensfähigkeit erziehen. Soziales und politisches Lernen als Unterrichtsthema.* München Berlin Wien, 1976; Volmerg U. Gesellschaftliche Verhältnisse und individuelles Verhalten in der Agressionsforschung. In *Friedensanalysen. Vierteljähreszeitschrift für Erziehung, Politik und Wissenschaft,* Bd. 5. Frankfurt a.M. 1977, pp.17-84
3. For the 1950s see: Genschel D. *Wehrreform und Reaktion. Die Vorbereitung der Inneren Führung 1951-1956.* Hamburg, 1972; for the 1960s see: Thielen H.-H. *Der Verfall der Inneren Führung: Politische Bewübtseinsbildung in der Bundeswehr.* Frankfurt a. Main, 1970; for the 1970s see; Hesslein B.C. (ed.) *Die unbewaltigte Vergängeheit der Bundeswehr: Fünf Offiziere zur Krise der Inneren Führung.* Reinbek b. Hamburg, 1977
4. This essay is mainly based upon Jopp M. *Militär und Gesellschaft in der Bundesrepublik Deutschland: Das Beispiel der Bildungsreform in der Bundeswehr.* Dissertation Universität Frankfurt am Main 1980
5. The period from 1969 to 1974 can be declared as the 'era of reforms', a time when, after the change from the conservative to the social-liberal government, major reforms of the social and educational fields were a topic on the political agenda. Since 1974 the policy of the *Inneren Reformen* has failed because of the lack of funds which as a consequence of the economic crisis were spent for other aims. This phase furthermore can be marked by the presence or the development of emancipation movements (students', women's, citizens' initiatives), which even today are (though sometimes opposed by police) to some extent established important parts of the political culture of the Federal Republic.

6   The definition 'reformers' includes the members of the planning committees during the processes of the reform. Such instances are mainly the Bildungskommission beim Bundesminister der Verteidigung and the Institut für Erziehung und Bildung in den Streitkräften, which had to design the curricula for the officers' studies. The Bildungskommission consisted of 25 military and civilian members in nearly equal proportions and had six secretaries for support. The members of the Kommission were leading representatives of the military, trade unions and educational system as well as of the public administration and the Defence Ministry. They designed a modern training system providing civilian degrees for limited service as well as professional soldiers and pleaded for the introduction of an academic university study for officers, which caused considerable public attention.

7   See, Fliess K. *et al. Partizipation als Lernziel.* Pullach b. München, 1975 (esp. pp.9-20).

8   The following explanations of this concept are based upon Bildungskommission beim Bundesminister der Verteidigung. *Neuordnung der Ausbildung und Bildung in der Bundeswehr. Gutachten der Bildungskommission an den Bundesminister der Verteidigung.* Bonn, 1971, pp. 50, 53 and 54. The Bildungskommission had not explicitly described civilian professions as a subject of the Anleitstudium, but their inclusion can be assumed because of the formulations of the expert opinion and the reference to the recommendations of the Wissenschaftsrat in the appendix of the *Gutachten* that military as well as civilian professions were concerned. See also: Massing O. *Reform im Widerspruch.* Giessen, 1976, esp. Chapters I and II; and Arbeitsgruppe 'Anleitstudium', 'Anleitpapier 72', in Fliess *op.cit.* pp. 21-58

9   Sozialwissenschaftliches Institut der Bundeswehr, Curricula für die Hochschulen der Bundeswehr. *Aus Politik und Zeitgeschichte.* Vol. 15-16, 1974; Fliess, *op. cit.,* pp. 9-20

10   During the education reform, the Wissenschaftliche Institut für Erziehung und Bildung in den Streitkraften, founded in 1970 − 71, took over the function of developing the curricula for the officers' studies. This institute, which since 1973 has been called the Sozialwissenschaftliches Institut der Bundeswehr (SOWI) employs approximately 30 - 40 scientists, mainly civilians, and during its first years covered a broad spectrum of philosophical stances (positivism, critical rationalism, critical theory). The curricula were planned by working parties, each relating to one subject. The interpretation of the concept 'participation' differed among the working parties depending on the theoretical orientation of the group concerned. Many conflicts arose, especially in the working group attending to the planning of the general educational goals, and those planning the curricula for specified courses, but these were partly solved by the withdrawal of certain individuals.

11   The separation of the reformers into *systemkritische* and *systemimmanente* groups does not correspond to the general usage in the literature. I have chosen this separation to distinguish clearly between the two different interpretations of the reform.

12   For interpretation and conception of the goals of the reform see also: Krause H.F. *Das Konzept der Inneren Führung und die Hochschulen der*

Bundeswehr. Bochum, 1979, esp. Chapter II; for the following see also: Sozialwissenschaftliches Institut der Bundeswehr: *op. cit.*

13   For this and the following see: Fliess, *op.cit.*, pp. 10 and 17; Nahamowitz P. Militärische Systemstruktur und 'erziehungs - und gesellschaftswissens- chaftlich dimensionierte' Hochschulausbildung für Offiziere. In: Fliess, *op. cit.*, pp. 134-174; Seiz P. Curriculare, didaktische und organisatorische Aspekte zur Realisierung von erziehungs -und gesellschaftswissenschaftlich dimensionierten Fachstudiengängen. In; Fliess, *op. cit.*, pp. 175-208

14   Arbeitsgruppe 'Anleitstudium', 'Anleitpapier 72'. In; Fliess, *op.cit.*, pp. 21-58

15   Ellwein T., Müller A.v. and Plander H. (eds.) *Hochschule der Bundeswehr zwischen Ausbildungs-und Hochschulreform.* Opladen 1974, pp. 24 and 25.

16   Sozialwissenschaftliches Institut der Bundeswehr, *op. cit.*, Dillkofer H., Ellwein T. *et al.*, *Wirtschafts -und Verwaltungs-wissenschaften. Curriculum für die Hochschulen der Bundeswehr.* Opladen, 1975

17   These figures reflect the status in 1979. See *Verteidigungspolitische Information für Politik und Presse,* No. 393, 18 Jan., 1979, pp. 6 and 7.

18   Ellwein, *op.cit.*, p. 25; Opitz E. Bildung in der Bundeswehr als politische Entscheidung. Referat vor der Evangelischen Akademie Tutzing anlässlich der Tagung 'Bildung in der Bundeswehr' vom 13. -15.4. 1973. (typescript), p. 15 ff, cited in: Liebau W.E. *Akademiker in Uniform.* Hamburg-Heidelberg, 1976, pp. 29 and 30.

19   These fears were expressed by among others the deputy Generalinspek- teur. Poeppel H. Die Situation an den Hochschulen der Bundeswehr. Lecture given at the closed conference of the heads of the departments of the Defence Ministry in June 1980 (typescript), cited in the follow- ing as the 'Poeppel Report'; published in part by *Frankfurter Rundschau,* No. 166, 2 Aug., 1978

20   Der Wehrbeauftragte des Deutschen Bundestages. *Annual Report 1977.* Deutscher Bundestag, 8. Wahlperiode, Drucksache 8/1581, 6 Mar., 1978, p. 15; Bornemann J. Bundeswehrhochschulen — auf dem Weg zu einer neuen Offiziersgeneration? In: Hesslein, *op. cit.*, pp. 90-109.

21   Potyka C. Die Kollegenschelte des Professors Ellwein. *Süddeutsche Zeitung,* No. 28-29 Oct., 1978, p. 8; Leonhardt R.W. Kreuz mit den Hochschulen. *Die Zeit* No. 41, Oct., 1978, p. 4; Streitkräfte und Strategien. Norddeutscher Rundfunk, 28 Dec., 1976, programme 21.30.2200 (manus- cipt of the programme)

22   See: Jopp M., *op. cit.*

23   Mackensen U. Dann lasst uns doch Juden verbrennen. *Frankfurter Rundschau,* 29 Sept., 1977, p. 2; Arens R. Bundeswehrärffare zieht Kreise. Offiziere grölten in der Wiener Judengasse. *Westfälissche Rundschau,* 4 Oct., 1977; Potyka C. Wie Soldaten Vergangenheit bewaltigen. *Suddeutsche Zeitung,* 7 Nov., 1977.

24   For the following see: Poeppel Report; Schaefgen H. Soldat und Studium. *Europäische Wehrkunde,* Heft 2, 1979, pp. 66-74; Politisches Forum. *Norddeutscher Rundfunk,* 27 Dec., 1977, programme, 22.10; on the interpretation of the position of this conference see also: Schultz-Gerstein H.-G. Das Anleitstudium an den Hochschulen der Bundeswehr. *Aus Politik und Zeitgeschichte,* 6, 1978, pp. 15-26

25   Poeppel Report; Genschel D. Erfahrungsbericht des Leiters Studenten-bereich der Hochschule der Bundeswehr Hamburg. December 1976 (type-script, 35 pages, unpublished, in the following cited as the Genschel Report); Mackensen U. Oberst warnt vor Verschlampung der Bundeswehr-hochschule. *Frankfurter Rundschau*, 20 Jan., 1977; Schaefgen *op. cit.*, p. 70.

26   For the following see also: Schubert K.v. Ansprache des Senatsbauftragten der Hochschule der Bundeswehr Munchen für das EGA-Studium anlässlich der Gründung des Fachbereichs Sozialwissenschaften, München 14 June, 1978 (type-script, unpublished); Bülow A.v. Rede anlasslich der Gründung des Fachbereichs Sozialwissenschaften an der Bundeswehr-hochschule Munchen, 19 June, 1978, Bundeswehrhochschule: Tech-niker gingen in den Fuhrerstand, *Sozialdemokratische Sicherheitspolitik*, 6, 1978, pp. 9-12

27   Schubert *op. cit.*, also Ohne Vergangenheit in die Zukunft? *Die Zeit* No. 44, 27 Oct. 1978, p. 12

28   For the following see also: Hochschule der Bundeswehr Munchen: Ergeb-nis der Beratungen zur Angebotsstruktur und inhaltlichen Ausgestaltung der gesellschaftswissenschaftlichen Komponente des EGA-Studiums im 2. und 3. Studienjahr. Neubiberg, 6 June 1978, p. 3 (type-script)

29   Schaefgen, *op. cit.*, p. 70

30   Potyka C. Sozialwissenschaften in Neubiberg. *Süddeutsche Zeitung*, No. 16 June, 1978, p. 2; see also the commentary, Eingriff in Neubiberg, *idem*, p. 4

31   One of the six 'Anleit' subjects was tested in the Hauptdiplom exams before the new department was founded. Bülow, *op. cit.*, Schaefgen, *op. cit.*, p.69.

32   For the following see also: *Atü* (students' paper of the Hochschule der Bundeswehr München) no 1 1978, pp. 21-24; Stabenau H.J. Ein erfolgver-sprechendes Modell der Ausbildung von Offizieren fur die Durchführung von politischer Bildung in der Bundeswehr. *Atü*, No. 4 1979, pp. 33 ff. The results of this paper by Stabenau were partly published in *Atü*, No. 2, 1978, No. 3, 1978, No. 5, 1979 and No. 6, 1979.

33   Schultz-Gerstein, *op. cit.* p. 23 is of the same opinion.

34   Schaefgen, *op. cit.*, pp. 72 and 73; Bülow A.v. Die Hochschulen der Bundeswehr. *Wehrwissenschaftliche Rundschau*, 4, 1979, pp. 103-106

35   See: Bornemann, *op. cit.*, p. 102; Langner V. Hochschule oder Militärakademie? *Druck*, (students paper at the Hochschule der Bundes-wehr, Hamburg) No. 1, 1979, p. 34-39

36   Some reports in *Druck* give this impression: see Langner, *op. cit.*, and Flöge R. Offizier - Quo Vadis? *Druck*, No 3, 1979, pp. 23-26

37   Flöge, *op. cit.*, p. 25

38   Langner, *op. cit.*, ref. 35, p. 35; see also: Gross W. *Studenten in Uniform! oder: 'Der Schoss ist fruchtbar noch . . .' Ein Bericht über die Bundeswehr-hochschulen in der BRD.* Karlsruhe, 1978, p.9; Bornemann, *op. cit.*, p. 102.

39   Mark K. Die Studenten an der Hochschule der Bundeswehr. *Atü*, No. 2, 1978, pp. 84-87

40   *Druck*, No.1, 1979, pp. 40-43

41   Langner, *op. cit.*, ref. 35, pp. 35, 36

42   The extreme peculiarities of the studies at Bundeswehrhochschulen are not
      denied even by higher civil servants of the Defence Ministery. See Bülow,
      op. cit., ref., 26, p. 11; also Schaefgen, *op. cit.*, p. 72

43   This definition is used in Ennenbach W. Probleme des Studierens an der
      Hochschule der Bundeswehr. Eine psychologische Analyse. *Gruppen-
      dynamik*. Special number, 8, 1977, pp. 225-241

44   The tactics of the Head of the 'Studies' Department, Oberst Genschel, have
      after all contributed to this because he had secretly collected censures of
      students' behaviour. See: Genschel Report; Streitkräfte und Strategien.
      Norddeutscher Rundfunk, 25 Jan., 1977, programme, 21.30

45   Bülow emphasized that, the students being civil servants, they were obliged
      to study eagerly and in an orderly fashion. A delay of studies could possibly
      bring about negative consequences for their future military careers. See:
      Bülow *op. cit.*, ref. 26, p. 11; Streitkrafte und Strategien. *Norddeutscher
      Rundfunk*, 14 June 1977, programme, 21.30-22.00 (interview with v.
      Bülow). Students therefore expressed the suspicion that the studies would
      not only have the function of mediating knowledge but also of selecting the
      students. See Flöge; *op. cit.,Druck*, No. 3, 1979, pp. 23-26; Schultz-
      Gerstein, *op. cit.*, p. 23

46   Ennenbach *op. cit.*, describes the traditional patterns of socialization, p.
      225-241. Ennenbach has the opinion that elements of this pattern of
      socialization of the officers' schools still exist in the structure of the Bun-
      deswehrhochschulen.

47   For this goal political education, derivable from civil rights, see Reuter
      L.-R. Grundrechte, Staatsgrundnormen, Grundwerte — Einige Anmer-
      kungen zu den Aussagen von Grundgesetz und Länderverfassungen zum
      Verhältnis indivdueller Selbstverwirklichung und gesellschaftliche Ver-
      antwortung. In Landzsentralle für Politische Bildung, *Selbstverwirkli-
      chung und gesellschaftliche Verantwortung in einer demokratischen
      Gesellschaft*, II. Rheinland-Pfalz, December 1979, pp. 42-79

48   Partly about this problem see Schubert K.v. Bedingungen des Überlebens.
      Sicherheitspolitik und politische Moral zwischen Militärstrategie und Waf-
      fentechnik. *Aus Politik und Zeitgeschichte*, 10, 1980

49   As an example, see the analysis of the history of the procurement of the
      MRCA-Tornado in: Mechtersheimer A. *Rüstung und Politik in der Bun-
      desrepublik. MRCA-Tornado*. Bad Honnef, 1977, (esp. pp. 155-187). It is
      made clear that if it had not been for private and European political
      interests, it would have been possible to procure a cheaper and more
      suitable aeroplane.

50   Salewski M. Die bewaffnete Macht im Dritten Reich 1933-1939. *Hand-
      buch zur deutschen Militärgeschichte 1648-1939* Vol 8, part 7, pp. 183-241
      (Blomberg-Affair, Fritsch-Intrigue, Beck's withdrawal/fall)

51   Bald D. Der deutsche Generalstab 1859-1939. Reform und Restauration
      in Ausbildung und Bildung. Sozialwissenschaftliches Institut der Bundes-
      wehr, Report No. 7, Munich 1977, (esp. pp. 87-103)

52   Hesslein *op. cit.*, Hauer I. (pseud.) Wer kontrolliert die militärische
      Führung? *Vorwärts*, No. 45, 1978, p. 6

53   Massing *op. cit.*, p. 33

54   *Op. cit.*, ref. 20; Potyka C. Neue Nahrung für ein altes Thema. *Süddeutsche Zeitung* 87, 15-16 April, 1978, p. 9 and Harte Kritik an der Inneren Führung. *Süddeutsche Zeitung*, 13 Feb., 1979, p. 5; Graf v. Baudissin W. Gedanken zur Inneren Führung. In: Lutz D.S. (ed.) *Die 'Innere Führung' auf dem Weg zur dritten Gestaltungsphase?* Institut fur Friedens - und Sicherheitspolitik Hamburg Diskussionsbeiträge, 10, 1978,

55   For the following see: Gessenharter W., Fröchling H. and Krupp B. *Rechtsextremismus als normativ-praktisches Forschungsproblem. Eine empirische Analyse der Einstellungen von studierenden Offizieren der Bundeswehrhochschule Hamburg sowie von militarischen und zivilen Vergleichsgruppen.* Weinheim, Basel, 1978, (esp. pp. 1-6 and 233-262)

56   Esser M. Neofaschisten an der Hochscule der Bundeswehr? *Druck*, No. 3, 1977, pp. 19 ff.

57   This definition is used by: Potyka C. Sozialwissenschaften in Neubiberg. *Süddeutsche Zeitung*, 16-18 June 1978, p. 7

58   Bald D. Innere Führung in der Bundeswehr. *Vorgänge*, No. 33, 1978, p. 89

59   Genschel Report; Mackensen, *op. cit.* ref 25; Poeppel Report, partly published in: *Frankfurter Rundschau*, No. 166, 2 Aug., 1978; Potyka C. Gegen offene Hochschulen der Bundeswehr. *Süddeutsche Zeitung*, July, 1978, p. 5; Mackensen. Werden die Hochschulen der Bundeswehr militärisch angekettet? *Frankfurter Rundschau*, 5 July 1978; Hauer I. Die Restauration zieht ins Manoever. Bundeswehrhochschulen auf dem Rückmarsch? *Vorwärts*, No 46, 1978, p. 8; Hauer I. Die miltärische Falle schnappt zu. Widerstand gegen Reformkonzept an Bundeswehrhochschulen. *Vorwärts*, No 47, 1978, p. 8; Palmer H. Straffe Zügel an Bundeswehr-Hochschulen . *Süddeutsche Zeitung*, Nov., 1978; see also; Wagemann E. (Major-General retired): Überlegungen zum Ausbildungssystem der Streitkräfte. *Forschungsbericht* 5; Sozialwissenschaftliches Forschungs-Institut, Konrad Adenauer Stiftung, 1980

60   Together with the change in direction of December 1978, it was decided to give the military as an education mission the enlargement of disciplinary competence and personal presence. See: Nur Kurskorrektur bei den Hochschulen der Bundeswehr? *Sozialdemokratische Sicherheitspolitik* No. 10, 1978, pp. 3 ff; Potyka C. Eine Kurskorrektur mit brisanten Details. *Süddeutsche Zeitung*, 16-17 Dec., 1978, p. 4

61   *Druck*, No. 1, 1977, pp. 40 ff

15. Education for peace and disarmament: a suggested sequence of learning objectives*

Betty Reardon, *Programme Coordinator, World Council for Curriculum and Instruction*

Education for disarmament and for peace is an integrally related process. One objective cannot be separated from the other, neither pedagogically nor politically. As there is little or no likelihood of achieving peace without disarmament, there is no way to educate for disarmament without educating for peace. Failure to comprehend fully that disarmament is not an end in itself, but rather the most significant structural change among various such changes which will be required to achieve peace, has been an obstacle to the achievement of both the ultimate objective, peace and the instrumental objective, disarmament.

Such lack of comprehension of the interrelationship of these objectives may also account for the paucity of curricula on disarmament, even within programmes of peace education. The paucity is especially lamentable in that the pedagogical means to educate for disarmament have, in fact, been developed within the past two decades of efforts to build and introduce the field of peace studies into educational institutions. Indeed, it is now possible to conduct programmes of education for disarmament within the context of peace education at all levels of formal education. What is needed is the integration of existing approaches into a comprehensive and appropriate sequence of learning objectives. Such integration of existing techniques, materials and theories of peace education around the task of education for disarmament would be a significant contribution toward both objectives.

The purpose here is to sketch out a comprehensive set of learning objectives for all levels of precollegiate formal education, and to suggest the requirements for teacher education to prepare teachers to achieve the objectives. None of the suggestions is original in that all have been previously advocated and most have passed the test of practical application. In short they comprise a selection and integration of existing, workable approaches and objectives, indicating that what is advocated is possible.

*Based upon a paper prepared for Network to Educate for World Security (NEWS).

While the organizational paradigm for formal education which provides the framework for the suggestions is that of the USA, the suggestions are drawn from a variety of countries. Transnational discourse among peace educators seems to indicate that while the instructional modes may vary from culture to culture, the learning objectives are cross-culturally applicable. Indeed, it is widely agreed that education for peace must be global both in its approach and in its application.

Most peace educators also agree that the teacher is the most crucial component of the peace education process. The shaping of a world view, and the values and professional skills of teachers should, therefore, be an integral part of any programme of education for peace and disarmament. The attitudes and assumptions communicated by teachers may be more powerful than the explicit instruction they offer. Since the achievement of disarmament and peace depends upon the assumption that they are possible and practical goals, and the rapidity with which they can be achieved depends upon a widespread attitude among citizens of responsibility for their achievement, these objectives are basic to all the suggestions offered here. Early education should lay the groundwork for these attitudes and assumptions. As young people approach adulthood they should be provided with the knowledge and skills to act upon these assumptions and attitudes.

The preschool suggestions which follow are based upon the central concepts of identity, conflict and violence as the basis for an early socialization for non-violence. In the primary grades this socialization process is continued around the concepts of alternatives, values and order, intended to encourage a rational approach to conflict and a valuing of justice. At the intermediate grades the children are to be introduced to a study of cultural differences as a source of conflict, and the concepts of war as an ancient human institution and history as the unfolding of human efforts to change old habits and invent new institutions. Instruction about these concepts is intended to open their minds not only to the harsh realities of war, but to the possibilities of overcoming it.

As children grow to adolescence and enter junior high school they should be prepared to face conflict with a repertoire of resolution skills, and should be instructed in the concepts of social and political systems. They should also be introduced to cultural and ideological conflict as obstacles to overcoming war and other global problems. In senior high school where many young people receive their final educational preparation for responsible citizenship, students should be provided with instruction on the most central issues of war and peace, the arms race and problems of disarmament, the consequence of military expenditures the dangers of contemporary warfare, and the possibilities for war prevention and peace keeping. These concepts might be summarized as the war system and alternative security systems.

The teacher education needs for the implementation of these educational objectives are fairly universal. The most effective approach to meeting the needs would be a world-wide programme, bringing together non-governmental educational organizations and peace groups, in collaboration with school systems, national ministries, and international institutions such as UNESCO. A proposal for a teacher training programme is offered to meet the needs. It comprises a series of planning and development conferences, training workshops and model experimental courses. The required funds, it is hoped, would be contributed by foundations, international agencies and national governments.

Early childhood and preschool education learning objectives

Identity/self interest, conflict and violence are three concepts which young children can learn to comprehend and which should provide the basis for the earliest peace education lessons. They can also learn to understand that there are more ways than one to pursue goals. These are the basic components of education for good peer relations and getting along with others, two essential social skills for peace-making. It has been widely documented that the formation of a 'positive identity' (i.e. understanding one's racial, religious background, personal traits and characteristics and feeling good about them) and believing oneself to be a person of value, is crucial to peace education. Persons who have a sense of self-worth, it has been demonstrated, are less likely to be violent and more likely to respect the rights of others.

Through games and stories young children can be taught that each one of them is a unique and special person, both different from every one else in the world and the same, and most similar to others in basic needs. Everyone has needs and desires, like needing food and wanting toys, which they try to fulfil. Needs and desires often lead to conflict. Sometimes two or more people think they want the same thing, and there is not enough for both to have equal amounts. It can be communicated to them that satisfaction of desires may not be as much in their self-interest as learning how to resolve conflicts and settle disputes — skills they will need all their lives.

The concept of conflict can best be introduced when it occurs, such as when a dispute erupts between two children. Although small children cannot comprehend abstract ideas about reason and justice, they can learn much from the way a teacher behaves in intervening in their conflicts. By using her own authority and sense of fairness as she provides a resolution, she communicates to the children the principle of the need to seek fair solutions to conflicts. More important, she has the opportunity to demonstrate that there are several ways to settle a conflict. The idea of multiple approaches to conflict is one that can and should be communicated to children at an early age. They should also be encouraged to think of ways other than force and violence to settle disputes. As early as possible children should come to understand that violence represents the admission that imagination and creativity have failed in the face of a problem. Only through non-violence can all parties 'win'.

Violence is another concept which in its abstract sense young children cannot comprehend. However they do experience it. Some have suffered it in severe forms, such as those in Northern Ireland, Vietnam, and Cambodia and other countries torn by warfare. Many children experience physical violence in the form of child abuse or when their own conflicts lead to fighting. The learning objective for young children in regard to violence should be that it is the least desirable of the various ways of dealing with conflict, and that it is often unfair. Teachers can help youngsters to understand these ideas implicitly by the attitudes they manifest, and explicitly by helping them to see the inequities that result from fighting between children of differing strength and size. Even very small children understand what a bully is. Teachers can also help students to see that damage and suffering always result from violence. Someone (usually both parties) always gets hurt in a fight. The main point here is that instruction about violence, not just simple discipline, should be the goal of teachers of young children.

Teacher education for preschool

In order for preschool teachers to achieve these objectives they will require training in the instructional techniques to be used with the children, and they will also need education regarding the concepts involved. It is essential that teachers of young children be sensitive to their influence on a child's sense of its self-worth and be trained to work with children to develop positive identities in them. Their training should provide them with a repertoire of stories, games and other techniques for developing a sense of self-worth and respect for others. They need also to receive education in regard to children's needs, their physical and mental development and how they perceive social relations and conflicts.

All teachers need education in conflict and its resolution and in understanding particularly its causes, and how it escalates. Teachers of young children should have special training in techniques for resolving conflicts within that age group and preparation in the ways in which incidents of conflict in the learning environment can be used as the basis for teaching children about conflict and non-violent conflict resolution. Teacher education about multiple alternatives to conflict resolution should include the study of the philosophy, theory and history of non-violence as well as an overview of the fundamental principles of non-violent conflict resolution and illustrations of techniques used in all types of conflict situation.

Learning objectives for primary grades

For the primary grades the major concepts which might be taught are alternatives/choice making, values/rights, and order/fairness. Understanding these concepts is a requirement for constructive social behaviour and, therefore, for peace-making.

Teaching about alternatives and choice making can be approached in a variety of ways, such as unfinished stories for which the children make up the endings and games which involve making choices and then dealing with the consequences. It is at this age that children can understand several important facts related to peace-making. They can learn that their behaviour produces consequences and reactions, that there are in most situations several different ways to respond. Every day produces choices to be made about how they will behave in different circumstances. They can be helped to understand the need for personal and social standards to guide individual behaviour and inter-relationships, and learn that standards and consequences are criteria for choice making.

Instruction about the concepts of alternatives and choices can be based upon the earlier lessons about conflict, and serve to deepen the understanding of the need to develop a repertoire of responses. It can also be used to initiate discussion of consequences. Asking simple questions like 'what do you think might happen, if . . .' and then engaging with the children in speculating on the possible outcomes of fighting *versus* other means of dispute settlement (and many other choices children could make at this age) lays the groundwork for reasoned consideration of consequences, and for a better understanding of the costs of violence.

Introducing the concepts of values and rights as standards for choice making is the first stage of explicit education about ethics. It should be emphasized that education for peace requires sound ethical education.

Children can be taught to comprehend values by raising questions about what is important and why some things are more important than others. By explicit instruction children can be taught some fundamental lessons about human values and their relation to peace. They can be taught that people are important, that the opportunity to make choices is important, that health and learning are important. The true value that society places on people, choice, health, and learning is most strongly communicated to the children by their social environment, especially the teacher's behaviour. Children can tell very well whether or not the teacher values such things, and learn through their own experiences what the society values. Teachers often need to deal with contradictions between the values articulated in the explicit instruction of school materials and the implicit instruction of the child's experience with the real world.

Like incidents of conflict among children, these contradictions can form the basis of important lessons in peace education.

Teachers can use these incidents as well as peace education materials to instruct children in the concept of rights as the entitlement of everyone to enjoy what is important, and as a means of demonstrating what is valued. Rights can also be linked to the concepts of conflict and self-interest. Many opportunities arise to point out to children that the rights of others impose certain limits on the pursuit of self-interest, This should be done in concrete terms arising out of actual experience, such as one child wanting to recite all the time, or keeping all the crayons for his own use.

Such incidents also provide an opportunity to teach the concepts of order and fairness as the basis for the fulfilment of rights and the maintenance of harmonious group living. The class itself can be explained to the children as the group in which they live for several hours each weekday. It can provide an example to demonstrate what order is and why it is needed for harmonious group living. The idea of rules as a social need, not the inexplicable whims of adults, can also be introduced, showing how the consequences of good rules lead to more group harmony. They can also be taught that rules can and should be changed when there is a need for such change. It is upon such foundations that instruction about law to maintain order, and as a possible alternative to war for resolving international disputes can be made more meaningful later in the secondary schools.

Fairness can be introduced as a consequence of good rules and a test to see if rules are indeed good ones. In this way children have the opportunity to learn that not all rules are uniformly good, that rules in fact must be changed or new ones invented when fairness requires it. They will thus acquire a background for later instruction about law and justice and their relationship to peace.

It must be emphasized that these objectives are to be met not through abstract preaching or even careful exposition of specially designed curriculum materials. They are to be achieved mainly through the skills and style of the teacher and will come as a consequence of her own knowledge of and commitment to the concepts.

Learning objectives for intermediate grades

At the intermediate grade levels, the ages of about 10 — 13 years, children can at last be introduced to some abstractions, and are able to engage in some problem analysis. Most important, they can begin to categorize, to understand more complex similarities and differences, and to comprehend historical time and geographic space, two very important understandings for peace education. Some key learning objectives for the intermediate grades might be understanding the multi-cultural character of the human family, knowledge of the nature and purpose of war and comprehending the historical capacity to change human habits.

Although many children will have had first-hand experiences of cultural differences by the age of 10, few will have any knowledge of the variety and geographical locations of the major human cultural groups. It is customary in most schools to teach some cultural geography in the intermediate grades (grades 5—7). Schools concerned with peace education also use this instruction to communicate two basic concepts essential to developing an interest in the achievement of peace; first, that all human beings share one finite planet, and second, that all human beings are members of a single species.

These concepts reflecting the oneness of the human family should underlie instruction about cultural differences and similarities so that children will develop an attitude of respect for other cultures and solidarity with other human beings. The concepts can be made concrete by teaching about the specific human commonalities, such as basic needs, and common social customs and practices such as families and celebrations. These commonalities provide the basis for instruction about cultural differences, demonstrating how people meet common needs and engage in common types of experience in different ways. As with younger children, games (now somewhat more complex) can provide a basis for instrumentation, as can stories, art, music, and dance.

Previous instruction on self-interest, conflict and values may serve at this level for an introduction to the nature and purpose of war and its acceptance as a social institution by most cultures. Children of this age, while learning about similarities and differences, can begin to understand some of the causes of intergroup and international conflict. They can also learn about value differences as well as cultural differences. They could receive instruction about war as a means of resolving conflicts between peoples who hold different values or who are competing for the same resources or land. They might also be taught how war is conducted; that its basic method is to exhaust or destroy the enemy; that no matter the cause nor the outcome, it always results in death, destruction and much human suffering; that war is violence in its most destructive and extensive form. The idea that war often seemed the only way to overcome an evil like slavery, as well as the only means to defend interests like food supplies and liberty, can be presented to the children as a challenge, a problem for them to solve. Can they think of a better way to overcome evils and defend the interests of their country?

Children usually receive their serious history lessons at this stage, so they might be taught that the historical experience of the human family has been affected by values, by what people thought to be important.

If enough people thought some goal was very important, human beings usually achieved the goal. They can be shown films about scientific inventions and the space programme; read stories of the adventures of explorers and persons who devoted themselves to the goals of making better lives for all like the abolitionists and the defenders of human rights. The basic idea to be communicated is that people have frequently changed their institutions and ways of doing things. Throughout history human beings have achieved 'the impossible'. The students could then be challenged again with the question of whether we can overcome the problem of war. Can this goal be achieved in their lifetime? Will war be outlawed before the mid-21st century? What new forms of conflict resolution might be tried in the future? Using history as a basis for future studies is appropriate here.

Teacher education for primary and intermediate grades

In order to teach about alternatives and choice-making teachers must have a clear concept of how multiple alternatives are derived and how they can be evaluated and implemented. They also need to be trained in decision-making, so that they have a reasonably full repertoire of choice-making skills and the capacity to select and implement those appropriate to a given situation and the age level of the children concerned.

In order to communicate a sense of the ethical nature of choices among alternatives, teachers of primary grades need more background than they have at present on the subject of ethics and on the concepts and history of human rights. In addition to education in this type of subject matter, teachers should receive more rigorous training in value clarification and analysis.

Achieving understanding of the concepts of order and fairness also requires some basic philosophic training, so that the teachers themselves have a full understanding of the concepts. They need, as well. training in group process and social dynamics. If such knowledge complements that of child development, teachers of primary grades will be well prepared to lay a foundation for an understanding of and commitment to an orderly and just world society that children can begin to perceive as an alternative to the war system, and as a humanly achievable goal.

Teachers at present receive little or no education about cultures outside their own countries. they need to study other cultures and traditions in some depth. They should be given an opportunity to learn anthropology to understand better the significance of culture and the potential for conflict inherent in cultural differences, but most especially to gain insights into the very basic commonalities which exist within the human species. Anthropological studies will also help teachers to achieve a better understanding of war as a social institution.

To provide the type of instruction about war appropriate to the intermediate level, teachers need some background in conflict theory and knowledge of the causes and consequences of war. It would be helpful for them to have, as well, some knowledge of past and present suggestions for alternatives to war, and the history of efforts to achieve lasting peace.

As with the case of cultures, elementary level teachers are at present unprepared to communicate concepts related to evolutionary or institutional change as they are not sufficiently educated in history. While their training in the 'three R's' and in child development and instructional techniques for pre-adolescent children is essential to their professional success, it is not adequate for peace education. Education for peace and disarmament requires a broader preparation for teachers of the primary and intermediate grades.

Secondary schools: learning objectives for junior high school

The most useful concepts upon which to base junior high school curricula for peace and disarmament education would be conflict resolution, social and political systems and cultural and ideological conflict.

The introduction of conflict resolution offers an opportunity through which the concept of alternatives suggested for the primary grades could be reinforced and further developed. Assuming that the students at this level have come to understand that conflict is a normal part of human life, they could be introduced to the institutions human groups have devised to deal with conflict, and begin to learn that there are various modes for its resolution. Three modes which might be emphasized are war, law, and mediation and arbitration.

Instruction about war should review its history as a human institution, its purposes, most frequent causes, attempts to regulate it and the possible future of warfare. This instruction can be offered in the social sciences and humanities, particularly within the subjects of history and literature. To develop further the concept of a multicultural world suggested for the intermediate grades, the historical context should be global and the literature on war should be drawn from all cultures.

Law as an instrument for the resolution of conflict and the maintaining of social order could also be taught in the social sciences, particularly in programmes of citizenship education. Students should be taught that just as all groups have rules, as they have already learned in the primary grades, all nations are governed by some form of law as a means to maintain order, limit violence and resolve conflict within the nation. As with warfare, they should be instructed in the concept of law, its functions, limits and possibilities, and the potential of law for maintaining order and resolving disputes in a global society. Instruction might also include consideration of the similarities and differences of law as it functions in different cultural traditions. This comparative dimension can be approached by such specific subjects as how courts function in various parts of the world according to the culture and form of law.

Arbitration as another non-violent method for dispute settlement could be studied through examples of how it can be applied to conflicts at all levels of social organization from the family to the international system. Some specific techniques of conflict resolution could be taught through study of the skills and methods employed by arbitrators. The case study method would be an interesting and instructive teaching approach to this topic, especially if it permitted students to see how particular techniques can be applied under different circumstances and at various social levels.

At this stage of their development students can be introduced to some abstract concepts related to social and political systems. Such understanding is essential to learning about the present international system and the possibilities for bringing about the changes which would replace the war system with a peace system. Proposals for peace systems from over the centuries might be considered, providing as background the historical context, the assumptions about the major causes of war, and the suggested system's mechanisms for maintaining peace. A more sophisticated form of values analysis might also be introduced through an inquiry into the values which guided the planning of the various systems. Through the use of scenarios and simulations students can be introduced to the possibilities of alternative future systems.

The concept of culture in the anthropological context should form the basis of an introduction to cultural and ideological conflict. Such instruction, while building on previous learning about cultural differences, values and systems, could through problem analysis provide the basis for studying the major global problems and how these, in combination with the cultural differences and competing ideologies, combine to produce a dangerous violence-prone world. Through this medium students can also be introduced to world order values, how they relate to the global problems and how different cultures and ideologies interpret the values and the strategies they propose for achieving them.

Senior high school

At the senior high school level students must be offered fairly sophisticated instruction in the nature and dangers of the present war system and some of the practical and 'utopian' possibilities for replacing it with a peace system.

Indeed, the practical application of utopian thinking may be the most constructive aspect of peace education which can be included at the secondary level. Confronting problems, the solutions of which may require changes in systems as well as values, demands the development of creative imagination. It requires the ability to envision a set of circumstances in which the preferred values obtain in a new system which has transcended the problem. The drafting of concrete images of alternative systems is an effective way in which to think constructively about the achievement of peace. Instruction to develop this type of thinking might be organized under three conceptual categories; arms races/disarmament, warfare/human survival, and war prevention/peace-keeping.

There is no more essential content for the peace education of young adults in senior high schools than the facts about arms races. The plural is used here to indicate the degree of detail advocated for such content. It should include information about weapons development, production and sales, from the small-scale simple weapons used by terrorists to the ever escalating development of nuclear and chemical weapons and the experiments with space weaponry. Here students should learn the nature and volume of weapon sales and production, the consequences of these sales and developments in the realms of economics, politics, their actual effects on the current quality of life and the potential effects on human survival.

Students should also learn the history of and distinctions between arms control, disarmament, and general and complete disarmament. Here, too, they might study and evaluate agreements, treaties and proposals for arms control and disarmament in terms of the values and the cultural and ideological factors they learned about in junior high school. As young citizens they should be prepared to evaluate proposals and policies and learn ways in which to work for the implementation of the most promising among them. Most important, they should be disabused of beliefs about the positive effect of warfare. They should know, for example, that World War II resulted in some outcomes not so desirable as the elimination of Hitler and the invention of 'wonder drugs'. American students should be encouraged to study some of the historical research that indicates that the independence of the USA could have been won more quickly and at less cost without revolutionary violence.

These subjects could be studied through the objective analysis of materials and arguments put forth to support various positions. Their citizens' education should teach them to analyse and evaluate such materials and arguments.

Subject areas in which the topics could be introduced include economics, political science, contemporary problems, global education, science (which could include the effects of testing and use of weapons and the principles of physics upon which they were developed) and mathematics, which might include computations of the costs of the arms race and the comparative percentages of national budgets spent on military as opposed to social needs.

Another essential understanding which might be included as a major learning objective at the secondary level is the potentially horrendous consequences of warfare in the 20th century. While it is questionable whether these stark and terrifying facts should be introduced at younger ages, it is without question that everyone reaching adulthood should be aware of them. High school graduates should know the basic facts of the destructive potential of the weapons now ready for use, as well as those proposed for development. They should understand the arguments for and against deterrents, and the limits of defence against or preparation for nuclear attack. Above all, they should know all aspects of the immediate and long-range effects of the detonation of a nuclear weapon.

In addition to learning about the potential effects of nuclear war, students need instruction regarding the actual effects of conventional war. The curriculum should include information about the regular incidence of armed violence used for political purposes, and students should be made aware of the contant negative effects of current and past wars on the daily lives of millions of people. They should know who is affected and how.

Essentially this necessitates education not only through prepared curriculum materials but through the use of public information media. Students could be given this instruction while learning to read and analyse newspapers and interpret the broadcast media. Contemporary literature, art and films which depict the true human experience of warfare can also be used to present these lessons.

As schools should not omit lessons about the realities of war, neither should young adults leave their formal schooling without sufficient knowledge of efforts, proposals and possibilities for war prevention. Courses in world problems and/or contemporary issues could include units on the United Nations efforts at peace-keeping and proposals for the revision of the UN Charter to provide for the establishment of permanent peace-keeping forces. The long-neglected concepts of and proposals for non-violent peace forces and peaceful means of international conflict resolution should be introduced into the curriculum. Students should have the opportunity to study issues and proposals for economic conversion to a peace system. Most important, the curriculum should include proposals for alternative futures and world order models, based upon images of a disarmed world.

These subjects could be most effectively studied through the use of materials prepared by peace groups in various countries which have developed pamphlets, books, films and film-strips for nearly all educational settings. Teachers could use these materials for culminating exercises in the range of skills which have been emphasized throughout the peace curriculum, such as cross-cultural interpretation, system evaluation, values analysis, conflict resolution. And a new skill of model-building and strategy and action-planning for peace could be added as the final essential lesson, communicating to students that all people have a responsibility to contribute to the achievement of disarmament and peace.

Teacher education for secondary schools

The teacher preparation required for junior high school instruction in conflict resolution, social and political systems, and cultural and ideological conflict could be based upon the same fundamentals advocated for teacher preparation for the elementary grades, and might include the addition of substantive knowledge of the topics and skills development for teaching introductory systems and values analysis.

In addition to the more simple forms of interpersonal conflict resolution, junior high school teachers should have some knowledge of the modes and sources of international arbitration services. They should be given, as well, some training in the philosophy and institutional history of law and the laws of war and war crimes. They should also become familiar with workers in these three areas who could be invited to classes to share first-hand experiences with students, opening their minds to the practical and real possibilities for non-violent conflict resolution.

Teachers at this level also need more substantive education in the social and political sciences and in systems analysis. Courses in futuristics would be helpful, too, in preparing them to teach these concepts. Training in the use of simulation games would provide one means of equipping teachers to present effective instruction about political systems and processes.

To deal adequately with the topics of cultural and ideological conflict, teachers need not only the previously advocated background in anthropology, but more substantive knowledge of contemporary ideologies and how they are influenced by culture. As ideology has been identified as a major obstacle to disarmament, it is important for teachers to be able to present ideological conflict in the more objective light of anthropological and historical contexts.

While senior high school teachers will also require additional general substantive background on these topics, the most significant substantive need in teacher education for this level is the subject of general and complete disarmament and the institutional changes it would require in the international system. It is absolutely essential that teachers understand the conceptional differences and political implications among and between arms control, disarmament, and general and complete disarmament. To gain such an understanding and to develop pedagogic competence on the subject of general and complete disarmament teachers would be well served by training in the use of utopias as heuristic devices.

To be fully prepared to deal with the topic of war in the 20th century teachers should become familiar with the general field of peace research, particularly findings that reveal the full consequences of contemporary conventional warfare and the potential holocaust of nuclear warfare. It is, however, equally important that teachers be informed about present efforts and proposals for war prevention.

Secondary school teacher's preparation, therefore, should include familiarization with the various peace groups, their ideological and philosophical bases, their assumption and world views, the goals they espouse and the strategies they employ. In addition to this information, they will need to acquire skills and techniques to evaluate these proposals and to pass on their ability to their students.

Most important, all teachers need to be made aware that there is a responsible, world-wide peace movement, that it has developed an academically sound and pedagogically effective field of peace education, and that they have a responsibility to know what comprises the field, whether or not they apply it. Even this much consciousness-raising among the teaching profession would constitute a worthwhile contribution to education for disarmament and peace.

Conclusion

The intention of the suggestions outlined here is not to advocate the specific exemplar approaches as the only or the best way to educate for disarmament and peace. The main purpose is two-fold; first, through the specific examples cited to demonstrate that sufficient means now exist to establish a comprehensive, sequential programme of peace education in all educational systems, and second, to put forth one possible conceptual framework in the form of objectives which have been demonstrated to be achievable. This framework is intended as the basis for further discussions to derive more detailed, and precisely defined frameworks suitable for a variety of cultures and learning systems. The whole exercise is to demonstrate a few possibilities for peace and disarmament education in the hope that knowledge of these will inspire educators to devise and implement practical and adequate programmes.

The major requirement for implementation is education of in-service and pre-service teachers on the appropriate conceptual frameworks and in the specific skills and approaches available for classroom application. Fulfilling this requirement, which most peace educators believe to be an urgent necessity, demands the collaboration and support of all individuals and institutions involved in education. Suggested below is a brief sketch of one possible model for such a collaboration.

An implementation strategy might be built on the United Nations Decade concept, with the declaration of a Decade for Peace Education from 1982 to 1992. The decade programmes could involve governmental and non-governmental international educational organizations, national ministries of education, professional and scientific associations, and various educational institutions from the local to the global levels.

An international body such as UNESCO, in collaboration with appropriate professional and scientific organizations, could develop a plan for a series of international and national conferences, workshops and model courses. Preliminary workshops could evaluate and select portions of existing techniques and materials for achieving learning objectives for peace and disarmament education such as those outlined earlier. International conferences could agree upon some common objectives. Another series of workshops could plan their implementation, and model courses would try them out prior to broad-scale dissemination through all teacher education institutions.

International world conferences and regional workshops for elementary grades would take place in different countries from the venues of those for preschool, and those for secondary level training would be held in still other countries. The special benefits and educational impact of hosting such an international event could be received by at least 30 countries. National workshops could be held in dozens of countries and through the collaboration of the professional associations virtually all educational systems might ultimately be reached.

The suggested implementation model, like the teaching approaches, is not unique nor the only way to achieve the implementation of universal education for peace and disarmament, but it is a practical and possible way. However, like all the possibilities sketched here it requires the commitment of all educational institutions to this purpose and the commitment of resources from public as well as private funds. No better demonstration of commitment could be made than to give our full support to the suggestion of the Secretary General of UNO that one-tenth of one per cent of the funds expended for military purposes be devoted to research and education for disarmament and peace.

16. Disarmament education in the universities: the case of Finland

Helena Rytövuori, *Institute of Political Science, University of Tampere*

The purpose of this presentation is to carry out a brief survey on the extent, forms and substance of what could be called disarmament education in Finnish university curricula[1]; to take a look at the extent and ways in which research carried out in Finland on questions related to disarmament is transmitted to university education[2]; and to evaluate the results of these and put forward some ideas of the further development of the ways and means in which issues of disarmament could be included in higher level education. In the last task the UNESCO recommendation adopted at the 18th General Assembly offers fruitful points of departure, especially parts III, V (14, 18-20) and VI (26-27). However, since the articles are of a rather general nature they are not repeated here but only referred to. By disarmament education is meant education dealing with issues of or related to disarmament, arms control and the arms race in university curricula (courses and textbooks). The term 'education' is defined as the UNESCO recommendation, i.e. in a comprehensive way, implying learning with the 'object' of developing one's personal capabilities within the context and for the benefit of the national and international community (I, a).

Disarmament education may take various forms: it may be a subject on its own (as is the case in some universities in the USA), it may be included in other subjects as a separate issue-area, or it may penetrate all the teaching. In other than the university context, the subject of disarmament as a rule — and also most naturally — is taught in the context of more comprehensive peace education, the function of which is to provide a general orientation to the international environment from the aspect of peace promotion. As to the universities, research on or related to problems of the arms race and disarmament is by nature interdisciplinary. The education, however, has somewhat differing functions and emphases in those disciplines or research areas which focus on the scientific explanation of phenomena, and those areas of the curricula in which questions related to disarmament are of a more generally educational and orientative nature. In addition, the case of natural sciences is somewhat special.

To sum up, disarmament education may (1) have the function of general orientation to the international environment from the aspect of peace education; (2) it may be related to basic theoretical and methodological questions of science in general and a discipline in particular; or (3) it may play a special role from the aspect of applying a science (natural sciences).

A technical division which must be made in this context is the separation of the so-called faculty studies (common to all students in a particular faculty) and those at a disciplinary level. The function of the former is usually more orientative, whereas in the latter the approach is more often determined by the theoretical and methodological criteria of the discipline in question. Levels of study in general are divided into first, second - third and third - fifth year studies.

As to the substance of disarmament education, the function of university education in general is not merely to transfer knowledge, but also to reproduce it. For this reason, even education of a more orientative nature should consist of 'fact kits', but instead provide analytical tools for an understanding and synthesisation of the phenomena as well as for taking new approaches to 'known' things.

To aim at a problem-oriented approach might seem somewhat ambitious, taking into account the relatively modest share of what could be called disarmament education in university curricula in general. But precisely for this reason the qualitative aspect should be emphasized. People in general, and for obvious reasons university students constitute a very special group in society, seem to be tired of hearing only how many times everything living can be wiped off the earth. The more abstract security or moral approaches need to be complemented by new means of argument which make disarmament questions more concrete (e.g. social and economic costs of armaments and the arms race, conversion/transformation). Fresh approaches in general are needed to penetrate and transcend the whole logic of the arms race.

These questions could probably be integrated in higher level education more efficiently, by emphasis on problem orientation and consequently interdisciplinarity, rather than by focusing on descriptive analysis of tendencies in the arms race, disarmament and arms-control negotiations. Problem orientation, of course, presupposes a certain level of fact orientation.

In the following discussion, the questions considered include:

1. How is the division of labour between fact and problem orientation realized?

2. What disciplines at present have the main responsibility for scientific explanation of the phenomena?
3. What kinds of approach are taken to the causes of war, conflict, armaments and the arms race;
4. To what extent and how are issues of the arms race and disarmament dealt with within national and international contexts (which we argue should be the case)?
5. What is the emphasis given to the socio-economic consequences of the arms race in various disciplines?

It should, however, be kept in mind that the survey is more illustrative than aiming at complete coverage.

Disarmament education in general international studies

Studies of an introductory and descriptive nature on the structure and functioning of the international system are realized most naturally through courses or textbooks required of all students in a particular faculty. Such faculty studies, where problems of war and peace are part of a more general education and orientation to the international environment, mostly appear in the curricula of social/political science faculties. The approach is often more that of an 'international community' than that of an 'international system', i.e. the focus is on common problems of mankind, the need for cooperation and international organization. Such faculty studies dealing with the international environment have to some extent been realized or are to be realized in Helsinki, Tampere, Turku and Jyväskylä.

The substantive emphasis varies at different universities. At some, such courses (usually for first—second year students) focus more on questions of global development and underdevelopment, whereas in some other cases, and perhaps in a less problem-oriented way, the main substance is the structure and development of the international system since World War II.

At Helsinki University a basic course on development studies, concentrating mainly on questions of development and the social and cultural systems of the less developed countries, is organized by the Institute of Development Studies which is affiliated to the university. A similar course is organized at the political science faculty of Turku University. The approach seems to be somewhat more structural, focusing more on the total international system which generates development and underdevelopment. With this emphasis, wars and conflicts are dealt with in an indirect way, i.e. they are related to the concept of structural violence in the international system. The faculty studies at Turku University also include a course on the international system, focusing on the development of different socio-economic systems and also their mutual cooperation.

At the Swedish university of Turku (Aabo Akademi), a course on the international system, in which questions of cold war and detente form one part, is included in the social science department studies. In Tampere, the elementary level faculty studies have included a course on the Finnish and the international system, with textbooks such as *From the cold war to detente* and *Our common world*[3]. In a similar study section at Jyväskylä University, issues of war and peace are also primarily dealt with in the context of changes in East-West relations since World War II. The focus is, however, more on questions of technological development and ecological problems.

To sum up, in social/political faculties, issues of war and peace are mainly dealt with as part of studies of a more general and educational nature in courses for first or second year students. These problem areas are not much dealt with directly; rather they are presented in the context of either development and underdevelopment, or the development of international relations since World War II.

In the humanities there are in general no faculty studies dealing with issues related to disarmament. An exception is higher level art education (Institute of Art Industries, Helsinki), where general studies include a course on ecology, with as one theme 'expanding international cooperation and permanent peace'. As to arts subjects in general, these disciplines could surely make a greater contribution to the 'soft approach' to these questions, an approach related to culture and human philosophy.

In the economic science faculties, the 'global approach' studies usually consist of textbooks typified by Tinbergen's *New international economic order* or RIO reports. Questions of the arms race and disarmament are in general not dealt with in economics — a question which will be considered later. In this context it is also worth mentioning that the curriculum of the faculty of theology at Helsinki University, includes a relatively extensive study section on 'global problems and international responsibility', also dealing with international conflicts. (The textbook edited by the Finnish National Commission for UNESCO is also in the curriculum).

In the case of the pedagogical fields the function of dealing with issues of and related to disarmament is primarily educational but also didactive. These questions are as a rule part of a more general orientation to the international environment. Only in one case (Oulu) was there special reference to peace education and the arms race in the curriculum.

In natural sciences which have a major responsibility for the development of arms technology (sometimes the sole subject of the arms race) these issues hardly receive any attention at university level. The curricula of natural sciences in some cases include courses or textbooks on the relationship between science and society, but questions of arms development and their societal use receive no attention as such in the curricula.

As to the textbooks used in such general or faculty courses, the only one directly dealing with the arms race, arms control and disarmament is that already mentioned, *Our common world*. The book provides a relatively comprehensive introduction to the international environment for early university or pre-university education. In addition to other issues concerning the development and functioning of the international community, problems of war and peace are dealt with in a comprehensive way. These include. *inter alia,* an analysis of the concepts of structural violence, peace and security, and the relationship between armaments and development. A review of tendencies in the arms race as well as arms control measures is also made.

In the evaluation of such general and orientating studies on international systems/communities in higher level education, an important criterion is whether such studies form an isolated entity of their own (which could be due to their descriptive nature) or act as a step towards understanding and being able to explain these phenomena from the aspect of one's 'own' discipline or field of study. In other words, are the issues related to the theoretical and methodological bases of science, in the sense of explaining the phenomena.

At the level of university education, the main function of presenting these matters should not be that of 'general peace education'. Orientation to these problems should instead be instrumental in aiding further study and research. This does not mean condemning the descriptive approach as such: being already acquainted with the problem is naturally a necessary precondition for further study. Mere description, however, is not enough; at this level, impetus should be given to a further activation of minds. This also means that the approach should be as interdisciplinary as possible. Such an intention is explicitly stated in connection with the courses held at Turku University. These should 'provide the ability to understand and theoretically comprehend (the functioning of) the international system in a later phase of study' and function as 'an introduction to later studies on problems of development in different disciplinary areas.'

In the social science faculty of Tampere University, instead of the elementary level studies of the descriptive nature mentioned above, a problem-oriented course on development studies and peace and conflict research is planned for third – fourth year students. Taking into account the function of university education and the need to expand

H. Rytövuori

the interdisciplinary bases of these research areas, this can be considered a major improvement. However, since the course held previously is now to be omitted, it may be wondered if the students can be introduced to problem-oriented and scientific research of these phenomena if they do not have sufficient information on the international system in a more general sense. It can, of course, be supposed that it is a task of pre-university education to provide the latter.

A preferable structure of studies would consist of first, orientation to the structures and functioning of the international system, including, among other things, issues of the arms race and disarmament, with not only a descriptive, but rather a problem-posing approach; secondly, an introduction to peace and conflict research, related to the basic theoretical and methodological questions of a group of sciences; proceeding finally to the aspect of a particular discipline or research area. Division of labour between these 'steps' may take various forms; the main thing is that both ends of the continuum are taken into account. The extent of the scientific aspect naturally has differing emphases in different disciplines. As is indicated below, attention paid to these problems is very much concentrated on a few disciplines.

Issues of disarmament at the disciplinary level

At this level, problems of war and peace naturally have to be approached from the criteria of a particular discipline or research area. As part of the substance of the science, problems of war and peace are mainly dealt with in history and social sciences.

In history (general and political) there has been some research interest in problems of the arms race and disarmament, although the history of war, conflict and powerful states clearly dominates the approaches. This is a natural historical outlook since the approach of peace is still young. (In Finland peace research only began to develop in a more active way in the early 1970s.) Only in the case of Helsinki University is one section of the general history curriculum called 'History of War and Peace'; in other cases the titles are 'History of International Crises and Conflicts' (Oulu), 'History of International Conflicts' (Turku, Tampere, Joensuu) or simply 'History of War' (Jyväskyla). In some cases such studies are obligatory, in others optional alternatives. In Helsinki the studies are of *approbature* (general) level, in other cases of *cum laude* (honours) level.

The 'peace approach' is most advanced in the case of Helsinki University. Although this has to be considered a major improvement, the situation at the same time seems to remain strangely schizophrenic: on the one hand the history of war (strategies and tactics) can be studied; on the other 'peace thought in history' can be chosen. More comprehensive approaches are planned in order to integrate these ambivalent aspects (e.g. by taking a historical aspect of war and its consequences in society). At Helsinki University, courses in general history have included peace education, peace movements, Middle East problems, war and society ('practicum on peace research') as alternative options at *cum laude* level.

In a more general sense any structurally oriented approach seems naturally enough to be better integrated in the studies of the history of colonialism and neo-colonialism. Problems of war and peace are approached more from the aspect of the behaviour and political interaction of dominant states. Literature on for example the history of the Third World has been on the increase, but especially in lectures (excluding the Helsinki case mentioned above) the interpretation of history which seems to dominate is based on power politics.

This approach is even more obvious in *political history* from which it originates. In the curricula studies of war and peace are usually included in international politics, concentrating mainly on international relations since World War II. The approaches typical of political history may perhaps be roughly characterized by mentioning some textbooks: e.g. Hinsley's *Power and pursuit of peace: theory and practice in the history of international relations* and Kahn's *On escalation*[15].

The traditional approach of power politics is naturally well presented in the field of international politics. However, approaches of this orientation seem to be less dominant in a general sense. In other words, power politics are more explicitly articulated as a particular tradition based on certain assumptions (the anarchic nature of the international system, states by nature engaging themselves in the pursuit of power, state behaviour based on national interest, armaments and the use of force as an instrument of foreign policy). To discern some basic features is not to deny the fact that the tradition comprises a rather heterogeneous set of approaches.

In the basic courses held in international politics, issues related to the arms race and arms control as a rule form an essential part. The extent to which these problems are taken up varies, sometimes including a thorough examination of tendencies in the arms race, disarmament and arms control measures, the arms trade, the role of military R and D activities, and also theoretical approaches to the phenomena of the arms race, conflict and war. In some cases (e.g. at Tampere) a section on peace research is also included in the course.

The standard textbook is in most cases Dougherty-Pfaltzgraff's *Contending theories of international relations,* which includes a section on conflict theories. In addition to this, the previously more popular work by Holsti, *International relations,* is in use at Helsinki and at Tampere. The textbooks used for studies on peace research and security policies

Table 1.

Level	University				
	Helsinki	Turku	Tampere	Oulu	Jyväskylä"*
1st year	Wiberg, H. *Konflikteori och Fredsforskning (Conflict Theory and Peace Research)*				
2nd-3rd year	Thee, M.(ed.) *Armaments and Disarmament in the Nuclear Age.* SIPRI OR Ruhala. *Security Policies of Foreign Policy and Strategy in the Nuclear Age.* Articles on European Security and Cooperation	Wallensteen, P. *Structure and War* (alternative)	Buchan, *The End of Post-War Era* Wiberg, H.† *Konflikteori och fredsforskning.* Alternative topics: social consequences of war; arms race and disarmament‡	Galtung, *Ar fred möjlig (Is Peace Possible)*	Galtung, *Ar fred möjlig* OR Senghaas, *Imperialismus und Strukturelle Gewalt.* Thee, M. *Armaments and Disarmament in the Nuclear Age.* SIPRI

3rd-5th year	Wallensteen, P. Structure and War	Dencik (ed.) Fred, våld, konflikt (Peace, Violence, Conflict) OR Schelling. The Strategy of Conflict Dedring, Recent Advances in Conflict and Peace Research	Green. Deadly Logic – the Theory of Nuclear Deterrence OR Gretcho. The Armed Forces of the Soviet Union Galtung. Strukturelle Gewalt (alternative)

* Jyväskylä University has already implemented a new study and curriculum system omitting the *approbatur – cum laude – laudatur* phase division.

† To be placed in 3rd year faculty studies (the course mentioned on p.0).

‡ E.g. following books may be chosen: Urlanis, *Wars and Population*; The UN Report of the Secretary-General on the Economic and Social Consequences of Arms Race; Pfaltzgraff. *Contrasting Approaches to Strategic Arms Control*; International Detente and Disarmament, Contributions by Finnish and Soviet scholars. Tampere Peace Research Institute 1977.

H. Rytövuori

are presented in Table 1.

As to the lectures, these are basically of two types. First, it seems that recent research carried out on specific issues (by the lecturer) has considerable influence on the subject. Secondly, lecturers have been held on the arms race and disarmament in particular. This pattern is in accord with observations based on a survey of Finnish research on issues related to the arms race, arms control and disarmament. Väyrynen concludes that although the research in Finland is relatively extensive, the nature of it is at the same time somewhat fragmented: viable and systematic research has been carried out on specific issues, whereas studies with a more comprehensive coverage are few[4].

The fact that research interests in Finland have to a considerable extent concentrated on relations between the major powers, in particular from the aspect of European security, can also be discerned in university education and teaching. Although the interest in for example Third World militarization and attempts to relate tendencies in armaments to the structure of the international system have been on the increase, such approaches have not been implemented more generally in research or teaching.

In other social sciences the share of anything that could be called disarmament education is negligible. In sociology and similar fields issues related to the arms race and disarmament internationally seem to be in a secondary position[5]. In Finland the input of sociological and sociologically oriented research has also been a minor one, excluding perhaps some studies of public opinion on the arms race and disarmament as strategies of security policy, and on the level of information concerning these issues in general[6].

In some cases the curricula of sociology (mainly at Helsinki University) and more particularly in social policy, have given more attention to problems of global development and underdevelopment in recent years. This does not, however, seem to have been related to issues of armaments and the arms race. The contribution of sociology and similar disciplines would indeed be needed for concrete national analyses on the internal factors generating the arms race, e.g. structural explanations (the military/industrial complex etc), bureaucratic politics and impacts of technological development, as well as on the internal conditions and restraints of disarmament policies.

In international law, the treaties and resolutions on disarmament and arms control measures as well as the norms applied in war and conflict situations form essential objects of study and research. The textbooks on international organization as a rule also deal with the role of the UN in the field of disarmament and arms control. An interest in problems of disarmament and arms control from a judicial point of

262

view, mainly from the aspect of the international law of treaties, has been taken in Finland since the early 1960s. These issues seem to be somewhat better presented at the Turku universities (Finnish and Swedish) than in Helsinki where the approach also seems to be more strictly judicial.

In arts subjects, e.g. in the field of philosophy, the roots of arms-based security thinking could be dealt with. In the final analysis, the whole construction of the seemingly sophisticated logic arguing for arms-based security and increased armaments relies on simplistic assumptions, (especially in the nuclear age) of the anarchy of the international system, endless pursuit of power by states and the evil nature of man. In order to present alternative security models, we need to transcend the logic of arming as an end in itself.

In this context the faculty of theology at Helsinki University might be mentioned, where lectures on the theme of pioneers of peace research have been held in the field of religion, philosophy and ethics. The lectures have dealt with ethics and politics in the thinking of Emmanuel Kant and Friedrich Hegel from the aspect of peace problems[7].

The case of journalism and journalism training is again somewhat special in the sense that issues related to the arms race and disarmament have a more generally orienting function here. The approach is not, however, merely educational, but rather that of learning to analyse the problems. As 'educators' journalists, of course, have a major responsibility for creating public opinion and the general approach of readers to the international environment. At Tampere University, the curriculum includes courses on 'Information in the service of peace and international understanding' and 'Global problems and communication'. Seminars are also occasionally held on communication issues related to disarmament. In other cases, and especially at lower level journalist training, such studies are generally lacking or only occasional.

In economics the interest taken in the waste of mankind's resources is almost nil. In view of the international research interest paid to these issues from the late 1950s, this is somewhat surprising[8]. The fact that the resources used for armaments in Finland in comparison with many other states, are of no major significance may have contributed to the lack of interest. Also, global or structurally oriented approaches in general seem to have challenged the liberal tradition of economic theory little in Finnish universities, the outstanding exception being the Swedish university in Turku. The emphasis in general is on liberal micro-economics, i.e. on the healthy functioning of firms producing arms, than on the socio-economic consequences of this activity. The more globally oriented approach and critique of traditional approaches has, however, been increasing, and textbooks by Tinbergen, Myrdal or Szentes have been included in the curricula. The only case to our knowledge in which the issues of the arms race and disarmament are touched on in economics is at Joensuu, where the book edited by the Finnish National Commission for UNESCO has been included in the elementary level national economics curriculum. Needless to say, in questions related to the conversion of arms industries into civil production, the contribution of economists would be essential.

In natural sciences the case of the Institutes of Radio- and Organic Chemistry at Helsinki University are somewhat exceptional in the sense that the research project on controlling the use of chemical weapons, financed by the Foreign Ministry of Finland and led by Professor Miettinen, has its impact on higher level education. The subject is not included in regular curricula, but has been integrated into the project, as a result of which theses from seminar papers to PhD level have been produced on the subject.

Conclusion

Special emphasis must be laid on the substantial aspect of disarmament education and teaching. At the university level, the solutions cannot be only institutional and quantitative, although sufficient resources certainly are an important condition for the fulfilment of the qualitative requirements.

In the generally oriented faculty courses held at some universities, issues of the arms race and disarmament are not much dealt with as such, but are discussed in the general context of East-West relations or are related to problems of development. In order to relate studies at this level to further study and research there is a need for problem orientation. It seems that this aspect can better be discerned in the courses dealing with development problems (where questions of the arms race are secondary), whereas in courses dealing with the international environment in general (in which questions of the arms race and disarmament are one part) the approach tends to be more descriptive and consequently not instrumental for further study within a particular discipline.

In various disciplines, issues dealing with the arms race, arms control and disarmament are primarily dealt with as a separate part of international relations in the curricula of history (general and political) and international politics. In history the 'peace approach' is relatively advanced in one case, but as a somewhat odd alternative to the 'war approach'. Explaining these phenomena by anything of a more complicated nature than the mere behaviour of states is by and large the field of international politics and peace research. These two cannot in many cases can be distinguished from one other, the latter also being presented in the context of the former in the curricula[9].

Partly due to the dominant position of approaches oriented towards power politics and focusing on the behaviour of states, issues of the arms race, arms control and disarmament have to a large extent been dealt with at the level of state interaction. Another contributory factor has been the fact that in courses oriented more towards peace research, descriptive and case type approaches have increased as a result of interest taken in current arms control measures and negotiations.

Different explanations of the origins of war and conflict are relatively well presented in the curricula of international politics (previously textbooks like Rapoport's *Conflict in man-made environment* and Waltz's *Man, the state and war* have been in use). What seems to receive considerably less attention, although it cannot clearly be separated from the causes, is the dynamics of the arms race, related to structures at both national and international levels.

In regard to all the disciplines, an even more apparent defect concerns study of the consequences of the arms race at various levels and dimensions. The lack of interest among economists in these questions has already been pointed out. As to the sociological viewpoint, it seems that the interest paid to this problem has in fact diminished since the 1960s in sociology and similar fields (and not all the sociologists were recruited to peace research).

Dealing with issues of the arms race and disarmament as a single field of international relations is to encapsulate the problem area, in fact, to forget that it has a multidimensional aspect, solutions to which cannot be found in international fora. Similarly, having peace and conflict research only presented as one specific research area within international relations is quite unsatisfactory and also, in fact, a somewhat strange state of affairs. As to the general context of detente, not underestimating it as such, this is far too fragile a framework to be alone responsible for disarmament arguments. (Furthermore, detente has also been interpreted as a means to legitimize armaments.)

In the final analysis, traditions in western political thinking do not have much to offer other than the power-politics model to explain armaments and conflicts. Perhaps even more so than in research, in education and in influencing public opinion, peace research still has to challenge this approach. To quote Spanier:

> To attribute wars to arms is to confuse cause and effect. An arms race does not obey a logic of its own . . . Military power serves the political ends of the state . . . Why then, besides the fundamental reason of seeking a power advantage, do states pursue disarmament? A second reason is propaganda.

Disarmament is like motherhood, the flag, and apple pie. Who can be against such things?[10]!

This short quotation does not do justice to Spanier's work but is nevertheless illustrative. Although it is true that the arms race cannot be divorced from the political context in which it occurs, and capabilities and structures cannot be separated from intentions and actors, it is much too simplified to attribute all this to behaviour at state level. Here peace research, with its focus on the internal mechanisms or invented external causes, has a contribution to make.

The approaches which are cited above could hardly be instrumental in promoting attitudes favourable to peace strategies and disarmament. On the contrary, they create assumptions of a deterministic development of the history of mankind which it would be naive to try to influence. In order to activate interest in and study of questions related to the arms race, disarmament and conflict phenomena in general, the interdisciplinary nature of the field needs to be strengthened. From the more specific point of view of research, the role of which is to develop new tools for reliable argument, this is even more important, and for this, again, university education and teaching are the most efficient means in the long run.

To present disarmament as an isolated issue area is to miss the point and also to leave unused the cumulative effects offered by higher level education. An important 'joint point' in university education is an introductory course on peace and conflict research for a group of disciplines having a somewhat similar theoretical and methodological framework. In the first phase, this could also offer a realistic starting point.

Notes and references

1. The information on disarmament education is based on the curricula of the academic year 1979-80.
2. See bibliography edited by Väyrynen, Tampere Peace Research Institute, Research Reports, 7/1977.
3. Yhteinen maailma, Suomen UNESCO-toimikunta. Espoo 1979 (Author's translation).
4. Väyrynen *op cit.*, p.12
5. *Ibid.*, p.3
6. *Ibid.*, pp.11 and 42-43
7. The lectures have dealt with Kant E. *Zum ewigen Frieden* and the critique of this by Hegel.
8. See also Väyrynen, *op. cit.*, pp.4 and 13.
9. In the Finnish universities there is no chair of peace research.
10. Spanier J. *Games nations play*, 3rd ed., New York, 1978 pp.315-8.

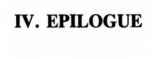

IV. EPILOGUE

17. Disarmament education: a partial answer

Johan Galtung, *United Nations University Project, Geneva*

The problems and the efforts to come to grips with the arms race through educational measures reported in this volume, are both very impressive. Today, we know perfectly well, or at least we ought to know, that it is within the human capacity to commit collective suicide. It is as if a giant, grossly mentally disturbed, is stumbling towards the suicidal brink. Is he able to stop before he reaches it, and even turn back? Is enlightenment, through education, the answer?

Partially, yes. But to press the analogy a little further, it is not that the suicidal candidate wants to leave life; it is usually because all alternatives seem even worse. This corresponds to the situation of humankind today: nobody, we are told, *wants* that big war capable of eradicating everybody, or at least not those of us living within and in the shadows of the superpowers. It is rather that no alternatives to armament and the arms race are seen, even knowing that the probability is high that an arms race leads to a war.

Hence, I am convinced that disarmament education cannot consist only of the tale of the horrors of a war and the enormous opportunity costs of the arms race. It must also contain at least two other messages:

1. a positive praise of life, an image of how beautiful life can be, what a gift peace is when it is real and not based on the threat of a future war;
2. an alternative to military armament as it is known today.

On this second point, fundamentally there is no substitute for solving a conflict if the conflict is real. Disarmament will not help if the conflict still remains: armament will only blossom as never before if the conflict takes on more sinister forms. Correspondingly, if there is no conflict, disarmament may not be strictly speaking necessary: there are many nations geographically neighbours which are very well armed yet do not go to war with one other simply because they have no reason to do so (Norway and Sweden being an obvious example). On the other hand, arms *are* costly and they *are* risky — but one should not exaggerate the peace building function of a disarmed world.

Even in such a world there will be conflicts, as there will always be as long as there are human beings in the world. That is not the problem: the problem is how to solve the conflicts without recourse to war, which ultimately introduces more conflict than it solves. This is not the occasion to go into detail, but if anything should be taught in school in this field then it would be the whole theory and practice of conflicts, how to understand them, how to handle them. One might even talk about *conflict imagination* as something to be developed. A much larger reservoir of people around the world who are capable of handling conflict constructively, would provide for peace what a reservoir of people capable of handling natural science problems constructively has been to economic and technical development.

However, regardless of how large an untapped reservoir there is for more creative approaches to conflict, the fact remains that efforts to dominate others through attack and conquest are hard to separate from the human condition. Hence, there is a need for what is conventionally called 'defence'. But for any move to be purely defensive it must be made in such a way that it has no provocative effect, that nobody in any way can feel threatened by it. For that to happen it should only be operational on one's own territory; it should even be meaningless outside that territory.

There are three forms of resistance that satisfy these requirements today, and it is hard to see what disarmament education can do without a thorough dialogue about their potential and actual usefulness. First, there are the softer forms of conventional military defence, on the ground, in the air, at sea. By 'soft' is meant, roughly that defence which is incapable of penetrating adversary territory. In other words, it is a border defence, equipped with ordinary weapons, not weapons for mass destruction and retaliation, even genocide and ecocide.

Second, there are the various forms of guerrilla activity. They are violent, and their effectiveness has been thoroughly tested in the period post World War II. This is capable of defeating big powers, even superpowers as shown, for example, by Mao Zedong.

Third, there are the various forms of non-military defence, such as non-cooperation, civil disobedience, positive action; forms associated with another of the giants of our century, Mohandas Gandhi. Their effectiveness is much higher than is commonly believed, as this is the normal way of counteracting dominance and repression — so normal that it usually passes unnoticed.

These three together constitute a type of defence that is neither provocative nor very costly. Obviously, they do not constitute a panacea in the sense of being capable of solving all defence problems: an enemy determined merely to destroy with some nuclear weapons could eliminate anyone within the active radius of the bomb. Our future is based on the hope that such powers are few and far between in human history and that the 20th century has already had its quota, since powers of that kind might also be tempted to use their weapons even at the risk of being obliterated themselves, simply because of the temptation to succeed with a first strike.

Disarmament education should therefore focus on conflict resolutions and alternative concepts and practices of defence. This means that the question of what offers a trustworthy defence in the case of war needs to be answered. Both pacifistic 'non-military defence' and militaristic 'military defence' are today sterile slogans. A mixed defence based on conventional forces, guerrilla forces and non-military components would be much stronger. The conventional defence could have as its task to serve in the front line. If it were defeated, the guerrilla defence and also the non-military defence would come into the picture as the normal forms. These would be effective even against occupation by superpowers and would be fundamental as a deterrent to convince possible opponents that a capitulation would only involve one of the three forms of defence, viz. the conventional part, and that the other two defence forces would continue. Such a defence would be a success on the day that a hostile power thinks 'this country would give me so much of a headache if I should try to occupy it, because they would never give in, that perhaps I should leave it alone'. A defence solely based on an easily defeated conventional force alone followed by total capitulation is an invitation to those who are militarily more powerful.

Such a mixed defence might be planned in terms of some form of division of labour in time (the conventional force would fight first, then the others), and space (conventional defence would be more strategic in non-populated but important areas, whereas the other two forms might be more important in the rest of the nation). The non-military defence would depend upon social imagination and energy: every municipality and small town, every firm, every farm, every factory would have a special defence plan, as of course would the central administration. And the same would be applicable to every organization, every branch of the trade unions, every association. In countries with a strongly built organizational apparatus this would be an enormous force, as was exemplified by the growth of the non-violent movement against the nazification of Norway during the German occupation.

What can and should be done now is at least to think in alternative ways about our concepts of defence. This thinking needs to be done at all levels so that it can grow out of the social imagination of all people as well as the official authorities. Not to do this is in reality a crime because it leaves a country defenceless if it should be pressured into capitulation. Only the enemies of defence can defend such an attitude. To begin such an educational effort would be to realize new defence forces going beyond those now existing.

Without a strong peoples' movement concerning defence problems, new signals of importance will not come to fruition, because the politicians are too often stuck in traditional concepts. *Military policy must be politicized.* It needs to be discussed with open minds: to be able to allow room for new opinions without becoming hysterical, to avoid an information monopoly in small expert circles, to call on social imagination and creativity. It is a tragedy that defence policy is discussed in such an undemocratic way as is the case in most countries, even when the purpose is to defend democracy.

This is an example of what disarmament education leads to when taken seriously: it leads beyond disarmament. Armaments are like the drug which pushes the suicidal candidate deeper and deeper into the abyss. What is needed is not a drug, but to give him — us — the wish to live fully and richly again.

Appendix: Extract from *Report and Final Document,* World Congress on Disarmament Education, UNESCO, SS-80, CONF. 401 REV/COL. 51

The last plenary meeting adopted the following Final Document by consensus, it being understood that certain stylistic improvements and modifications based on observations and proposals made during the final session would be incorporated into the final version by the Secretariat in consultation with the President and the General Rapporteur of the Congress. The Final Document contains: (A) Guiding principles and considerations for disarmament education, and (B) Recommendations addressed to the Director-General.

II. Final document of the congress

The World Congress on Disarmament Education, convened by the Director-General of Unesco and meeting at Unesco Headquarters in Paris from 9 to 13 June 1980, in accordance with resolution 3/2.1/1 adopted by the General Conference at its twentieth session.

1. *Deeply concerned* by the lack of real progress towards disarmament and by the worsening of international tensions which threaten to unleash a war so devastating as to imperil the survival of mankind,

2. *Convinced* that education and information may make a significant contribution to reducing tensions and to promoting disarmament, and that it is urgent to undertake vigorous action in these areas,

3. *Taking into account* the Final Document of the Tenth Special Session of the General Assembly and in particular paragraph 106, according to which the General Assembly urged governments and governmental and non-governmental organizations to take steps to develop programmes of education for disarmament and peace studies at all levels, and paragraph 107, according to which the General Assembly welcomed the holding of this Congress and urged Unesco to step up its programme aimed at the development of disarmament education as a distinct field of study,

4. *Bearing in mind* other pertinent resolutions of the General Assembly, such as resolution 34/75 according to which the General Assembly declared the decade beginning in 1980 the Second Disarmament Decade, and resolution 33/73 by which the General Assembly adopted the Declaration on the Preparation of Societies to live in Peace,

5. *Considering* resolution 11.1 adopted by the General Conference at its twentieth session concerning the role of Unesco in genera-

ting a climate of public opinion conducive to the halting of the arms race and transition to disarmament,

6. *Considering* further the Declaration on fundamental principles concerning the contribution of the mass media to strengthening peace and international understanding, to the promotion of human rights and to countering racism, apartheid and incitement to war, adopted by the General Conference at its twentieth session (1978),

7. *Desiring* to promote the implementation of the Recommendation on Education for International Understanding, Co-operation and Peace and Education Relating to Human Rights and Fundamental Freedoms, adopted by the General Conference at its eighteenth session (1974),

8. *Recalling* the Expert Meeting for the preparation of the World Congress on Disarmament Education held in Prague, Czechoslovakia, on 4-8 June 1979 at the invitation of the Czechoslovak Socialist Republic.

A. Believes that disarmament education should be guided by the following principles and considerations.

Relation of education to disarmament
1. Disarmament education, an essential component of peace education, implies both education about disarmament and education for disarmament. All who engage in education or communication may contribute to disarmament education by being aware and creating an awareness of the factors underlying the production and acquisition of arms, of the social, political, economic and cultural repercussions of the arms race and of the grave danger for the survival of humanity of the existance and potential use of nuclear weapons.

Definition of disarmament
2. For the purposes of disarmament education, disarmament may be understood as any form of action aimed at limiting, controlling or reducing arms, including unilateral disarmament initiatives, and, ultimately, general and complete disarmament under effective international control. It may also be understood as a process aimed at transforming the current system of armed nation States into a new world order of planned unarmed peace in which war is no longer an instrument of national policy and people determine their own future and live in security based on justice and solidarity.

Role of information
3. Disarmament education requires the collection and dissemination of

reliable information from sources offering the highest degree of objectivity in accordance with a free and more balanced international flow of information. It should prepare learners, in the strictest respect for freedom of opinion, expression and information, to resist incitement to war, military propaganda and militarism in general.

Relation to economic and political realities
4. Disarmament education cannot, however, confine itself to the dissemination of data and information on disarmament projects and prospects nor even to commenting on the hopes and ideals which inspired them. It should recognize fully the relationship disarmament has with achieving international security and realizing development. To be effective in this regard, disarmament education should be related to the lives and concerns of the learners and to the political realities within which disarmament is sought and should provide insights into the political, economic and social factors on which the security of peoples could be based.

Research and decision-making
5. In addition to reaching the general public, disarmament education has a more specific and equally crucial task of providing rational arguments for disarmament based on independent scientific research which can guide decision-makers and, to the extent possible, rectify perceptions of a potential adversary based on incomplete or inaccurate information.

Substantive approaches
6. As an approach to international peace and security, disarmament education should take due account of the principles of international law based on the Charter of the United Nations, in particular, the refraining from the threat or use of force against the territorial integrity or political independence of States, the peaceful settlement of disputes, non-intervention in domestic affairs and self-determination of peoples. It should also draw upon the international law of human rights and international humanitarian law applicable in time of armed conflict and consider alternative approaches to security, including such non-military defence systems as non-violent civilian action. The study of United Nations efforts, of confidence-building measures, of peace-keeping, of non-violent conflict resolution and of other means of controlling international violence take on special importance in this regard. Due attention should be accorded in programmes of disarmament education to the right of conscientious objection and the right to refuse to kill. Disarmament education should provide an occasion to

explore, without prejudging the issue, the implications for disarmament of the root causes of individual and collective violence and the objective and subjective causes of tensions, crises, disputes and conflicts which characterize the current national and international structures reflecting factors of inequality and injustice.

Links with human rights and development

7. As an integral part of peace education, disarmament education has essential links with human rights education and development education, in so far as each of the three terms peace, human rights and development must be defined in relation to the other two. Moreover, disarmament education offers an occasion to elucidate emerging concepts such as the individual and collective rights to peace and to development, based on the satisfaction of material and non-material human needs.

Pedagogical objectives

8. Whether conceived as education in the spirit of disarmament, as the incorporation of relevant materials in existing disciplines or as the development of a distinct field of study, disarmament education should apply the most imaginative educational methods, particularly those of participatory learning, geared to each specific cultural and social situation and level of education. It aims at teaching *how* to think about disarmament rather than *what* to think about it. It should therefore be problem-centred so as to develop the analytical and critical capacity to examine and evaluate practical steps towards the reduction of arms and the elimination of war as an acceptable international practice.

Values

9. Disarmament education should be based upon the values of international understanding, tolerance of ideological and cultural diversity and commitment to social justice and human solidarity.

Sectors of society concerned

10. Disarmament education should be the concern of all sectors of society and public opinion. Indeed, schools, non-formal and informal education circles such as the family, community organizations and the world of work, universities and other research centres and information media, all have a part to play in this task. Educators and communicators should strive to develop the most appropriate and effective language and teaching methods for each situation. The challenge is all the greater as the stakes are so high.

B. The World Congress on Disarmament Education, *Considering* that in this initial year of the Second Disarmament Decade special impetus should be given to the development of disarmament education, Accordingly *requests* the Director-General to:

(a) set out, on the basis of the aforementioned principles and considerations, elements to be included in the Declaration of the 1980s as the Second Disarmament Decade aimed at making disarmament education one of the vital means of achieving the objectives of the Decade, and transmit them to the United Nations Secretary-General for submission to the General Assembly at its thirty-fifth session;

(b) encourage initiatives designed to make adequate funds available for the significant development of disarmament education, by supporting, *inter alia,* the suggestion of the United Nations Secretary-General that one-tenth of one per cent of military spending should be devoted to national and international efforts in favour of disarmament, including disarmament education and information;

(c) strengthen social science research activities on disarmament, peace and international relations with a view, *inter alia,* to improving education and information programmes in these fields, in collaboration with the United Nations, in particular with the Centre for Disarmament and the Institute for Disarmament Research, with national and international research bodies, and with appropriate non-governmental organizations;

(d) investigate the possibility of drawing up standard clauses whereby States parties to arms control or limitation agreements would undertake, on the one hand, to foster the dissemination of the instrument in question and, on the other, to promote, to the greatest possible extent, and by appropriate means, disarmament education in general;

(e) examine, in collaboration with the Secretary-General of the United Nations, the possibility of setting up a United Nations-Unesco Radio Station, to provide information and to promote the objectives of the United Nations relating, *inter alia,* to disarmament, human rights and development;

(f) draw up, on the basis of the work of the Congress, a detailed, phased action plan, on the understanding that this plan will coincide with Unesco's next Medium-Term Plan.

For the purpose of implementing this final recommendation, the Congress took note of the recommendations contained in the working papers and of the points proposed by the rapporteurs of the commissions on the bases of suggestions submitted by the participants and observers.

About the authors

Robert Aspeslagh. Born in Indonesia 1940. Taught history and geography at secondary school (1965-1975); and since 1975 has worked at the Netherlands Institute for Studies on Peace and Security as a peace educator. Council member of the Peace Education Commission (1977-79); member of the Dutch National UNESCO Commission (1978), council member of the Dutch Association for Studies on Peace and Conflict (1979); executive secretary of the Peace Education Commission (1979).

Elise Boulding. Holds Chair of Sociology Department, Dartmouth College; member of the Program Advisory Council of the UN University's Human and Social Development Program; member of US Commission on Proposals for a National Academy of Peace and Conflict Resolution. Former editor IPRA newsletter; organizing secretary and first chairperson, CORPED. Publications: *The underside of history: a view of women through time.* Westview Press, 1976. *Children's rights and the wheel of life.* Transaction Press, 1979. *Bibliography on world conflict and peace,* (with R. Passmore and S. Gassier), Westview Press, 1979.

Birgit Broch-Utne. Born 1938, lecturer at the Institute of Educational Research, University of Oslo, Norway. *Cand. polit.,* University of Oslo and MA, University of Illinois. Chairperson, Norwegian Educational Research Association (1974-75), council member, Nordic Society of Educational Research (1975-81). Recent publications are two books on educational action research, and on women as teachers and pupils (with R. Haukaa), University Press, Oslo 1979 and 1980.

Robin Joan Burns. PhD, La Trobe University, Melbourne, lecturer in that university's Centre for Comparative and International Studies in Education since 1973, following three years as member of Australian Diplomatic Service. International officer (1966-75) and member of the international executive (1972-74), World University Service in Australia, executive committee member, Peace Education Commission, International Peace Research Association (1979 to date). Numerous publications on development education and cultural studies.

Narayan Desai. Spent his first 20 years with Gandhi, taught for 7 years in rural Gandhian school, walked 8000 miles collecting and distributing landgifts before joining Indian Peace Army. As General Secretary of National Peace Committee he mobilizes and trains peace-volunteers. Has written numerous books including *Towards a nonviolent revolution* and *Handbook for Satyagrahis.*

Jaime Diaz. Born 1932, founder and Director of Corporation for Social and Cultural Development. Bogota, Colombia, a non-profit civilian organization dedicated to education for justice and peace in Latin America, executive committee member, Peace Education Commission, International Peace Research Association, Vice President Elect, World Council for Curriculum and Instruction. Numerous writings on education for peace and justice in Latin America.

Antonino Drago. Has been active in many grass-roots movements in Naples, particularly those involving informal education, and has written many papers on them. Engaged in the practice of and theoretical reflection about non-violence and peace research. Member of Italian branch of IFOR and of Italian Peace Research Institute (IPRI), Naples. MSc in physics; assistant professor of History of Physics, University of Naples: papers cover foundations of science and the teaching of science.

Philip P. Everts. Assistant and research associate (1962-1970), Polemological Institute, University of Groningen, Netherlands. Since 1970 Director, Institute for International Studies, University of Leiden. Since 1968 has engaged in the activities of the Interchurch Peace Council (IKV) in the Netherlands. Publications on the institutionalization of peace research, problems of European security, South East Asia, the role of the churches in foreign policy-making, domestic sources of foreign policy.

Philomena Fischer. A native of Seoul, Korea and naturalized Swiss citizen. Currently doctoral student, Fordham University, New York, writing a dissertation of 'Self-dissatisfaction as a determinant of changes in student's peace value and attitude towards war'.

Johan Galtung. Director of the Goals, Processes and Indicators of Development Project, UN University, and professor, Institut Universitaire d'Etude du Development, Geneva. In addition to books, many of his other works are currently being published in five volumes of *Essays in peace research*. Christian Ejlers' Forlag a-s, Copenhagen.

Gerd Greune. Chairperson, German Peace Society (DFG-VK). Executive member, International Peace Bureau, Geneva, and War Resisters International, London. Publications on arms trade, Southern Africa and international politics. Teacher working in the field of disarmament education, 1977. Since 1979, in Paris as NGO consultative of UNESCO.

Guido Grünewald. Born 1952, historian. Member, national board, German Peace Society (DFG-VK) and of Working Group on Peace and Conflict Research (AKF). Publications on conversion and history of peace movement in Germany. Currently working on doctoral dissertation dealing with the pacifist movement in the Federal Republic of Germany.

Amalendu Guha. Born 1935, Chittagong (now in Bangladesh) educated in Calcutta, obtained DSc in economics and PhD in petroleum economics, in 1965 and 1966 respectively from the University of Bucharest. Has taught international economy in several universities in Asia, Africa and Europe, and has been research fellow in institutes in Asia and Europe. Associated with chair in Conflict and Peace Research, University of Oslo, 1974-76. Now Executive Director, Institute for Alternative Development Research, Oslo. Has written several books and more than 60 articles on social sciences topics, including conflict and peace research.

Magnus Haavelsrud. Born 1940, lecturer, Institute of Social Science, University of Tromsö, Norway. Holds PhD from University of Washington and *Cand. Polit.*, University of Oslo. Executive secretary, Peace Education Commission, International Peace Research Association (1975-79). Editor of *Education for peace:*

reflection and action, IPC Science and Technology Press, 1975; *Indoktrinering eller politisering,* Universitetsforlaget, 1979 and (with J. Galtung and V. Wiese) *Education for peace and development: form – content – structure,* Christian Ejlers Forlag, Copenhagen, forthcoming.

Mathias Jopp. Born 1950, studied public law, political science and economics. Since 1976 researcher, Peace Research Institute Frankfurt/West-Germany. His major research interest has been the relationship between the military and society in the Federal Republic, specially looking at the reforms in educating military officers. He received his PhD at the University of Frankfurt in 1980.

Alva Myrdal. Most recently held Tom Slick Peace Professorship, University of Texas, 1978-79; former Director, UNESCO Department of Social Science; member, Swedish Parliament; Cabinet Minister for Disarmament; Ambassador at Large. Chief of Swedish Delegation to Geneva Disarmament Conference; Board of Directors of Stockholm International Peace Research Institute. Among numerous books: *Disarmament: reality of illusion* (1965); *The game of disarmament* (1977); *Women's two roles: home and work* (1955); *Nation and family* (1941).

Betty A. Reardon. Programme Coordinator, World Council for Curriculum and Instruction; former Chairperson, CORPED; founding member, Peace Education Commission of IPRA; former Director, School Program, Institute for World Order, Inc. Publications: Human rights and educational reform, *Bull. Peace Proposals,* V. 8, (3) 1977; *A teachers guide for global studies.* Rockefeller Foundation Educational Publishing Program, 1977; Disarmament and peace education, *Prospects,* 8, (4) 1978.

Helena Rytövuori. MSc. Lecturer in international politics, Department of Political Sciences, University of Tampere. Major fields of interest and study: development studies and peace research. Publications on interdependence in the international system, the changing order for the oceans and the economic uses of the seas and the New Ocean regime.

Ben J. Th.ter Veer. Social psychologist/peace researcher, Polemological Institute, Haren, Netherlands. Main field of interest, peace education. Published in 1980 the final report on a 6 year curriculum development project for pupils of 14 and older. President, Interchurch Peace Council from 1977 (the year in which the campaign for nuclear disarmament in the Netherlands was started).

Haakon Wiberg. Born 1942. PhD in sociology, associate professor and director, Department of Peace and Conflict Research, Lund University, since 1971. Books: *Konflikteori och fredsforskning* (1976), *Visions of the future* (1977), *Images of the world in the year 2000* (with H. Ornauer et. al., 1976), *Dragkampen pa Afrikas Horn* edited 1979.

Veslemøy Wiese. *Cand.polit.,* University of Oslo, 1976. Teaching adult education and sociology of education in Rauland, Norway. Connected to the chair of Conflict and Peace Research, Oslo, and Department of Peace and Conflict Research, Uppsala. Member of the Executive Committee, Peace Education Commission, 1979 to date.